The Wooden Walls of Thermopylae

Nick Brown

Clink Street

London | New York

Nick Brown has an archaeological background and is the author of the highly acclaimed *Luck Bringer*, *Skendleby* and *The Dead Travel Fast*.

Praise for Nick Brown's books

Luck Bringer

"This is a fascinating and entertaining book and makes the reader feel as if he were present together with Mandrocles, the Luck Bringer." Antonis Mistriotis, author of *507-450 BC- The 57 Years Which Gave Birth to Democracy*

"Fleshes out the life of the true historical figure, Miltiades, and brings the ructions of the Arab Spring crashing into life." *Cheshire Life*

"Fast paced and based on meticulous research it tells it like it most probably was, stripped of the hype, but none the less moving for that." *Indie Author land*

Skendleby

"Something creepy afoot." *Big Issue*

"Gripping and genuinely creepy." *New Edition*

"Echoes of the ghost story master, M.R. James." *I Like Horror*

"A heartily recommended read for all thriller and horror fans." *Horror Cult Films*

"I wish the book had been longer." *Sexy Archaeology*

The Dead Travel Fast

"Sent chills down my spine; a thrilling read from start to finish." Jessica Ward, author of *The Path of Destruction* series

"It's crying out to be made into a movie!" *Spectral Times*

"A fantastic genre bending experience." *Web weaver*

"An imaginative chiller mixing horror and thriller fiction with a twist of quantum strangeness." *Indie Author Land*

Also by Nick Brown

The Ancient Gramarye series:
Skendleby
The Dead Travel Fast

The Luck Bringer series:
Luck Bringer
The Wooden Walls of Thermopylae

For my lovely sister, Liz Spence

Published by Clink Street Publishing 2014

Copyright © Nick Brown 2014

First edition.

ISBN: 978-1-909477-61-2
Ebook: 978-1-909477-62-9

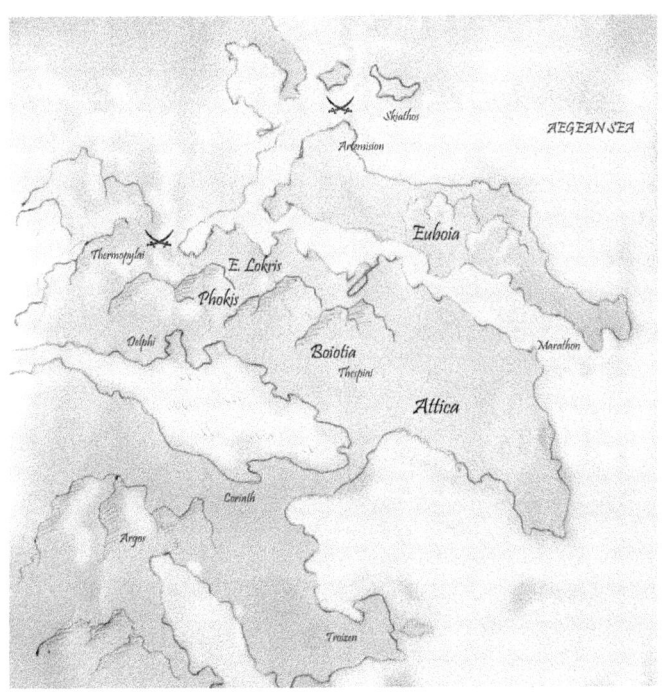

AEGEAN SEA

Skiathos

Artemision

Euboia

Thermopylai

E. Lokris

Phokis

Delphi

Boiotia

Thespini

Marathon

Attica

Corinth

Argos

Troizen

Map by Gaius Brown

Glossary

Agora: Greek for market place. In Athens it was the main square and centre of city life

Andron: Room for entertaining in the male section of a Greek house

Areopagus: Ancient criminal court with powers to supervise entire public administration. Regarded as too conservative by democrats and had its power reduced in 462 BC.

Archon: Group of aristocrats with authority for power over the state. At the time of Marathon open only to the wealthiest class and serving for one year with a president called the named Archon

Boule: Council for Athens representing the Athenian tribes

Ceramicus: District of Athens originally of potters' workshops. At the time of Marathon seedy, drinking, red light district

Choregus: Wealthy citizen who finances a play

Chorus: Performers of the plays at religious festivals

Chou: Measure of liquid used for ordering wine

Deme: Administrative district

Demos: Greek word meaning the people. Democracy means sovereignty of the people

Dionysia: Spring drama festival in honour of the god Dionysus

Ephors: A board of five elders elected to supervise all activities in Sparta including the actions of the two kings.

Ephibatai: Hoplites serving as marines on board a trireme

Hekaton: Representation of the goddess Hekate, found at crossroads

Heraion: A temple in honour of the goddess Hera

Heroon: Landmark monument to legendary hero

Hetaerae: Courtesan or up-market sex worker

Hoplite: Heavily armed foot soldier

Krater: Jug for mixing wine

Kottabos: Drinking game involving flicking dregs and wine from a wine cup

Nike: Greek goddess of victory

Panonium: Sacred place for Ionian Greeks at Mycale

Polis: City state

Pornoi: Sex worker

Strategos: A General. In Athens there was a board of ten generals who were elected

Symposium: Greek drinking party

Thalamioi: Bottom tier of rowers on a trireme

Thranitai: Top tier of rowers on a trireme who rowed through an outrigger and were the rowing élite

Trierarch: Captain of a Trireme

Trireme: A fighting ship with three banks of oars

Tyrant: A ruler with full power of a city state or territory. The term did not have quite the modern day pejorative implications and some tyrants were regarded as benign

Zugioi: Middle tier rowers on a trireme

Major Historical Characters in the *Luck Bringer* Series

Aeschylus First great Athenian dramatist and poet. Fought at Marathon and probably Salamis

Aristides Aristocrat of the Alkmaionid faction known as "The Just" rival of Themistocles

Aspasia Intellectual and controversial mistress of Pericles.

Aristonice Phythia of Delphi in 480 BC

Callias Wealthy Athenian and suitor of Elpinice

Callimachus Athenian general killed at Marathon

Cleinias Aristocratic Athenian politician, father of Alcibiades

Cimon Son of Miltiades

Cleomenes King of Sparta until deposed on the charge of mental instability

Darius Great King of the Persians at the time of Marathon

Elpinice Strong willed daughter of Miltiades

Euripides Athenian dramatist

Eurybiades Reluctant Spartan Admiral

Gorgo Daughter of Cleomenes and wife of Leonidas, a striking, ambiguous character.

Hipparchus Athenian aristocrat who defected to Persia in the wars

Kallixenos Aristocratic Athenian, opponent of democracy

Leonidas King of Sparta who commanded at Thermopylae.

Leotychidas Joint king of Sparta with Leonidas

Mardonius Persian general

Megacles Alkmaionid opponent of democracy

Metiochus Son of Miltiades, linked to the Persians during the wars

Miltiades Deposed Athenian tyrant of the Chersonese who commanded the Athenians at Marathon

Pericles Son of Xanthippus who later became leader of Athens

Phrynichus Athenian dramatist; only fragments of his work survive

Sophocles Athenian dramatist and contemporary of Pericles

Themistocles Athenian politician, promoter of democracy and sea power

Xanthippus Athenian politician of the Alkmaionid faction

Xerxes Great king of the Persians following the death of Darius

"Most hateful name of all-
Athens! Who can forget
Our Persian women's debt-
Innocent tears that fall
For husband lost, or son,
Long since at Marathon?"
　　　　Aeschylus: "The Persians"

Clytemnestra: "You speak as to some thoughtless woman:
You are wrong."
　　　　Aeschylus: "Agamemnon"

Part One

Chapter One

"Now watch as it falls apart."

He leant back on the bench miming a gesture of resignation, or maybe disgust, and spat the fruit stone onto the beaten earth floor. Both the gesture and the denunciation were aimed at me. I couldn't reply, because a part of me agreed with him, so I just sat silent watching the dark juice from the fruit trickle down into his beard. We were in the bar Cynegeiros had built out of driftwood in the Piraeus; except of course he wasn't there, his remains were under the mound at Marathon while his shade lamented over the spot where his blood soaked the sand.

The bar now belonged to Aeschylus but his heart wasn't in it despite the fact that Cynegeiros had been right to speculate on the new port. Below us on the water we could see the rapid expansion of Themistocles's project but also the cause of his anger. Bobbing on the water by the short stretch of new harbour wall was the Athenian war fleet, its polished bronze rams flashing in the sunlight. Within the hour I'd be boarding its flagship: The Athene Nike.

"You can't be such a fool that you don't understand what I'm saying, boy."

I'd seen Themistocles take apart the most senior aristocrats in the city, seen him reduce their arguments to shreds so there wasn't any point in contesting it.

"I thought you had more sense, thought you could be useful. But look at you, dressed up and ready to go and play at pirates."

I sat in front of my friends, wanting to be out of there, feeling sick and ashamed, even though I knew I was only a proxy for his anger: the real recipient was making his triumphal procession down to the harbour. We could hear faint cheering in the distance. Aeschylus opened his mouth to speak in my defence but at the last minute thought better of it. It would have been futile: you can't stop Themistocles.

"At Marathon we changed the world because we agreed to unite. That's what saved the city. You were there, Mandrocles, you saw it. Because of that, because of that decision which no other city could take, we beat Darius. Beat him and forced him to flee with his fleet. We were part of it, the three of us; we were there when those up themselves Alkmaionid buggers stood in the line next to honest tradesmen from the Ceramicus. Stood and fought for each other. Look."

He pulled the tunic down off his shoulder exposing a livid and barely healed scar running from just below the neck round under his left armpit.

"Look, see this? I took this sheltering Aristides with my shield; I saved his life that day, we fought shoulder to shoulder. Days before he was my enemy and would have done me down same as I would him."

He replaced the tunic, muttering,

"To be fair, he saved me too."

I knew what was coming next; it wasn't the first time I'd heard this speech.

"The finest men in the city died that day. Died for our freedom, the freedom of all Greece. Callimachus, the most honourable man amongst us, Stesileos, both generals, both in the front line. Cynegeiros, your brother in whose bar we're drinking, Aeschylus. Killed at the sea's edge trying to take the Persian ships; a hero like Hector."

There was a period of silence, deliberate silence. You could take the man out of the city but you couldn't take the politician out of the man and Themistocles was the best politician we ever had. Once satisfied that the silence had created its dramatic effect, he moved to the point he made many times each and every day.

"And what was all that sacrifice for?"

Like all his other questions this was rhetorical; he had no intention of giving his friends, never mind opponents, a space to speak.

"If Callimachus were here today he'd place a curse on the city. He understood that Marathon was only the first race in the games. He knew the Persians would be back and with a much bigger army. He knew that our only chance was to use the time we bought with our blood at Marathon to prepare. To prepare for a war at sea, not on land. He knew we needed a fleet of three hundred triremes and a safe harbour to protect them."

He gestured with his empty cup towards the stalled work on the new harbour and then refilled it. Both Aeschylus and I knew that in all probability Callimachus would have vetoed any such projects. He had been a man of honour but also a man of conservative principles and it had taken Themistocles a great deal of effort to get him to Marathon. But there was no point in saying so.

"Callimachus's bones must be turning under the mound because of what we've done. Because of the way we've let vested interest come before our duty to the city. The way we've forgotten about the Persians and the lessons of Marathon. Now the great families are attempting to restore things to the way they were: the way they were before the Demos showed us how to be great."

The cheering outside was now much louder; the procession must have been close, but Themistocles wasn't talked out.

"And now your master, the man I pardoned and supported in his rightful policy of fighting the Persians, is throwing it all away. And we know who's supporting him, don't we? Aristides, the man whose life I saved at Marathon."

There'd always been bad blood between Themistocles and Aristides. Some of it was to do with politics but according to gossip most of the animosity dated from before and stemmed from the fact that they were both rivals for the affection of the same youth.

However now there was another rival who Themistocles hated and feared more than Aristides and his clique. Hated with such intensity it was rumoured he was no longer able to sleep at night. This man was Miltiades, hero of Marathon and my master. The man who would lead the expedition against the island state of Paros, and whose procession towards the ships was being loudly cheered. So loudly that Themistocles had to raise his voice to be heard.

"So now, instead of preparing to defend our homeland against the greatest power on earth, our aristocratic masters are wasting our men and resources on a pointless act of piracy for reasons which no one understands. And we don't understand them because the great Miltiades refuses to explain himself other than to say that the city must give him a fleet and money and in return he'll make us rich."

He paused again on the verge of the climax of this peroration, milking the moment for the greatest effect. I'd heard it before so knew where it was going and was numbering the deliberate bits of misinformation that he'd included in his argument. But that's the way with politicians, isn't it? The ones today are much worse: Pericles the onion head regards it clever to dissimulate and he's a pillar of rectitude when compared with some of the demagogues; Cleon for instance.

Sorry, reader, I've started to ramble. Anyway I got no further time for reflection and Themistocles never reached his climax. He'd just said, "Well Miltiades had better be careful," when two things happened almost at once. First, there was a burst of cheering loud as a thunderclap from right outside and second, the door opened.

"And of what had I better be careful, son of Neocles?"

Miltiades in full armour walked in looking like the god of war. His success at Marathon seemed to have made him taller. He was at ease with himself and brimming with confidence that flowed out towards anyone near. How much the tables had turned since we'd been chased to Athens by the Persian navy. Then, Miltiades had been forced to beg and wheedle to survive. Now it was Themistocles who looked the supplicant.

"Perhaps you can enlighten me. But you'll have to be quick because I have an appointment with the fleet to carry out the City of the Goddess Athena's business."

Themistocles must have been surprised by Miltiades's entrance but he was too much the politician to show it.

"I could enlighten you if you chose to divulge the nature of the enterprise, son of Cimon."

I wondered what could have happened so quickly to change the relationship between these men. The two who had worked so closely to deliver us the victory at Marathon. I should have been thinking about what was going to happen as I was witnessing, without knowing it, the prologue of a tragedy. Aeschylus watched: he said nothing but he missed nothing either. Those of you who love his plays will recognise the content if not the context of what followed.

"And why should I divulge the nature of the enterprise to

you, son of Neocles, when there is no need for you to know it? For you, it should be sufficient to be told only that it is in the city's interests. But because of the work we have done together I will indulge you more than I choose to indulge others of your rank. I am prepared to tell you that the enterprise is essential because I consider it to be so."

I still often wonder what causes great men like Miltiades to behave the way they do. At that moment in his burnished armour with his hair and beard freshly dressed he looked like a god. Perhaps he even considered himself to be one. But it was tempting fate: the gods hate hubris and punish it accordingly. Themistocles, a much better manipulator of men and certainly a far more accomplished dissembler, kept his self-control, replying quietly.

"That is most gracious, son of Cimon, and I am sure it is the best of reasons. However I still fail to understand the threat that Paros presents us with. If it were Aegina, that nest of pirates, then I could see the reason but not Paros."

He paused a second favouring Miltiades with his most ingratiating, yet irritating, smile – a smile I'd seen provoke even moderate men to wrath – then added,

"Unless of course there is some private agenda between you and the citizens of Paros. Is that the case perhaps?"

Miltiades, despite the strength of his position, began to colour up; I could see the veins on his forehead swelling. Never a good sign. But Themistocles continued in honeyed tones.

"And why the considerable sum of money granted you by your erstwhile enemies but now close friends, the Alkmaionid clan?"

Miltiades rasped out,

"That again is something you don't need to know."

"But it's something I do know and something that the whole city will know once you've sailed."

Miltiades, angry as he was becoming, realised he was being bated and there was nothing he could gain from the exchange. He turned away from Themistocles with a glance intended to convey lofty disdain, saying to me,

"Mandrocles, there's no time to waste so unless you intend to drink away your life in the company of agitators and scribblers, get yourself moving."

He swept out of the tavern and I stumbled to my feet and began to say my goodbyes, but Themistocles cut across me, speaking cold and controlled.

"That man who marches under the shadow of nemesis better be warned: it's time to make your choice, Luck Bringer. Last chance, so you'd better think clearly."

I remember shuffling from one foot to the other in indecision for what seemed an age. Then, with a brief nod towards Aeschylus I turned and followed the General out of the door.

Back then the Piraeus was nothing like the great port and hub of empire that you know today. Then it was little more than a ragged bay, patches of sand interspersed with rock pools and headlands. A few scattered fishermen's shacks, grazing goats and that was it.

The building had only just started: a few cubits of wall but you could see the future. Some bars and dwellings were springing up and those with the aptitude for it understood there was money to be made. I caught a glimpse of the future that day looking down at the fleet preparing to set sail. Small compared with our modern fleet, reader, but exciting all the same.

So I was caught up in the noise and bustle of embarkation and any worries about Themistocles's words dispersed. It was a great adventure; but then that's both the advantage and the drawback of youth, isn't it? You go from one thing to another and embrace change like a lover.

Cimon and Elpinice were on the harbour wall by the Athene Nike. He was wheedling Ariston into letting him stow away onboard and she was somewhere between woman and girl. A woman in appearance and dignity but still a girl in that her reaction to her father's departure was so transparent. The sailors made a great fuss over Cimon, who had always been their favourite, but stayed well clear of Elpinice out of respect.

So we grabbed a shared moment. Even back then she was wise way beyond her years and if she'd been born with the rights of a man, she'd have given Themistocles a run for his money like she did Pericles all those years later. Now looking back on the conversation, what obviously escaped me then seems clear: her analysis of the expedition was as clinical as Themistocles had been.

"Do you find anything strange about this expedition, Mandrocles?"

I was about to reply but there was another similarity between her and Themistocles: she didn't want an answer either, merely a listener.

"Because the men who he had to fight with to persuade them to fight the Persians are falling over themselves to see him off; look."

I followed where she pointed and saw them in a group clustered round the General: Megacles, Aristides, even Kallixenos, friend of the Persians who was lucky not to have been exiled after Marathon.

She turned her gaze back towards me and muttered,

"And yet his own brother Stesagoras who counselled against this has chosen not to be here I see."

She was right; there was no sign of him, which struck me as odd. But how could a girl like her, excluded from the affairs of men, know what was counselled when I didn't?

Miltiades broke away from the group of well-wishers

come to see him off and, ignoring the helping hands, leapt with the grace of a young warrior onto the deck. The crew erupted into a loud cheer. He turned and acknowledged it as his right as leader and I saw on his face that same expression of command and confidence that he wore at Marathon when he ordered the charge. Theodorus shouted to me from the deck.

"Better jump too, Mandrocles, if you don't want to be left behind."

I was about to but I felt a cool hand grip my arm and Elpinice said,

"Keep your eyes on him, Mandrocles; I think he will need your luck. Now go well."

I turned and jumped down to the deck just in time to see the General lead the singing of the Paean and pour the libation. Then the Athene Nike was moving, pulling smoothly away from the harbour wall. Moving to the heartbeat of the stroke that Theodorus called. And I was truly alive in a way that only those of you who have served with the fleet can understand.

But later, as I stood by the trierarch's chair and watched the Piraeus recede into the distance, the melancholy that follows pulling out to start a new adventure set in. But this time it was more than just that. Something was troubling me, something that must have gnawed away deep inside since Themistocles had said,

"It's something the whole city will know once you've sailed."

Now out on the open sea with twilight approaching it came to me that this was no empty threat; Miltiades had no real friends in the city and certainly none he could trust. He'd been given the money and the fleet for this expedition because after his leadership at Marathon no one could refuse him. However, as with most things in this city, there was a big but. Some days before Aeschylus had filled me in as a warning when I told him I was sailing with the fleet, but I hadn't really been listening.

"Don't be fooled by the apparent closeness of your master with Aristides, Megacles, Xanthippus and all the rest of that high born clique. For the moment they have similar interest in restoring the old principle of Eunomia and ending the stirrings of the Demos. Now the danger's gone they want Themistocles and his new ways shut back up in their box. His talk of a new port and sea power leads to change and that's the last thing they want."

I hadn't understood the real significance of what he said and had replied.

"But the Persian danger hasn't gone away, it's ..."

He cut me off.

"You're missing the point, Mandrocles. I'm talking city politics, not the real world. Of course Themistocles is right about the Persians and the fleet: but that's not the priority right now. The priority is to marginalise Themistocles. That's not easy so they link themselves to the great popular hero Miltiades. But the great thing about the Paros expedition for them is that it gets Miltiades out of the city."

I must have looked baffled because he interrupted his flow to ask a question.

"Do you understand the objectives of the Paros expedition?"

"No, but ..."

"Does anyone? Does anyone understand how it will work?"

"The General knows. It's his plan, it's a secret."

"Exactly, and how will that look in the city when it fails?"

"And that's what Themistocles thinks?"

"Of course."

"Then why hasn't he warned the General?"

"Why indeed?"

He must have seen the bewilderment, then gradual understanding, cross my face because with a smile he answered.

"Exactly, Mandrocles. Exactly now you begin to understand what goes on beneath the surface of our scheming city."

Chapter Two

We could see he was a dead man as soon as they let us into the court chamber. What I remember most is the smell of the wound: anyone who's been in battle recognises that stench. He'd never taken the time to get the bone reset, splinted and cleaned on Paros. By the time he was back in Athens it was too late for the doctors to do anything and the gangrene was taking its slow and agonising course. Consequently when he tried to defend himself against the spite of his political enemies he was a dying man, barely conscious on a stretcher. He could scarcely draw breath, never mind speak for himself. So it was a death sentence for the General, whatever the court decided.

Who would believe that something as ridiculous as jumping over a field wall could cause the death of such a hero? But it just about summed up that ill-conceived and badly executed expedition. Things had gone wrong from the start. We'd delayed too long securing bases and plundering smaller islands and by the time we reached Paros they were ready. After a siege of several weeks, we ran out of money and provisions and had to slink off home, having achieved nothing.

When we got back to Athens they were on him like a pack of jackals: they'd stitched it up while we were away. Themistocles and the democrats accused him of wanting to establish a tyranny and the conservatives charged him with defrauding the people. They'd even done a deal on who would be the chief prosecutor: Xanthippus.

A small group of us, those who loved him and were brave enough, walked to the court in the armour we'd worn at Marathon. His brother Stesagoras led us hoping it would shame the jurors into remembering what they and the city owed to Miltiades. But they were beyond shame.

Thus within a year of being hailed victor of Marathon and saviour of Greece, the great man was brought down. The charges were politically motivated and if they hadn't have got him for this they'd have found something else. Democracy of vipers: the bile still rises in my throat all these years later.

I don't suppose he helped himself though; his raid on the island of Paros would have been foolish even if it had proved successful: it gave his enemies their opportunity to pull him down. But even they shouldn't have brought his family down or tried him in the public way they did. It was like trying a walking corpse. Dragging him to court, incapable of speaking in his own defence, on that filthy stinking stretcher was deliberate. They intended to rub his nose in the dirt of public shame.

Not that a defence would have done him any good: the trial was rigged. Rigged by the same men who fought beside him at Marathon. Once the Persians had gone, they left off being heroes and reverted to type, fighting each other for power in the sewers of the new democracy. We should have thanked the Persians for attacking us; they were the threat that made Athenians stick together. The only great thing this city of the Goddess had ever done was to stand together at Marathon and it was Miltiades who gave hope and leadership.

The trial took no time; I suppose they didn't want him to die in that chamber and embarrass them. He was outlawed and his family's rights and property forfeited. Then they celebrated: all together men that hated each other but hated the General more. Even Themistocles. But the real cruelty, which by the way was the earliest indicator of what a monster democracy would become, was the fine they levied: fifty talents.

By imposing that fine the court ensured Cimon not only lost his father but he lost his future too. Those bastards, that was the real cruelty; fifty talents levied on a penniless nine year old boy condemning him to a life of poverty and debt.

Not only Cimon but Elpinice, because for her there would be no dowry and so no marriage thus depriving her of the only future fit for a respectable Athenian woman. As for Stesagoras, there was no official punishment: nothing you'll find in any of our papyrus or stone records, just a warning.

"Be on the first ship out of Phaleron."

You will understand the consequences, reader, whoever you are. I know as you read this you too will choke with anger. Miltiades saved Athens, saved the Demos and all free Greece and was rewarded by a painful death in a stinking gaol and the ruin of his son. The fools: they should have known the Persians would be back with the greatest army the world had ever seen

After, when it was over, I walked back towards the house in my father's armour, now too small and chafing my shoulders and neck. Where would I go? What would I do? As I turned the corner to Miltiades's house I saw the answer to at least one of those questions. Athenian justice had been expedited quickly. The slaves and valuables were being taken away and there was smoke rising from the roof. I was homeless and alone in a vengeful city.

The children were gone. But even there, watching the pillage of the once great home of the Philiads with the smoke stinging my eyes, I didn't have the clarity of vision to foresee the full tragedy. The effect on the boy: his homeless state and the reputation for wildness that followed him because of the way he was forced to live as a pariah outside society.

And worse the foul slanders about the unnatural sexual relationship with his sister. You know the stories, reader, you probably enjoyed hearing them. Well, none of it was true. None of it. I was there, I know!

Ironic, isn't it? Eight years after I sat there watching my home burn, every single home in Athens was destroyed by the Persians. Thank the Gods we can't see the future. I remember that I slumped down onto a low wall and put my head in my hands. Round about me men were carrying off what they'd looted from the house, shouting to each other and laughing. After a while it grew quiet, the only sound being flame scorching timber and the cracking of plaster and stone. To most people the sound of a fire reminds them of hearth and home but to me it's the sound of ruin.

Amongst the knot of idlers watching the flames there was a face I recognised, a free man of Miltiades who bossed the stable hands. There were tear tracks smearing the grime on his smoke-blackened face. I caught his eye and he shuffled across.

"Master Mandrocles, are you mad sitting there in armour? The Archon's guards will have a warrant for you. They've already taken Master Cimon and Mistress Elpinice. Once these bastards are tired of watching the flames they'll turn on you. Get going quick; get lost."

That's what he did: he must have thought talking to me endangered him. But where was I to go? I'd kept myself together pretty well until then but when I tried to think where I could put my father's armour the tears began to flow. It's always the little things that get you: the big blows you see coming you can ride out, but the small details that sneak up unexpected, they're what sink you.

I think I would have sat there weeping in my father's armour until the guards came for me if it hadn't been for a strange intervention.

I felt a hand shaking my shoulder and looked up expecting it to be one of the Archon's men. But it wasn't. It was someone I'd seen before: I recognised him from a brawl in a bar some years back. One of Megacles men called Eubulus if I remember right. Theodorus had re-arranged his face but he'd fought with us at Marathon. Even so there was still no love lost.

"You are to come with me."

The words were softly spoken, cajoling rather than threatening but I was too far gone to want to listen. He put his arms under mine and dragged me to my feet.

"Come on, get moving; we need to be away from here."

I noticed he was carrying a sack like itinerant potters cart their wares around in.

"Come on. In this armour, you stick out like the prick on the satyr at the Dionysia."

I still didn't move.

"Come on help me for fuck's sake or the guard'll have both of us."

He started to unbuckle the straps on my shoulder guards. I just followed his lead and shrugged off the armour as quick as possible and he stowed it in the sack. Then he put it over his shoulder and set off towards the Ceramicus. Life had lost most of its meaning and I had nowhere else to go so I followed.

The streets were crowded and noisy, the bars full and working girls were plying their trade on the roadside. It seemed like the striking down of Miltiades had covered the city in a cloak of madness. But, as you know reader, in Athens that's often the first cloak out of the cupboard. We were in a city living on borrowed time which had defied the

Great King and then struck down its own leader. Notice any similarities with today?

Eubulus didn't speak and stayed a few steps ahead; maybe he thought that made him safe. Suddenly he dodged down a foul narrow street at the far end of the Ceramicus, weaved his way through a warren of rough sheds and kennels before coming to a stop outside one of the city's most notorious taverns: "The Bald Man's".

I followed him in, noticing he was looking over his shoulder to check no one was tailing us. He pointed to a three legged table and bench hidden away in a shadowy corner. The bar tender brought over some greasy country sausage stuffed with gristle and a flask of thin wine. There was only one cup.

"Stay here until someone comes to fetch you. Don't talk to anyone and don't move."

He dumped the sack with my father's armour by my feet and disappeared. I sat there as the sausage gradually cooled and congealed into a pool of grease, and I drank the wine. It stung my throat and burnt my stomach but I drank it all, it took the edge off my anxiety. Then I ate the mess of sausage and realised how hungry I was.

I drifted into a daze; the table had become my only refuge and I didn't know what else there was. Does this surprise you, reader? If you've stuck with me through my memoirs up to now you'll know that I can fuck and kill with the best of them. But that's what life does to you while you're making plans. It plays with you then reduces you to nothing.

I must have been aware of my surroundings at one level because suddenly the room went quiet. A hooded man had entered, not tall but with a bruiser's body. He paused to give his eyes time to adjust to the gloom. Then he saw what he was after: he began to cross the filthy floor towards my corner watched by everyone in the bar. His hood was pulled low so he couldn't be identified but as he drew closer there was something in his walk I recognised.

He didn't say anything, just picked up the sack and headed for the door. I got up and staggered after him; no payment was demanded for the food so all this had been pre planned. The hooded man didn't hang about; he lingered just long enough to see I'd followed him then set off at a loping trot towards the Hangman's Gate.

The only person I knew who lived near there was Themistocles but we didn't pass his house. Instead my guide left the road and followed a weaving path through the tombs that ended in a gap in the city walls. We called them walls back then but they weren't, they wouldn't have stopped anyone. Not like the monsters we've got now.

I had no idea where we were going; was I being taken to the border and sent into exile or had I been lured out into the fields to be murdered beyond the range of prying eyes? I began to consider making a run for it. It was nearly dark and despite the food and drink I was pretty quick on my feet back then.

We seemed to be heading for the sacred road to Eleusis the site of the mysteries and I reckoned that made it more likely that I was going to be killed. It never occurred to me that the fate of a young man of no account like me wouldn't come very high up the list of the politician's priorities. But at that age you think you're the centre of the world and everything is just a part of your personal journey. As you get older you discover how far from the truth that is. Anyhow, I decided I'd slip off the path and leg it downhill towards Piraeus and maybe find Aeschylus or try my luck on one of the ships.

Strange how often the most minor actions have the greatest consequences. Just as I was about to slip off the track the hooded man did the same. He turned his head to check I was still following then loped off down towards the bay. So we both ended up turning at precisely the same instant and I followed him. There was no more to it than that. He'd stolen my plan and I didn't have another. It wouldn't have worked anyway because it turned out that we'd been heading for Piraeus right from the beginning. Whatever you do, you can't outrun your fate.

Today, if you tried to slip into the great port that Piraeus has become carrying a sack and wearing a hood the guards would have you within seconds. Then no one bothered unless you tried to mess with one of the boats; it was a sort of non place. It was changing but except for Themistocles no one knew what it was mutating into. In that sense it was rather like one of those newfangled plays young Sophocles keeps bashing out.

At last as we neared our destination my mind started to work and I began to guess who my hooded guide was and where he was taking me. I bet you've guessed already, reader. We pulled up at the quay and followed it to the third ship docked by the new wall to be greeted by a gruff voice from somewhere inside.

"Took your time."

"Things were lively for a while in the Agora so I was late getting the boy but he followed quiet as a lamb."

He pushed his hood back and cuffed me lightly round the head.

"You dozy little bugger. I'll make sure we never put you up as a look out. Who did you think you were following?"

I still don't know if I felt more embarrassed or relieved as I followed Ariston over the side and down onto the deck to join Theodorus, who also gave me a slap. I think that's about as close as they ever got to showing affection. I felt safe, I didn't know what was happening but I was onboard Athene Nike with two of the only men I knew I could trust even though they weren't finished mocking me.

"A chicken would have shown more intelligence than Mandrocles did leaving the Bald Man's: he didn't even question me."

He grinned across at me.

"And don't try telling anyone you knew it was me either. You had no fucking idea, cluck cluck cluck."

Theodorus and he started imitating chickens in a farm and clucking till tears ran down their faces. Simple creatures, seamen, amused by simple things, but I gave in and laughed with them. Eventually they grew tired of laughing every time one of them said Cluck Bringer and we settled down in the stern with a flask of wine.

"Don't worry, this isn't the stoat's piss the bald man deals out to the customers he's not scared to cheat. You can consider yourself lucky this comes from the amphora of a great man."

I was too tired for riddles and it must have shown.

"Okay, you're safe here boy. If we'd got to you earlier and you hadn't gone missing I'd have put you up at my place. What made you do something as stupid as go back to the house and draw attention to yourself. You got noticed; that's why we had to go through all that play acting with Eubulus. I bet you were surprised when he turned up."

I didn't know what to say, didn't understand any of this.

"We thought you be sensible and go and hide up with Aeschylus or your little pornoi, that's where we looked, the house was the last place and as we daren't turn up there we had to come up with someone who could; Eubulus, hates us and hates the general. But then again Athens is a surprising place. Not that you're going to be seeing much of it for a bit."

I asked why.

"Because the man whose wine you're drinking says you're to sail with us on a little mission at dawn tomorrow."

"Why? Where to?"

"What's the most dangerous place for an Athenian, especially a democrat, outside of the Persian Empire?"

I answered, remembering what Themistocles had said before the Paros debacle.

"Aegina of course."

"Got it in one, the chicken's using its brain at last."

Chapter Three

The boy Ephialties, named after the rabid democrat by his radical grandmother, has just brought me a lamp and some wine so I can continue to write as the light fades. It is necessary to use all the time there is: I don't think there's a great deal left to me.

The boy has gone now, a wild lad although he means well – but something familiar about him disturbs me. He reminds me of his grandmother when she was younger, the same eyes. But something else, something that slips away every time I get near; retreating to the back of my mind where it sits and stirs echoes.

His grandmother was a flute girl I used when we were younger. No, that's not fair or true she meant something to me and gave me much more. There was a time when I thought we would, perhaps be together: well if Pericles, onion head, can live with a pornoi openly then why shouldn't I? But then she got with child and was secretive about it. Got with child when I was almost ready to ... well what's the point in raking it all up, all the hurt and anger. She came to talk to me about it, about the child, but I was about to sail and decided to forget her.

Perhaps I should have listened, perhaps if it had been a decent man's child I could have ... but I sent her away then joined the ship. It was for the best. When I got back wounded she sent to me asking to bring the child, wanted to show him to me. I was wounded; confused, I refused to see her.

He was killed, the boy, her boy, in an action years later during the Eurymedon campaign. Strange that was my last fight too. Ephialtes wasn't born when his father sailed and his mother died in labour so she, the grandmother, Lyra, brought him up. When he'd grown a bit I was sickening and she suggested he come and help out. He reminds me of someone but it keeps slipping away. I can't write any more. These memories tear at me.

Forgive me for those ramblings I wrote last night, reader; it happens to men who live too long. But this morning I feel better and remember that trip to Aegina like it was yesterday. I slept long and deep that night, so much so that the first rowers climbing on board just before daylight failed to wake me. It was Ariston pushing his foot, none too gently, into my ribs that did that.

"Wake up and get ready to hear the bad news."

He passed me a cup of weak wine and a crust of flat bread.

"Eat this; it'll stop you interrupting while I tell you something you won't like."

He waited until I took a bite; then,

"Xanthippus commands."

I spat the bread out.

"Xanthippus? He's the worst of them, he prosecuted my master; you weren't there you didn't hear what he said: the lies; if that bastard steps on this boat I'll stick my knife in his lying throat."

I didn't get any further as Ariston slapped me hard, made my teeth rattle, certainly made my head swim.

"There'll be no talk like that on this boat whatever the reason, understand?"

He pushed his scarred face close up to mine.

"That was for your own good, stop you saying anything that'd get you hung. Now listen to these three things and don't forget them. First, Miltiades was my master before you were born so don't talk to me about grief or revenge. Second, you talk mutiny on a trireme and you die and no one will speak for you, talk like that and even your mates agree when you get the drop. Final and most important, you don't understand the politics, you've no idea what's been going on. Lysias will fill you in when we sail, he's trierarch."

He must have seen my expression because he said,

"What? You don't think Xanthippus would be stupid enough to command from Miltiades's own flagship? You may hate him but better respect his intelligence. Now eat your bread and get your head thinking."

I finished the bread and watched as the rowers squeezed themselves onto the three tiers of benches. The sun was just visible, rising from below the night black waters. We pulled out of Piraeus with the figure of Lysias silhouetted in the trierarch's chair.

Theodorus set a slow pace and the chant of O op op op O op op op from the rowing benches was little more than a sigh. So smoothly did we leave that our wake resembled a murmur of gentle ripples. I discovered that four ships would travel to Aegina but we left alone: a fleet from Athens, however small, would be unwelcome. So my first glimpse of Xanthippus would be on hostile ground.

Lysias called me over and I threaded my way gently between the rowers, taking care not to rock the boat.

"Ariston tells me you are unhappy with our mission, Mandrocles."

He raised his hand to prevent me replying.

"While you were away on Paros there were many changes, some of them unexpected. For the moment Xan-

24

thippus makes common cause with Themistocles. This mission's his idea but even you can understand that there's no way he'd be an acceptable presence on Aegina; so Xanthippus commands."

Way behind us I could see a tiny speck pulling out of the harbour, perhaps with Xanthippus in the trierarch's chair.

"These are strange times, Marathon changed everything; even a handful of the most conservative aristocrats. While some of them: Megacles, Kallixenos, maybe even Aristides want to turn back to the old days, men like Xanthippus know that's not possible. Darius, if the rumours aren't true and he's still alive, won't let us. He'll be back and this time he'll be even angrier."

He motioned to Theodorus to increase the stroke and maintain the distance from our fellow conspirators.

"So even though Xanthippus and Themistocles remain enemies they're prepared to cooperate until they fully understand how the land lies."

This was the longest conversation I'd had with Lysias even though I'd sailed and fought with him for six years. He was a taciturn man and if it weren't for his love of poetry, wine and rich food he'd have made a good Spartan. And he hadn't even finished.

"But be very clear about whose side you're on, Mandrocles, because you're treading the deck of his ship."

I was about to tell him I'd never ever be Xanthippus's man but he beat me to it.

"No, not Xanthippus. Use your brain, boy; do you seriously think he'd arrange for you to be brought on board? The Athene Nike sails under Themistocles now; it's his pay off from the trial."

All I could remember was the warning Themistocles gave me before Paros. Again Lysias read my mind.

"But don't think that all is forgiven, there's a score you

have to settle and a debt to pay before that."

He had only one more observation to make and not a comforting one.

"So while we're on Aegina we work together: after that who knows? Which of us will go over to the Great King and which of us will stay and fight?"

The morning breeze had sprung up so the sails were fully unfurled and the rowers pulled in their oars. It was only a short way to the pirate island of Aegina and the men had hardly worked up a sweat. The wine skins were broken out and food shared. Soon the buzz of talking spread across the deck. Athenian triremes are crewed by free men who choose to be there, not slaves, and they behave accordingly. You'd never die wondering what someone's opinion was on a trireme.

Other Greeks and the Persians, of course, used to laugh at us for this. For letting men voice their opinions and behave like equals in their down time. They regarded it as weak, ill-disciplined and against all the laws of sea craft. They're not laughing now.

Aegina was like a war zone: not the hot war of blood and battle but the cold war of intrigue and treachery. The arena of war where no man can trust even his neighbour and where loyalties are bought and sold several times each day. Who would expect anything less of Aegina, a nest of vipers? An island where they offered earth and water to the Great King almost before he demanded it. The Persians were made welcome if only because they would destroy Athens. Because then their rival in trade would be no more. It didn't matter to them that it was their fellow Greeks the Persians would be killing.

Back then Aegina looked like an island inhabited by Greeks but it didn't feel like one. The fighting war may have temporarily ceased but the intriguer's war was in full swing and the island was unstable and unsafe. It reminded me of Athens while we were waiting for the Persians. Every morning the dead were collected by the city guard. They were found in alleys, middens, watercourses and sometimes left naked and mutilated on their own doorsteps as a warning to others.

No one saw the killings or who wielded the knives, all was done under cover of night. The dead man's last thoughts must often have been surprise. Surprise that with no warning it was a friend doing the cutting. A man who maybe just minutes before had suggested a last drink or a quiet walk to discuss a proposition or deal.

So no one knew what to expect and who they could trust and the miasma of fear sweated off by this hung like a metaphysical pall over the city: see, reader, I wasn't born on the island of philosophers for nothing.

We pulled slowly into the harbour and after the customary hostile welcome were made to wait and then overcharged for one of the worst moorings. So it was near dark before we got our first close up look at the city. It could have been anywhere in the Persian Empire rather than Greece. The harbour housed ships from all over including many Phoenician war ships in the service of the Empire lightly disguised as merchantmen. The bars, stalls and brothels on the quayside were crowded with the mixture of Greeks and barbarians being roughly equal. Not what I'd expected after Marathon.

You could sense the ferment and treachery from the boat: the island was seething. The excitement was infectious, I was eager to get ashore and knew the crew felt the same even the steady greybeards. Perhaps that's what prompted Lysias to what he did next. Something I'd never seen him do before and can't remember him ever repeating. He called the crew together and spoke to us as a body. He spoke well, which surprised me.

"Listen carefully, lads: you're in the service of the city of the Goddess even though I can't tell you what we're here for. I know most of you were at Marathon and that the ones who weren't wish they had been."

Lysias had fought in the front rank as an officer and carried the wound scars with pride; wounds that had, luckily for him, kept him away from the debacle on Paros.

"I know how you feel about Strategos Miltiades who led us there because I feel the same. Don't let that anger guide your hands or tongues. What we do here is important so keep out of trouble, don't attract attention and be ready to obey orders."

He stopped speaking and deliberately ran his eyes across the faces of every man. I knew we'd arrived at the difficult bit.

"There will be four other Athenian triremes arriving here tonight and some of them will be crewed by men who I know aren't friends of yours ... particularly after what has just been done to our leader by the men they follow."

They knew what was coming, particularly the Thranitai: elite top deck oarsmen; the bowels, heart and stomach of the Demos. There was a sharp intake of breath starting with them and spreading across the Athene Nike. Lysias gave this no time to gestate rather pushing on to his main point.

"So let's get this out of the way now."

He paused; it was like watching as man teetering on the prow of a rammed pentecontor.

"The man who accused him, condemned him to wretched death, penniless in a filthy cell leads our mission."

A series of howls and curses filled the air aimed at one name, which Lysias had to shout out to be heard.

"Xanthippus. Yes, Xanthippus – now get over it. Remember the man who fought beside us at Marathon, not the one who prosecuted Miltiades."

Not an easy thing to quieten sailors though. It was then that Lysias displayed an aptitude for oratory I'd never suspected.

"Well, answer this then. Who leads the city now? Come on, isn't a difficult question. Who puts these men in power? I'll give you a clue; you're on this ship. Yes you, you rowers; democrats to a man blame yourselves for who we're now led by."

I don't know what he'd intended to say but it was apparent that whatever it was he changed his mind at the last instant shouting out the new word.

"Politicians. It's all fucking politics now. Your fucking politics, the monster you've created."

They'd mostly stopped howling him down now, they were interested and slipped back into their Agora mode. Strange that a word that doesn't really mean anything should have that effect; politics or citying? What does that mean? But they didn't take it literally: they knew he was talking about the men who led the city and how they made up the rules as they went along. And it seemed he saved his best Kottabos flick for last.

"And I'll tell you this. I'll tell you which fucking politician dreamed up this mission and gave Xanthippus his command."

I'm sure I was wrong but for a moment I thought he was enjoying himself, thought maybe he wouldn't do too badly in the Agora himself if he fancied a change in occupation. He spun out the expectant silence before uttering four syllables,

"Themistocles."

He let that settle in before he landed the killer blow.

"Themistocles put Xanthippus in charge so that's who you take your orders from, understand?"

Once he'd finished, Ariston spoke for the crew: for all of

29

them and order was restored.

"The trierarch's explained it all to us now, mates, hasn't he? So let's be getting onto the harbour for a few drinks orderly like and stay close to the barky and in range of the whistle."

They started to troop off deck mild as lambs. So brilliantly Athenian: couldn't happen anywhere else; imagine a Spartan officer explain a decision to his men. The Ephors would have him flayed alive in one of those temples dedicated to the cults of mindless cruelty they love so much.

But it wasn't just their minds Lysias appealed to, it was their hearts. That's one of the best things about democracy but it's also the most volatile and worst. Ariston wiped his knuckle across his forehead by way of salute and said,

"Don't worry, Sir, you can rely on the lads, we know what we have to do"

I was about to follow but Lysias held out his arm.

"You have to stay with me, Mandrocles; you're attached to the expedition leader."

He nodded his head towards the harbour mouth where I saw the lights of another trireme gliding towards us. I didn't have to ask who was commanding it: the crew had accepted and so would I. If I'd any idea what Xanthippus had in store for me I'd have argued right enough. But that's life, isn't it? Just like Aeschylus says, a joke to amuse the Gods.

Yet when I look back at those terrible days following the trial and death of Miltiades it all returns with a terrible blinding clarity. But for all that if I could go back to those days I'd swap years of my comfortable old age for just hours of my youth, hard as it was. Those of us who built this city were both blessed and cursed. Stick with me, reader, and you'll see what I mean, it's well worth your effort.

Oh, just one other thing I must set down before the lamp flickers and dies and I turn to my bed to take whatever broken sleep is granted me.

A couple of hours later I followed Xanthippus with the other trierarchs and an escort to a house in the city where we were to eat. Even though Xanthippus hadn't offered me one word of explanation I had a pretty good idea what we were up to. We were going to take soundings from the Persian agents in Aegina.

We were briefly searched at the door then shown into a room where a group of men were waiting, gathered round tables. I'd never been to Aegina, didn't know anyone there and was wondering why I was included. Turned out I was wrong: Leading the Persian delegation in the room there was one face I had good cause to recognise and at the same instant I saw that he recognised me: Metiochus.

Chapter Four

He'd changed. Looked leaner, harder and there were scars from recent wounds on his arms and face. He looked less of the sybarite; Marathon hadn't been kind to him. I knew I'd changed too, but only outwardly I think. Inside the wider shoulders and layers of muscle of my early twenties I was still the same boy I'd been on Samos: more experienced, that's all. It wasn't the same with him, his exterior was only a toughened up version of the man I'd known: but the eyes. The eyes were something different, the man inside was changed. When I last saw him in Sparta I tried to kill him; now from the first glimpse I feared him.

Something else too, something that Xanthippus must have realised set his plans back to nothing. I wasn't a boy anymore and from the stare that Metiochus directed towards me it was obvious he'd no lust for a twenty year old warrior. Any sympathy I might have cultivated for his altered state was counteracted by the venom in his eyes.

The way it turned out, none of that mattered; Metiochus and his contingent got up and left as we entered. Their message couldn't have been plainer and Xanthippus got it loud and clear.

Today Xanthippus is best known as the father of Pericles

but back then he was one of the men that determined the fate of Greece. A good commander and not one to be taken lightly as was evident by his cruelty in the campaign following Mycale. He was slow to forget and slower to forgive. But he was subtle enough to know when to forgo his principles or change direction. Hence his strange mis-alliance with Themistocles which would be renewed several times before it finally fractured. The two of them shared some of the same qualities, something best illustrated by that ridiculous story about the dog that he went to such pains to propagate and which I'll come to later.

We didn't stay long either and whoever set the evening up had made a piss poor job of it. There was some polite conversation with the local great men present then Xanthippus in foul humour stood up and walked out, walked all the way back to the harbour in a towering rage. All I could make out was that it had been a gathering of Persian agents and locals who favoured them and that we had been invited only to be snubbed; what game were we playing? I wished Aeschylus were there to explain the significance of the events. But there again it wasn't long before I was to find out.

Things weren't any better back by the ships: the crews hadn't followed instructions to cooperate if the cuts, bruises and sour looks were anything to go by. Xanthippus dismissed me sneering,

"Lot of use you were, Mandrocles the beautiful."

Then he stalked off to his own ship. The harmony and euphoria following Marathon hadn't lasted long! I asked after Ariston and Theodorus and was directed to a tavern: from the look of them they hadn't obeyed orders either. I noted that the only seamen drinking with us were from the two triremes crewed by men whose trierarchs and owners were democrats. We disobeyed another order and got drunk.

The last thing I can remember was singing the old Marathon favourite "The arse and ass of Kallixenos".

The next day we were confined to the ships, all of us, as a punishment. So five crews of divided hungover Athenians spent the day being growled at by officers whose mood was even worse than theirs. It was clear, even on the quay, that the Athenian navy wasn't popular. The boats were spat at and we were mocked which hardly improved matters. That night Xanthippus led out another group; I wasn't included. The rumour was they were meeting democrats to offer Athenian help in a democratic coup.

The evening couldn't have gone any better than the first one because although they got back late we could hear the cursing. Sitting alone by a small fire I watched as Lysias picked his way towards our ragged collection of shelters grouped round the Athene Nike. He looked unhappy, which was to be expected, but I got the impression that he wanted to talk, which wasn't. If he needed someone to talk politics with he was out of luck on our boat. He couldn't share anything with the crew and even had he wanted to they weren't of the social standing to discuss matters of state.

So if he was minded to talk there was only me. Not that I was sure of my social standing; Miltiades afforded me the respect due to the son of his old shield companion and often in moments of uncertainty unburdened himself to me. He knew he could trust me, and more to the point, I was of no account and would never be a threat. But the great Miltiades had most likely succumbed to the agonies of gangrene in that filthy lock up by now. So again I was a nobody.

But maybe Lysias took his lead in this, as he had in so much else, from the dead hero: he came and joined me by the flickering flames. Even so I needed to prompt him.

"Why we are here, trierarch? Aegina is Athens's enemy; they burnt the harbour at Phaleron during the great revolt, they offered earth and water to the Great King and aren't we meant to be still at war with them?"

"Don't you think that I don't ask myself the same questions every day, Mandrocles? Every day the answer slips further away."

He poked the fire with a piece of driftwood. I knew better than to speak, I was no longer the raw boy who first boarded the Athene Nike on Samos. So I waited watching the flames till he was ready.

"I don't know why we're here; I don't even know what we're after. I don't think Xanthippus knows much more. I wish General Miltiades was with us but maybe he couldn't have made any sense of it either."

The speech surprised me; it showed how uncertain and alone Lysias was. He'd been trierarch, but on Miltiades's flagship, under Miltiades's watchful eye now he depended on his own judgement. Command is lonely, that's why I've never wanted it. For me it's always been enough to watch a great man's back and faithfully carry out orders. I think Lysias felt the same; he was a brave man and a good fighter but no leader. Hence his next faltering words.

"There's nothing we have to offer here and with what authority do we speak?"

He didn't expect an answer.

"It's as if we've set out to fail. The democrats here don't trust us, they're no better than pirates who prey on our shipping. They don't want accord with us and why should they? The rest have thrown themselves into the hands of the Great King. They backed the wrong side at Marathon so they need the Persians back. That's why there's so many of them here with Metiochus."

He scratched at a knife scar across his lip that he'd picked up fighting on the right flank at Marathon.

"Are we here to sell our city? After all we went through

are we here to become Medisers and betray our city to the Persians? Is this all part of some great man's bid for power? Perhaps Hippias wasn't the only one who wanted to rule the city of the Goddess as tyrant in the name of the Great King."

I didn't say anything, just watched as he stared into the fire struggling to control some inner emotion.

Finally he said softly,

"I don't think we've heard the last of Metiochus and his Persian friends. But after how we stood together at Marathon, who would, who could betray?"

He stumbled to a halt and went back to watching the flames. He made as if to speak a couple of times but must have thought better of it. Then he scrambled to his feet and walked off towards the sea, leaving one word hanging on the night air:

"Themistocles."

The invitation from Metiochus when it finally arrived was surprising in many ways, not the least the request that I attend. According to Lysias it made no reference to the first night when Metiochus and the Persians walked out as we entered. Rather it was couched in honeyed words inviting named Athenians to a meeting, not in the house of some local man of status but in the temple complex of Aphaia, the island's jewel and site of Godhead. The implications of this were clear: if Metiochus could play the host under the same roof as Aphaia then the sentiments of the island were with him.

Now the rumours of traitors and the ambition and treachery of politicians were the talk of the camp. Xanthippus was the only great man amongst us; Themistocles was safe back in Athens. Here Xanthippus was the leader of our clandestine and ambiguous mission and however it turned out he was unlikely to come out of it looking good. From his surly manner it was apparent this had occurred to him. He'd been manipulated: if this went wrong he'd be the fall guy. And I was his immediate target.

"You're coming with me tonight and this time you'd better make yourself useful, not just stand there simpering like a Theban goat fucker."

Then something strange occurred. I was looking straight at him in the way my father had taught me. It was hard not to stare; the dome of his forehead drew your eyes. In that respect he was similar to Pericles, his son, but less touchy. Perhaps that's why he never got called onion head like his son does; or maybe it was because the comic poets back then hadn't yet realised what rich material there was to make fun of in politicians. As I stared I saw his expression change, soften would be too much to expect from a man like him. He said,

"Forgive me, Mandrocles, I should not have spoken to you like that, we fought together at Marathon and we're on the same side now."

Not all his asperity vanished for he followed up with:

"And I don't suppose you like Themistocles's little plan any more than I do. He'll no doubt be laughing himself sick in his hovel by the Hangman's Gate at what he's sent us to do."

With that he turned and set off on the long walk up to the temple complex of Aphaia. It was near dark when we arrived but I was glad there was enough light to study the temple. I've always liked these houses of the Gods, they speak to something above and beyond and yet we can touch them, feel the cool stone. The temple of Aphaia is the pride of Aegina, but like most temples it was being renovated to bring it into line with modern tastes. But you could still see the simple beauty of the pure clean lines the ancient builders had conjured into the stone.

But the temple itself wasn't our destination: I realised that when I saw I was alone and the others had disappeared into an adjoining warren of buildings booths and stalls. These were strangely deserted, devoid of drink, food, charms and temple prostitutes. Out of breath at running after them I found myself in the gloomy anteroom of a solid stone house. Xanthippus was entering the reception room and I followed him into one of the most dangerous nights of my life.

To be fair to Metiochus he didn't keep us wondering; from the start he shot his dice straight. He was sitting at the far end of the room on a raised chair with arms carved in the shape of sea serpents. Arranged on benches and stools either side of him were a collection of men, most of whom looked to be local worthies. One of them looked familiar. There were none of the customary trappings of hospitality visible. No drinks, dishes of nuts and fruit, no ewers of water to wash our hands and feet, no slaves to perform the service.

There were five of us: Xanthippus, two of his trierarchs, a man who seemed to perform the duties of a secretary but looked a killer, and me. Only three men had accompanied us as an escort. We'd been asked to travel as a small party for the purposes of secrecy. These three guards had been detained outside. My four companions had begun to mutter words of surprise and alarm. I heard the assassin secretary hiss to Xanthippus.

"We're tricked, look who's here; all of them."

I didn't know what he meant but the anxiety behind the message was crystal clear. I didn't have long to wait for clarification because after a deliberately prolonged period of silence intended to extend our discomfort, Metiochus said,

"You've guessed correctly, there'll be no wine, sweetmeats or fine words wasted on you."

Xanthippus made as if to protest but controlled himself; better to see how the land lay first. Metiochus favoured him with a chilly smile and continued.

"Neither will introductions be necessary because, of course, you've met before, haven't you?"

Looking round I realised there was nowhere for us to sit. We would have to stand like men do before their masters. The light was fading in the room, lit only by some small lights placed on small tables arranged round the seats of our hosts.

"Not that you would have expected to see us all together. Not when you sought separate and secret meetings to which you brought different though equally dishonest propositions."

Metiochus smiled again as he offered up this last sentence containing as it did every possible offence to the customs of hospitality. What the others realised as soon as they entered the room I now grasped. "All of them" had been a literal statement. They were all here: the oligarchs, democrats and Persians, all together all in on the plan. We'd been played; there had never been the possibility of a deal with one of the factions it was a set up. I was trying to think how Themistocles could have been so misled but Metiochus hadn't finished.

"But despite contempt for your pathetic low bred attempt at duplicity, my friends and I will maintain our respect for the traditional values of the host. Values which you so thoroughly traduced. We will favour you with an explanation."

There are times in life when you are so thoroughly mastered that there's no response. This was now the case with Xanthippus. Metiochus, sensing it, enjoyed the moment before delivering his explanation which was little more than the leeching out of his poisonous nature.

"Athenians. How you love treachery. You betray the trust of the Great King in your support for the Ionians. Then you betray the Ionians, next you betray your rightful leaders, then you betray the man who led you at the skirmish at Marathon: my father. Even he, Athenian to the core, betrayed his wife and King. Now you. You are here to lie and deceive your hosts on this island, both oligarchs and democrats. Even they prefer to unite than listen to you."

Xanthippus, shaking with rage, had had enough; he turned to leave.

"Stay where you are if you wish to leave alive."

I don't think it was fear that made Xanthippus hesitate, I think it was common sense. Like all guests we'd left our weapons outside in the anteroom.

"I've not come to the explanation yet, I'm sure that having walked all the way to this cold dark room you wouldn't want to miss it."

I wanted to kill the man just for that sneering delivery, and I noticed the assassin secretary reach for his missing sword.

"I see your manners are no better than your span of attention so I will be brief. Two things. First; when I saw you the other night so great was my disdain that I couldn't stand to be in the same room that you polluted and I had to leave. In so doing I failed to deliver my message. Second. Here it is. We have toyed with you on this island. You were betrayed to us before you left home. There was never any hope of an accord on this island. Here they hate Athenians as much as I do."

If he was acting it was a performance worthy of winning the prize goat at the Spring Dionysia: his face was a rictus mask of hate.

"One last thing for you to think about before you slink off home to that great rock that sits high above your poor stony land. Aegina always beats you at sea. How many triremes have you got left in that rocky harbour you're struggling to build? Forty? Forty-five? Perhaps even fifty? Yes, I thought so, and Aegina has?"

He turned to his companions then answered his own question.

"What, ninety? A hundred?"

He acknowledged the nods with a grin before his closing remarks.

"How do you feel, Athenians? Not only has your mission failed but Aegina is now an ally of the Great King. You'd better scurry back to your unfinished harbour: you'll not have it for much longer. Go while you still have your lives."

Not once during the whole performance had he deigned to glance at me and I wondered if this had been a part of his revenge.

There was no attempt to prevent us leaving. The ante-room was empty but our swords and knives were there. So were our guards, waiting nervously outside. The booths and stalls were still empty as we picked our way through them. We were defeated, unnerved and silent. No one spoke as we moved through that ghostly landscape. What was there to say? All I could think of was that I was hungry, but at least you have to be alive to be hungry. I think for the others it was worse: the humiliation and shame, particularly for Xanthippus. Whatever conclusions he'd drawn he was keeping to himself.

We'd reached the point where the track begins to slope down towards the city when it happened. It was clinical, like the way a skilled surgeon will swiftly cut an arrowhead from a man's flesh. The path forked and the shanties on either side faced right on to it making it darker. We never saw them.

It was like men cutting out a goat from the herd for sacrifice. They had no interest in the others; they were herded like a flock downhill by about twenty assailants. They probably didn't get time to notice I wasn't with them. I think even in that moment of terror I knew they weren't in any danger.

For me the path downhill was blocked by three burly men; they hadn't even bothered to wear hoods, must have known there'd be no one to identify them when it was done.

As they were forcing me back against one of the sheds I understood this was Metiochus's reckoning.

He was too high-born to involve himself: this way I got shame and death. Fear gives you wings, I slipped round the side of the shed evading their hands into the mouth of a foul dark alley. I ran, screaming for help. Me, I'd fought next to Miltiades at Marathon; now there was just terror, never occurred to reach for my knife or fight, just squeal and run; it's all about context.

I ran, slipping and sliding over rough ground through the shit and refuse littering the earthen track. I didn't know where; I ran stumbling blindly. I'd no plan, I just wanted to live; I'd have let Metiochus do whatever he'd wanted to me if I'd known this would happen. I think I was screaming his name when they caught me like they were always going to do.

They knew the ground; one had taken a different path and came out in front. I saw him, massive and threatening, blocking the way. Out of instinct, nothing else, I backed against a wall as they closed on me. Whatever they say about last thoughts isn't true. I didn't think of my mother, Elpinice or Lyra. I'd have given any of them to these men if it saved my life.

I just wanted to live, to see another day. So I blubbed and begged but saw in their eyes there'd be no negotiation – just death. Perhaps that made it easier, it certainly made it simpler. I fumbled for my knife, felt it slip from my sweaty palm. They crushed me back into the wall; I smelt their reeking breath, felt their callous hands. Then I felt the bronze knifepoint against my throat and my bladder emptied.

Chapter Five

My face was splashed by gouts of blood but there was no pain. The man with the knife stumbled, grabbed at my shoulder for support, then his legs gave way and he slipped to the ground fumbling at me weakly as he went, leaving a trail of blood on my tunic to mark his passing. Right where he'd been close up by my face, there was another man looking no better disposed towards me. Seemed I must be already dead of the wound and this was a frightening antechamber of Hades where you were assessed for punishment.

"Don't think that I like you any better than he did, boy. Just thank whatever daemon watches over you."

His hood was pushed back exposing his face; it was vaguely familiar but in my dazed state I couldn't place from where. Behind him, on the ground, was another man, deader than my most proximate assailant who was making the kind of whooshing noise a squid does after it's been lying on a dry deck for a few minutes. My interlocutor turned the body with his foot and the whooshing rose a pitch. Then he picked up my dagger and put it in my hand. I followed all this in a dream like it was happening to someone else.

He closed my hand round the knife handle then closed his own massive hand over that. I remembered where I'd seen him before but before I could make sense of any of this he grasped my wrist with his other hand. Then with a strong jerk he pulled my hand and the blade down into the upturned stomach of the man still wheezing for air. With the full force of his strength behind it, my hand and the blade slipped in easily. I tried to withdraw but he held fast and began to stir my hand round inside like he was checking the consistency of oatmeal porridge. I think I was sick and maybe blacked out momentarily because the next thing I remember was him shaking my bloodied hand in front of my face, saying,

"There that looks better, the hand of a hero fighting against odds."

The whooshing noise came to an end with a sigh that sounded almost peaceful – not that I looked down to check.

"Just the finishing touches, hold him tight."

Two men who I hadn't registered grabbed me and forced me back against the shed wall and I began to believe this was a punishment of the Gods; but theological reflection was pushed out of my mind by memory. Must have shown on my face because he leered at me saying,

"Wondered how long it'd take you to place me."

I noticed he had my dagger in his hand and was holding it close to my face. I gasped out.

"You were with ..."

But he made the first cut, slicing through my cheek between my jaw and left ear. So quick and clinical it just felt cold. I tried to bring my hands up to my face but they were held too tight. There was a slight shift in his balance and he gashed me from shoulder to forearm. So I was going to die after all.

"Now this next bit's going to hurt a bit more."

I didn't see it coming. He headbutted me and I felt my nose splinter and blood flow down over my lips. All I could think was why do this to me? It's not fair.

"Everything has to end, boy, even for you."

I felt something hard smash into my lower ribs, heard them crack, knocking all the breath out of my lungs. The men released me and I began to slide to the ground. He grabbed me by one hand beneath the chin and held me upright, blocking my windpipe.

"No sleeping now, Mandrocles: if you can't walk you're no use to us. So make your choice. Stand up or die gasping for breath like your friend down there."

I didn't know what was happening, I think I was crying but I got enough force into my legs to keep me upright.

"Good lad; see, it gets better when you cooperate."

He turned back to his henchmen. There were more than two of them. How had I missed them?

"He doesn't look so beautiful now lads, does he? Be no more jobs for you as a catamite."

They laughed the way men will laugh at cruelty. I knew he'd broken more than just my body.

"Now listen carefully, you little shit, because I'm going to explain this and once I've finished you'd better start running."

I knew who he was: one of the democrats. Why would a democrat want to kill me?

"You must be wondering why after I'd chased you so hard with my two mates I killed them and not you."

He was right, I was wondering that, amongst other things.

"Well, when Metiochus said he wanted you killed on the way home I volunteered to join the men he detailed to do it. I could see this puzzled him so I told him it was to show that when it came to killing Athenians, the Persians could trust all the factions on this island."

He took a bit of time out to enjoy my reaction, then,

"And under normal circumstances that'd be true. But these aren't normal times: war's coming and when it does our Persian friends might not have the political subtlety to distinguish between Athenian democrats and those from Aegina. So I prefer to back both wrestlers in this particular bout. That's why I did you this favour, see?"

I didn't. It must have been obvious.

"Hades boy, how dim are you? Your little expedition here was about much more than looking for support. In fact it wasn't about looking for support at all. So you tell your master."

I was confused and asked,

"Xanthippus?"

This time he laughed with genuine amusement while his men looked confused.

"I'm surprised you've lasted as long as you have, you witless idiot. Of course not Xanthippus. He's probably only just begun to work out what I'm telling you. I mean the man who's played you all and us. Fucking Themistocles. When you get back you go tell him what happened to you tonight."

To my amazement he doubled up laughing and it took a few moments before he could carry on.

"You tell Themistocles that once we finish our war with Athens there may well be men here who will be prepared to fight the Persians alongside them, providing we get the right terms."

"Who shall I say sent the message?"

"You shan't; he'll know. Oh I won't pretend I didn't enjoy messing you up. But it was necessary. If you'd come back unscathed who'd believe you'd killed those men by yourself? Now I hope you can move because you're going to stumble off down the hill. After a while you'll come to the track where, if they have any balls, you should find some of your mates heading up to rescue you."

I must have just stood looking at him, too stunned to respond, because he turned me round towards the slope and gave me a sharp push, shouting,

"Go on, get going or we'll give you some more scars to take back with you."

That was enough for me: I turned and legged it down as fast as I could but had to stop and slow to a crawl because of the pain from my ribs. If you've rowed on a trireme you'll know what I'm talking about, I doubt there's any rower on a war ship that hasn't had his ribs cracked a few times. It's not just the agony, it's the lack of breath. I turned and looked back up but they'd gone. Aegina's a dark and frightening place and I made a mental note never to come back until we'd crushed them and taken their fleet.

I was lucky on two counts: I didn't have too far to stumble and my mates did have the balls to try and find me. To my surprise they were led by Xanthippus, sword in hand. I was almost touched.

"Hades Mandrocles, what have they done to you? You're covered in enough blood to have been killed three times over."

By now I'd recovered my wits sufficiently to remember my script.

"Most of it's not mine."

"We feared you were dead."

He even looked like he meant it. Speaking with broken ribs, smashed nose and flaps of your cheek hanging loose isn't easy so I kept it short.

"If you really want the answer you'll find a couple of bodies up there, you can send them the cleaning bill."

Writing this after all these years it sounds so glib. It's certainly not the language that those who suffer in Aeschylus plays chant out to the masses packed into the Agora. But it was an act: there are things that befall you in life you never recover from. The body recovers but not the inner daemon, the bit that's only you and no one else.

You keep going, keep living but there's less happiness, less confidence and less trust in the world and its occupants. That night on Aegina was one of those things and I don't think I ever fully recovered. Immediately after the world seemed darker, more anxious and for months after I woke every morning with a dry mouth and fear of what the day would bring. Fear that only abated in the evening with the third cup of wine.

I disappeared inside myself, closed myself off from other people. Maybe if they hadn't done what they did to me I'd have been able to respond to Lyra properly when she tried to say those private things when I got back to Athens. Maybe if I hadn't been taken apart on that shitty little island I could have ... if only ...

I couldn't write after that: it brought back something best kept buried. Now after three days I'll try to scratch down some more. They helped me back to the ships and treated my wounds. Xanthippus paid for the best surgeon he could find, a Persian strangely enough. He straightened my nose and kept it that way with a couple of small splints which hurt and irritated for days. Sewed up the flaps of my cheek, telling me I'd always have the scar. He just laughed when he examined the ribs.

"You're lucky they're not broken, just cracked, so no danger of puncturing the lungs and dying painfully of the complications."

I wasn't laughing, just asked him,

"So what can you do about them?"

He found this even funnier.

"Nothing. I can do nothing; they will hurt for weeks, every time you move there will be pain. Even when you don't move and the worst will be when you move in your sleep."

He must have seen from my expression that he was enjoying himself too much, and he moderated his tone.

"But then after some weeks you will think something is

missing, and it will be because the pain is less. Now I will give you something that will take away the agony and send you into a strange dream-filled sleep."

He mixed a potion and watched while I drank it then helped me to find the least painful position to lie down on the camp cot Xanthippus had provided for me. All this time he'd been silently mocking me as if he knew the real cause of my wounds. Before he left he stooped over me and said softly,

"I have a message from the man who did this to you. Your life is still in danger; your enemy knows you are not dead. You must get off this island before it's too late."

He walked away but then turned back and I think began to say something about remembering my message but I can't be sure because already the potion was taking me off to very strange lands.

I woke late next day and wished I hadn't; my head ached, my mouth was dry and that was about the best of it. It took some time for my eyes to focus but when they finally settled down it was to a scene of great activity: we were leaving, it seemed, and quickly.

"Oh, so you've deigned to wake up at last?"

Theodorus handed me a cup of wine.

"Drink this then get up, they've rigged a seat for you on deck. Things are getting too hot for us here, we sail in one hour."

Less than an hour, as it turned out: an angry crowd gathered on the docks, its numbers growing larger by the second. They cursed and jeered us; as more arrived they became confident enough to begin to throw things. It was clear that before long they'd rush us and we weren't going to wait for that to happen.

Ariston blew his whistle, there was a burst of activity and I found myself standing groggily on the quayside watching as the rowers, bottom tier first, filed onto the Athene Nike.

As they passed, some of the long established crew members touched me for luck. It was some time since that had happened; the story about how I'd survived the previous night must have been circulating.

The seat they rigged was by the trierarch's chair where an agitated Lysias sat fidgeting. I knew there were things he wanted to get off his chest and wasn't surprised that after we'd pulled clear of the harbour mouth and the rowers settled to a steady stroke, he said,

"I'll never come back here unless it's to burn the city and fleet and scatter the ashes."

He paused as if he'd said too much and sat there silent, choking on his anger. I'd spent too long with the General and Themistocles to imagine that he'd stay silent. Men get to a point where they have to let all the rage and bile spill out, it's just a case of when. So I sat patiently waiting; it helped take my mind off the pain in my ribs. I wasn't surprised when a few moments later,

"Now we're sent off before the others because we're Themistocles's men. Athene Nike, the ship with the best fighting record in the whole Athenian fleet, driven home in disgrace. Us a disgrace? The men on this ship fought their way through the Persian fleet to get to Athens then stood in the front line at Marathon. And now fucking Bubblehead Xanthippus ..."

He realised his voice was rising in pitch and that this was not the way a trierarch should behave in front of his crew. I knew that if I said anything, even one word, he'd clam up for good so I just sat; eyes averted, staring out to sea. I didn't have to occupy myself with the placid waters for long.

"I don't know, maybe that's unfair. Xanthippus thinks we were sent on a mission designed to fail. But what's the point in that? Why send us out here to an island we'll soon be at war with just to be humiliated? Xanthippus believes Themistocles wanted him out here to get him out of the way: he thinks that him being humiliated on Aegina was part of the plan. So now he's angry, he wants revenge. Why would Themistocles want that? Xanthippus could re-unite the whole Alkmaionid clan."

He paused again then mumbled,

"I don't know, it's beyond me."

I knew there'd be no more. Lysias wasn't a great thinker, a good companion or a particularly skilful trierarch, but now looking back I'm inclined to think that he was a better man than he was ever given credit for.

It's only a short trip from Aegina to Athens and before long we sailed into the rocky bay that was beginning to transform itself into the great harbour of Piraeus. Standing on the only completed scrap of harbour wall waiting for us was Themistocles. Next to him was the year's named Archon with, behind him, armed men. Next to me Lysias muttered,

"So it begins."

As we disembarked, apart from a cursory nod towards Lysias the welcoming party ignored us. Themistocles blanked me when, remembering my message, I tried to make eye contact. He was wearing the expression he'd worn at Marathon; his killing face. It was directed beyond us out to sea where in the distance the ships of Xanthippus's squadron were bobbing on the water.

Chapter Six

My plans to stay with Ariston changed the moment we stepped ashore. Aeschylus was there waiting. He was Themistocles man, in so far as a free thinking poet can be said to be anyone's man. I'd assumed that he was there with the official welcome party but I was wrong: he had reasons of his own.

"If it's true that life is sweet to him who suffers grief then your life must be steeped in honey, Mandrocles."

Typical of Aeschylus to open our first conversation since my anger at him over Miltiades's death with a quote, probably from a work currently being written. I didn't respond, I hadn't forgiven him.

"Come on, you can't afford to cut yourself off from the few remaining friends you have. I've come to offer you a temporary home. It's close by, which from the look of you must be its main attraction."

He didn't wait for an answer: just bent down, picked up my gear and walked off. I hesitated a moment then hobbled after him. He was right, it wasn't far, but far enough because by the time he walked into his brother's bar my ribs were agony.

"I've moved in here, hadn't the heart to stay on the family

farm so I help out here when the muse deserts me. It's changed a bit since you last saw it. Look."

He pointed to a staircase of unseasoned mountain pine with sap oozing from its crevices.

"Once it dries out and twists into position it should last forever."

I followed him gingerly up the steps to a newly built first floor with a balcony looking down over the harbour. It smelt of the sea, I liked that and the view over the waters. This was my first room in Piraeus and it's only a stone's throw from where I'm sitting now as I write this.

He pointed to the bare ceiling, chanting,

"Come! Let someone work out in the ceiling a lesbian moulding in triangular rhythms."

"And what's that from?"

He'd drawn me back into life, almost made me smile.

"Just a fragment from an idea I'm thinking over about the chamber where the Danaids killed their husbands, long way from being worked out but seemed appropriate."

He pointed to a chair and I sat while he poured two beakers of wine from a jug on the table. He sat on the cot, which was the only other piece of furniture. Sparse but the largest and best lit room I'd ever had. We sat in silence drinking and after a while I asked,

"What's Themistocles up to down there?"

"He's waiting for Xanthippus."

"Why?"

"To demand that the Archon insists that he answer to certain charges levelled against him by true citizens of the Polis."

"What charges?"

"Charges that he led an expedition to an enemy Polis in order to betray the interests of the city of the Goddess."

"Fuck off Aeschylus: everyone knows the expedition was

Themistocles's idea. What do you think the Athene Nike was doing there?"

"I think it was there because Themistocles sent it to keep an eye on the men who would betray the Demos and the Polis."

"Don't be stupid: Lysias and I were there. We know what went on."

"And that's why you will both end up testifying before the Areopagus that it was only Themistocles's prescience in rooting out the treachery that prevented the city of the Goddess from being sold to the enemy. I'm sure you will both remember having seen agents of the Great King on Aegina."

I couldn't think of anything to counter this. He was of course right: the whole thing was a set up. But I wasn't prepared for what he said next.

"I suppose you're unaware that while the Athene Nike was away, we declared war on Aegina."

This was too much. I opened up my lungs to shout at him but with the first sound doubled up in pain. The pain intensified and I tried to sit back up and find a position where the agony was less acute; as the tortured gasps wheezed out of my chest and tears of pain streaked down my cheeks, Aeschylus started to laugh.

"Gods, I'd forgotten how much I missed you, Mandrocles; it's like having my own personal chorus of rustic idiots in the Satyr plays. Without you and Cynegeiros life was even bleaker than the Gods intend for us. Here get your breath drink this."

I did what he said. The truth was I'd missed him too, in spite of what had been done to my master. We finished the jug then he helped me onto the cot and left me alone. I fell asleep to the murmur of voices but whether they were from the harbour or the bar downstairs I couldn't tell.

I woke next morning to a room full of light and life felt

a little better, but I still hadn't much idea what I was meant to do. I sat up and slowly got out of bed as painlessly as possible and was searching for the pot to piss in when Aeschylus breezed into the room. Framed in the bright sunlight streaming in through the window, I could see that the recent years hadn't been kind to him either. His face bore not only the scars from Marathon but also a series of lines grooving their way down from the sides of his nose towards the edges of his mouth. The jet back hair now held streaks of grey and showed signs of receding. I've noticed that men with hair of that particular blackness seem to lose it early. I could see then the first sign of the man that you will recognise from the cheap busts of him for sale in every market place, fashioned during the fame of his later years.

"You look even worse in daylight, Mandrocles, and you stink. Make yourself look as good as you can and have a wash. We're going out."

He must have seen the look on my face because he added,

"Don't worry, you won't have to walk. I've hired a cart."

"Where, where are we going?"

"It wouldn't be a surprise if I told. Get yourself ready then meet me outside."

I did what I could then staggered down the stairs. Outside there was a small trap attached to something that looked like the cross between an ass and a giant Molassian hunting dog. Aeschylus helped me into it then handed me a cup of warm spiced wine and a honey cake. I was touched that he'd remembered my love of those.

"These should help to take your mind from the jolting of the cart."

"Tell me, where are we going?"

"No, but you don't need to worry, it's not to see Themistocles."

As we drew closer to Athens I realised we were heading

for the Hangman's Gate into the Ceramicus where Themistocles chose to live close to the heart of the Demos. We
passed through the gate and didn't stop at the great man's
house. By now I knew where we must be going and my
heart was pounding. I hadn't said goodbye and now I was
back: disfigured and smelling rank. Aeschylus helped me
down from the cart and hammered at the studded door. A
panel opened, revealing the boxer's face of Demetrius. Time
hadn't improved him: since I'd last seen him he'd acquired a
new scar across his mouth and lost a couple of teeth. Seeing
me seemed to cheer him up though.

"Well, what's happened to you? Not such a pretty boy
now are you?"

I knew it was only rough banter and not ill-meant but
it hurt. My confidence was already shot through, would
she still want me? I didn't have long to wonder: Aeschylus
slipped him a coin, the gate opened and we walked through.
It was just as it always was, a neatly swept courtyard with
a line of doors like stables at the far end where sitting on a
shaded veranda a group of girls were playing dice.

"Go on, Mandrocles; she's not going to bite."

I wasn't so sure and was about to ask him to wait with
the cart when I saw him walking back out through the door
which Demetrius slammed shut behind him. Lyra left the
dice players and floated off the veranda towards me, her smile
made me want to break down and blurt out all the things that
had torn me apart since I last saw her. I reminded myself that
she was a flute girl and the smile went with the trade.

She kissed me gently on the lips then took my hand and
wordlessly led me through the door and into her quarters.
Pushing the door closed with a practised back flick of her
heel the noise from the dice players receded and we were on
our own. It was then that I discovered the real reason for my
visit. She pointed to a small table by the window.

"There, recognise that?"

I did: it was the drinking cup that Metiochus had given me back in the Chersonese before we had to make a run for Athens. The one he had given me in his attempt at seduction. Fitting that it had turned up again after he'd tried and failed a second time, this time to kill me.

"Where did you get that?"

For a moment I hoped that Elpinice had sent it and that she and Cimon were somewhere I could join them.

"It was sent by a great man."

She was being playful, seeing this as a joke.

"Who? Which great man?"

"You should have asked your friend before he left; he delivered it a couple of days ago."

Then I understood what all this was about, all this pretence at friendship, it was to show me who owned me: whose man I was whether I liked it or not. Themistocles was reminding me through the people I loved that I was his dog. Aeschylus was a false friend, a panderer and she – well, she was the whore the world took her for.

I told her that and a lot more, struggling to get the words out through the pain in my ribs and anger in my heart. I looked round at the room: the whore's workplace. Saw she'd had a bath filled with scented and oiled water, saw the jug of wine with the two lovers' cups by the bed. The Gods do this to drive us from our wits. Offer you something you crave then turn it to shit before your eyes. That's how they make us mad.

Everything that I could see in that room I wanted so much, yet all of it was false and tainted. I don't know how long I raged at her. Let her have all the spleen and hatred I felt for the world. It wasn't all aimed at her, but she was there and they weren't so she got it. Stood and took it, said nothing. Said nothing, stood there arms by her sides, tears slipping down her cheeks. Stood there with a look of surprise on her face. Not anger, just surprise, hurt surprise.

For a moment I thought maybe I'd got it wrong. I wanted to have got it wrong but I'd gone too far: poured it all out, said things that couldn't be unsaid. Hurt surprise: but then whores are the best actresses there are: every minute of their lives is an act. So I carried on – couldn't stop – and she stood and listened, arms by her sides. Stood and listened with the hair that she'd let down as we entered that room falling almost to her waist. Stood and said nothing with tears on her cheeks. Hurt surprise.

"You pornoi bitch."

I stumbled out of the room across the yard to the gate. The dice players had been listening; they backed off as I came out. Demetrius opened the gate; there was no jibe or leer this time. Just a look of surprise and something that resembled pity. The door slammed behind me and I knew I'd cut myself off from everyone who mattered to me. It had all happened so quickly – I'd gone from Mandrocles the Beautiful, hero of Marathon to Mandrocles the disfigured friendless nobody. Worse, I was Xenos, a foreigner in a town where foreigners without friends or a particular skill weren't welcome. I wanted to go back: try and start over again, but I couldn't. I couldn't.

I shambled around the Ceramicus for a time; even the pornoi avoided me. I was tired, heartsick and sore so lurched into the dingiest, empty bar I could see. I found a shelf sticking out from the wall in the corner, pulled up a rough stool and ordered wine. Wine uncut: the madman's ostraka and the quickest route to oblivion. The wine was vinegar, the place stank and my arm stuck to the filthy shelf but I was beyond caring. I poured the wine down as fast as I could; I think I hoped it might send me into a sleep from which I'd never wake.

But even here I was out of luck. As I was vomiting back up the first foul jugfull, a gang of men, sailors and drunk by the sound of them, staggered in. Not only drunk but angry, sounding like they were after someone's blood. I slunk back as far as I could into the shadows of my corner: I'd recognised one of them. Eubulus: Megacles's man. Didn't take me long to work out who his companions were. Their anger gave them away. They were from Xanthippus's trireme fresh back from Aegina and their grievance was legitimate.

They'd been detained in Piraeus whilst Themistocles had arraigned Xanthippus for crimes against the Polis. But it wasn't Themistocles who was top of their list for vengeance. As I listened, I realised what danger I was in. Their speech may have been slurred but the meaning was crystal clear.

"You fucking expect it from politicians but not from men who sail with you. Fucking Athene Nike, never trusted those bastards."

I couldn't recognise who was speaking but no one disagreed and he ploughed on.

"Look at who's commanded her first Mil-fucking-tiades, the pirate and now Themistocles, that slippery bastard who would rather walk fifteen miles to tell a lie than speak one word of truth to the man sitting next to him."

He paused to empty his cup, which he then slammed down onto the table. It smashed; all his mates laughed and he shouted at the misshapen lump tending the bar before getting to the point of his peroration.

"So go on then, tell, tell me what type of man chooses to sail under shits like them? Yeah, you know don't yer mates, you know. Cos there's no one who could get a berth on a decent barky who'd sail with them; am I right?"

From the noise that followed it was pretty clear that he was right.

"Men who'd betray anyone, men who betrayed us on

Aegina then slunk away early to get back with the dirty news to their new master, who's the same bastard as stitched up their old master."

He paused to shout again at the barkeep.

"Hurry up with that cup or we'll drown you in a jar of the filthy piss you sell as wine."

His mates liked this and urged him on.

"We've all seen 'em swaggering round with their noses in the air like they're better than the rest of us. Like they're the only real seamen. They fought in the revolt, they were in the front line of Marathon. If I hear that liar Themistocles talking about Marathon any more I'll stop believing it happened even though I was there meself."

This got the best laugh of the night.

"So it's time we settled with them boys, time we brought them down. Time we got revenge for our mate Eubulus. Start with that swaggering bully Theodorus, see how a smashed jaw and broken nose look on him when they find his body in the Eridanos one morning."

He turned to shout at the barkeep but he was already on his way. This is when my day got even worse. On his way with the new cup he stopped off at my corner to collect the empty jug. The seamen watching became aware of my presence and their spokesman said in a friendly tone,

"Let's ask our mate over there if he agrees with us. Hey mate what'd you ..."

He never got any further: I heard Eubulus say,

"Hang on mates: you know who that is, don't you?"

Chapter Seven

The game was up, I'd cast the last die and landed the dead man's throw. The room went silent: I saw the greasy innkeeper slink out of his filthy booth. The orator was the first to reach me; I sat cowering, which it seemed was now my only role in life's tragedy.

"Well, well, look who we've got here mates; the bum boy Xanthippus took along as bait. Looks like life's not turning out too well for you, Mandrocles the fucked up."

He laughed so hard at this he almost choked. Now they were all crowding round hemming me into the dirty corner. I hadn't the room to stand up even if I'd wanted to. In my state I couldn't resist. Scared as I was, a part of me was saying, "Why not let them: get it over quickly, then at least the peace of oblivion." Wasn't only me thinking that; someone said,

"No need to wait for Theodorus, let's start with him. Won't take us long, then dump his body in the great sewer."

I didn't even bother to object, I was finished whatever happened so just prayed they'd be quick.

"Don't let the wine run off with your wits, mates."

The speaker was Eubulus. Why was I always running into him? It took him some time to divert their attention from killing me but he got there eventually, otherwise this tale would have ended in the filthy squalor of that bar. The world wouldn't have been changed much but you'd have been deprived of my story, reader, and without it you'd have never heard the truth about what really happened back then. The true story of how the Athens you're so proud of came to be built.

"I don't think we'll get much thanks for killing him before our masters have a chance to question him. A chance to find out what went on with Themistocles before we landed."

Even I could see the sense in this once he'd spelt it out, and so could they. It was a tight run thing though. Pulling drunken men back from the verge of killing is no easy task and I've seen it fail too many times. They pushed a none-too-clean hood down over my head and marched me out of the bar. I don't know how long we walked; it felt like hours and with every step the pain in my ribs got worse. They didn't handle me gently.

Eventually, after an eternity of stumbling, I felt a better constructed path under my feet as we struck upwards on a steep gradient. If you've ever had your ribs cracked badly enough you'll know what it's like having to walk up a steep path at an uncomfortably quick pace, even without a greasy hood pulled down over your face. Then we stopped.

I heard someone hammering at a door, and from some-where inside a voice demanded to know who we were. I heard it swing back on creaking hinges and we moved for-wards. I lost track of time then, we were left to wait, in a courtyard I think from the smell of blossom. The sailors weren't so confident now; the walk had sweated some of the drink out of them. I think they were beginning to wonder if what had seemed a good idea in the tavern had really been such a smart move.

Then everything changed. I could tell that they were in

the presence of someone they feared. As soon as he spoke I knew where we were.

"Let the eagle see the rabbit."

There was no response to this.

"Take his hood off, idiots."

It was twilight but it still took some time for my eyes to focus in the light – but when they did I found myself staring into the face of Xanthippus. He offered me a sad and strangely sympathetic smile.

"I'm sorry you've been handled this way, Mandrocles, seems to happen every time I see you. Accept the apologies of my house."

He turned to the sailors.

"This man fought at Marathon, he won his current hurts under my orders. Whatever Themistocles brought down on us was none of his doing. Consider yourselves fortunate you didn't serve him worse."

A retainer tossed a purse of coin to Eubulus and they shambled out, touching their foreheads in deference, leaving me alone with Xanthippus. He put out an arm to help me and thus linked we walked slowly into a room where I presume he received his clients. A slave helped me onto a finely carved chair with arms inlaid in ivory while another handed me a wine cup. I recognised the cup's provenance: Wild Goat style; delicate, ancient and rare. My father had some which had been handed down by his grandfather. I turned it in my hands, examining it carefully; it was a fellow refugee. Xanthippus noticed and laughed.

"What, Mandrocles, did you not consider I might be a man of taste who could appreciate things fashioned far from Attica?"

Strange how something so trivial can transform mood; a simple exchange about a cup altered my perception of Xanthippus and, I think his of me. No, I can't explain it any further, reader, but you know what I mean: something similar must have happened to you.

I sipped the wine; the mix was delicate and honeyed. For a moment we sat in silence: me sipping wine and trying to regain a measure of what old Pythagoras used to call equilibrium; as for Xanthippus? Well, I think he was considering what the basis of his relationship with me was to be.

He was a crueller, harsher man than his modernising son, the onion headed Pericles, but easier to understand and predict. We spent our lives alternating between being on opposing and then the same side but in spite of that I found it easy to get close to him in a way I never could with his, admittedly greater, son. Silence is, however, only temporary.

"I'm sorry for the way you were brought here, Mandrocles, but not sorry that you are here. I have a use for you."

He must have seen the look in my eyes.

"No, I give you my word; this time you'll come to no harm."

I must have looked unconvinced.

"Neither will I make you perform a task injurious to those you currently serve."

He clapped his hands and two slaves entered the room, one carrying another less fine cup.

"But now we will have your hurts dressed before showing you your bed; drink from that cup, it will help you sleep."

They led me off; I was in a daze but knew I needed sleep. As we left the room he added,

"Tomorrow I'll tell you about the task: I think it's one you will like."

Minutes later I was still trying to make sense of that as I fell into a pleasantly drug induced sleep.

I don't know what they'd put in the drink but it worked:

when I woke next day, the morning was half gone. It worked another way too. My body still ached, I felt bereft and lost but I realised I didn't want to die. I got up and wandered out of the small sleeping cell to try to get some bearings: I didn't want to blunder into the women's quarters and be expelled with a beating. I got no further than a few paces when a slave, obviously instructed to watch for me, escorted me to the andron.

The house of Xanthippus was elegant, light and airy, very different from most. The statues were few but exquisite; the man had an unexpected discernment and love for the modern ideas of beauty. It was clear where Pericles, with his fondness for sculptors and artists, inherited his tastes. Curiously there was no sign of the faithful hound that Xanthippus presented as a legend in the later wars. Why do I make so much of this, reader?

Because in those early days of the great changes consequent upon the rise of the Demos, leaders of men had to change ahead of the times. They had to begin to consider the opinions of those whom they previously instructed or employed. They had to grow a public face acceptable to the new force. In those early days few either tried or, if they did, succeeded. Themistocles was the best: you could almost believe he was born for the role but Xanthippus in a more subtle way wasn't too far behind. He would of course deny this, but in his manufactured tale of the faithful hound you can see the true genius of the politician.

Xanthippus was in the andron concluding business with the last on his list of clients.

"Good to see you looking better than you did last night, Mandrocles."

He rose; this signified the meeting was at an end and his client, who looked like a wealthy peasant farmer in his best festival robes, gushed out a few rapid sentences of thanks and praise then backed out practising a strange bobbing and bowing movement.

"You slept longer than I anticipated, the draught must have been strong. I have business to attend in the Agora but I have a task for you. Take this message to a house you will find at the end of a lane if you take the left fork at the crossroads of the hekaton just below the great ramp. Go and eat in the kitchens before you leave. Oh, and Mandrocles, I will require a full account of what you find in that house."

Like his client, I was dismissed.

Finding a house for the first time in Athens isn't easy. The city works on the basis that if you don't know the house-holder well enough to know his house already then you have no business there. The city's littered with hekatons, heroons and shrines and most of them look the same. It took me several false turns before I ended up in front of a house that more or less fitted the description I'd been given. They should give the streets numbers or even names; it would save a lot of time. All Athenian houses look poor from the street, everything is focussed on the inside, but it didn't take long to figure out this one had genuinely hit hard times.

The door opened after I'd hammered on it long enough to scuff my knuckles and then only by a couple of inches. A voice – I couldn't see a face – said,

"The master's out."

"Open the door and I'll come in and wait."

"We don't open to any we don't know."

"You'll open for me. I come on the orders of Xanthippus, son of Ariphron Strategos of the –"

The door started to close and would have done so but for a woman's voice inside shouting: a voice I recognised.

"Mandrocles, Mandrocles, is it you?"

The door opened; fully this time, and I found myself face

to face with Elpinice. I don't know which of us was more surprised. Her, probably; I looked different last time she set eyes on me. Then I was inside and the ancient crone door-keeper dispatched to her quarters. I won't record those first minutes, it was kept close then and it's kept close now.

She escorted me to the andron, or what passed for an andron in that cramped dwelling. No other lady of noble birth in Athens would have done that. But then Lady Elpin-ice wasn't like the others and we had history. I sat on a shabby chair, my ribs aching from the recent pressure.

"Cimon won't be back before dusk, he's hunting beyond Lykabetos. Yaya will stay in her room and sleep so we are alone."

We had so much to say but didn't know how to begin. I could feel myself shaking. Then she said,

"I'm to be married."

Just that. I waited as if it was a joke that she'd soon admit and laugh. But she didn't; she cried and I didn't know what to say. Then it all spilled out.

"Married to Callias, a rich man. Not a bad man like they insinuate to slur us further. Not a man who's bought me to further slake his lusts now my brother's enjoyed his fill, as the scandal sheets say."

It was said with such bitter sadness that despite my fury, I too wanted to weep. I'd heard the slanders about the illicit relationship. About the way that Cimon, grown feral on strong drink, and his promiscuous sister copulated not caring which of the servants saw them. Typical of the lies that spread in a free city where the Demos enjoys undue license. But a particularly cruel lie.

She was intact, I know it.

There were other lies spread as well. I'm sure you will have heard them, maybe even enjoyed them. Like the story of the painter Polygnotus: how he introduced the face of Elpinice into the portrait of the Trojan women he painted for the Peisianacteum in return for sexual favours. Only someone who didn't know the man or the lady could believe such lies and only a liar cursed by the Gods would tell the story.

Even her most twisted enemies admitted she was a strong woman but that afternoon she sat and wept for hours. But behind the tears was the strength. Strength and courage to equal any possessed by those who stood in the front line at Marathon.

"Because of what we feel for each other even though neither of us dare speak it and so that you will understand, Mandrocles, I will tell you why this marriage has to be."

She dried her eyes, pushed back her long hair which had earlier come undone and fallen to her waist, and told me a tale of sacrifice and heroism. Told it like a Spartan would: few words, no emotion.

"My father's enemies did more than just bring him down. They ruined the family, killed off any chance of greatness for Cimon while he was still a boy. A fine of fifty talents and the confiscation of the estates reduced us to this."

She indicated the small shabby room.

"We have only one thing left to sell: me. I can bring no dowry so the marriage brings us shame. Callias is a shrewd investor but one prepared to gamble: he pays the debt and marries into an ancient and noble family. One that, freed of debt, may rise again. That's all there is."

She paused a moment, considering her next words carefully.

"Except perhaps that I think he might have been encouraged in this by someone playing an even deeper game."

"But how?"

"No, no questions my love, that is what happened: there is no more to say."

I couldn't resist one last try.

"But married to such a man?"

"Do you suppose an Athenian woman, particularly of my pedigree, has any choice? If father was alive I would have still been married off."

"Yes, but to someone of higher ..."

"Callias works hard, his money frees the family. This is my role in the struggle. There is no more to say."

She was right, there wasn't. We sat in the uncomfortable room for a while in companionable silence until she said,

"The house will be empty for some hours yet; we will move to a room of greater comfort and I'll redress your hurts while you tell how these last months have treated you. No better than they have me, I suspect."

She stood, helped me up and walked me to a chamber deeper in the house near to where crone Yaya had gone.

"We have never had time like this before, have we? Although I know it is something you always wanted. And be sure there will never be a time like this again." She took my hand and led me through the ill-fitting door.

Some time later I was roused by the barking of dogs. I must have slept; there was no sign of Elpinice. Perhaps it was all a dream. I heard voices outside, one that I recognised although the timbre was now much deeper. I left the chamber rapidly and hurried down the darkening corridor to the andron. Inside, spinning goat's wool and wearing the most traditional peplos with shawl and veil, was a young Athenian matron. Elpinice. She gestured for me to sit. Down the corridor there was the sound of knocking at the door.

A short while later we heard it open and the sound of voices moving towards us. Two men only, from the sound of it. Then the door frame was filled by a well-muscled youth of about the age I'd been when his father rescued me from the life of a farmer on Samos. He was streaked with sweat and dirt from the hunt; long shaggy hair framed his face which, despite the covering of wispy hair, was instantly recognisable. Cimon!

I hadn't managed to fully get up from the chair before he was on me, embracing me, re-breaking my bones. I can't remember what either of us said; it doesn't matter. But what I do remember is the lightening jolt at what I saw standing in the doorway when I lifted my head and looked beyond his shoulder.

Pugnacious, bull necked and grinning: Themistocles.

Chapter Eight

My father used to teach me that the stars turn and spin; he picked this up from some cracked philosopher at the court of Polycrates. Well for a moment everything stopped, stars included.

"Brother, Lord Themistocles, now you are returned I can abandon my obligation of guest host and return to a modest occupation more fitting to my station."

She said it straight-faced and it flummoxed all three of us; none of us believed it was a genuine expression of her thoughts but it was said with such icy rectitude that we couldn't smirk either. She rose and left with her distaff, head bowed in an attitude of meek respect. Looking back now, I recognise it for the stroke of tactical genius it was. In one simple sentence she had thrown me and Themistocles into the same boat. I wished she'd been there when I'd spewed out my rage at Lyra.

Themistocles understood and he wasn't going to waste an opening.

"You see Cimon and I have been companions in the hunt. Do you think your young master would have behaved so with a man he believed had brought down his father, the hero Miltiades?"

So I was back in the fold: betrayed, bitter and bewildered,

but back all the same. I said nothing, just stood with my head bowed, after all I had spent the afternoon with a highborn Athenian lady so the sooner the conversation moved on to other matters the better. Anyway I did not wish anything that would detract from Cimon's high spirits. From what I'd heard they'd been in short supply recently. He clapped his hands and shouted for wine. It duly arrived; a draft of poor provenance. Cimon mixed and poured the libation then looked to Themistocles.

He tasted and looked satisfied with the vintage and for a moment I saw clear as day Miltiades in Themistocles's house before Marathon asking him if he always drank such piss. I think maybe Themistocles was thinking the same; he nodded to me over the rim of the cup before saying,

"I've heard how you received the cup I'd saved for you, Mandrocles. Unlike the Spartans and the Great King, I think it an ill thing to spear the messenger. "

He paused, holding my gaze a moment before concluding,

"Particularly an innocent who feels nothing but affection for you."

I think he'd been going to say love but, of course, a flute girl doesn't feel love.

"She didn't deserve it."

He'd played his cards skilfully as usual: all I felt now was remorse, all thoughts of anger and betrayal evaporated.

"So think next time, boy, now drink. Cimon son of Miltiades, what shall the pledge be?"

Cimon, with a political grasp I'd never suspected and without hesitating, replied,

"First Aegina, then the Great King."

We drank and Themistocles breathed out, almost too quiet to hear,

"If he still lives."

Strange, but back then – however parlous your own life

– even the slightest mention of the Great Persian empire dried out your mouth with fear. Particularly coming from Themistocles, whose ability to predict their intentions must have come from the Gods themselves.

So we drank and as I watched Cimon down his first cup in one I saw how experience and age had transformed him. He wasn't a boy anymore and I would become his man like I'd been Miltiades's. Now he'd order and I'd obey even were it to cost my life. Not that it stopped me noticing that he drank too quickly and enjoyed it too much. Then the thread of life changed stitch again.

"The arrangement with Callias concerning your sister progresses well?"

"Very well, to my surprise she accepts without complaint."

He spoke like the head of the family conducting the normal marriage business but I could see in his eyes traces of the boy who had relied on his sister as the one constant in his life. Themistocles was oblivious to any such niceties.

"Good, I think considering what is soon to break over us we move quickly. I suggest to avoid further slanders Elpinice move for a time to my house. My wife will collect her before dark."

Cimon nodded; I felt a twist of anguish wring my guts. She'd been correct as always: she was finally lost to me. He asked,

"And the wedding?"

"Quick as possible: best for everyone. Once the settlement's handed over you can establish a respectable household and move towards your ambitions."

Cimon nodded; I didn't know he had any ambitions: last time I'd seen him he was still a boy.

"For now though, best that you go to ground like a fox sensing the hunt."

From his face it was clear Cimon hadn't followed this particular stream of logic and I hadn't the faintest idea what Themistocles was talking about. He looked at us with the expression of an Athenian dealing with slow-witted yokels from the hills. Then he spelt it out.

"Things are going to be quite lively over the next few days: maybe worse than lively. Starting tomorrow, if you need to understand further then get to the Agora early in the morning, you'll be safe and in good company; it'll be packed with democrat patriots. After that there may be a few scores settled and a few cracked skulls so you take Master Cimon somewhere safe, Mandrocles."

I stared at him open mouthed.

"Take him home with you."

"Home with me?"

"To the Piraeus of course. It's all seamen living there so where could the son of the hero of Marathon be safer?"

I wanted to tell him about Aeschylus and Lyra but he forestalled me.

"The poet won't mind anyway, he's not there; he's gone away for a few days to attend to some business of mine, and you won't see the girl again unless you're prepared to crawl on your hands and knees to her. So you take Cimon home with you tonight, best to be out of the city and avoid the prologue of this particular play which is going to start after dark."

So that night we slept in the room above the bar overlooking the sea at Piraeus. There was no need to fear oversleeping: next morning, before Apollo's chariot dragged the sun up out of the waters and into the sky, the whole of Piraeus was on the move. We dressed rapidly, snatched a cup of wine downstairs then joined the crowd moving towards the Agora.

As is often the case on these occasions, in Athens there was a festival mood but I'd learnt enough to know it could very quickly turn ugly. A group of rowers carrying oar loops to signal their democratic credentials recognised Cimon and burst out cheering, which was carried out into the wider crowd by people who could have no idea what the cheer was for.

So it seemed we walked in the middle of an army of friends. By the Ceramicus our numbers were swelled by what appeared to be the whole artisan population of the city, and the ill-kept narrow lanes slowed our progress to a crawl. Eventually we could smell the stench of the Eridanos, the foul drain that moves across the Agora, and knew we were close to the action. All the seating in the Orchestra was taken so we stood near the back and waited for things to start. We'd learnt by now that this meeting had been called by Themistocles and his supporters to inform the people of close and present danger.

Themistocles was able to do this as his position of Strategos gave him the right. Since Marathon the role of the Archons had been circumscribed. They were now appointed each year by lot, so it was not a role from which a man could build a power base. The role of Strategos, the men who led the armies, was too important to be chosen by lot so were elected by tribe and could be re-elected. In this way there had been a subtle shift of power from the Archonate to the generals and many saw the hand of Themistocles behind this.

We hadn't long to wait; in fact if my memory serves we'd just brought some honey cakes from a street seller when a tremendous shouting broke out near the dais and rolled backwards through the crowd. Themistocles.

He climbed up with a pronounced limp and a series of playacting facial grimaces intended to convey his pain clearly enough to those standing right at the back.

"Forgive me, Athenians, the spear and sword wounds I took fighting for the city of the Goddess make it hard for me to move as quickly as I once did."

I knew this for a lie: he'd been moving easily enough

the day before. Most of the crowd loved it, however, and cheered. Not everyone though; someone shouted back angrily at him. I couldn't make out what but Themistocles's reply was crystal clear.

"Well, no one could accuse you of that, Kallixenos, the only place a spear would ever pierce you would be up the arse and then only because you asked for it."

The roar of laughter at this drowned out anything else for minutes. Themistocles put up his hands for silence and then, exaggerating his limp even further, moved to the speaker's post and began to explain what we were really here for.

I was told later by friends who were nearer the dais about something that was different about this assembly. There was a type of organisation to the way the great men arranged themselves, which was new.

In the past, with all the pushing and jostling, people were all mixed up. The speakers sat with their family and friends who would mainly be members of their tribe. Since Marathon even this had been relaxed as most of them had fought together there. When they'd held the stitched up assembly that decided to arraign Miltiades, the proposers were scattered all across the range of the benches.

Not now. Those who supported Themistocles and his ideas for the Piraeus and a larger fleet to combat Aegina and the empire sat together. Men from different tribes, many of them new men, interspersed with merchants and some of the city's best trierarchs. They sat as a block and must have arrived early to manage this. On the other side, not quite as organised but recognisable, were Hipparchus, Megacles, Aristides, and Kallixenos with their supporters. Interestingly Xanthippus was close to them but not quite with them.

This wasn't the arrangement for a debate about land, family and status. It was about power but also about something else: about something that Themistocles had begun to call decisions of the city, or policy. So they sat together in ranks the same way they would have lined up in hoplite armour to fight a battle.

Looking back, reader, you can see a pattern to the way things changed but when it's all new and you're in the middle of it there is no pattern: just excitement and confusion.

Once the crowd finally went silent Themistocles waited a further moment to extenuate the suspense then began.

"I'm, as you know, a simple man who speaks his mind so I beg my Alkmaionid friends who stood with me at Marathon to forgive me for my simple message and failure to match their fine and elaborate speeches."

Everyone knew this was a gibe but no one knew where it was going.

"The city of the Goddess is in grave danger. Danger made worse by the fact that we can only see the tip of it. But behind that tip, stretching away into the dark is a force far greater than any we have seen. You know the tip is that nest of vipers Aegina. But do you also know that the surface of Aegina is crawling with agents of the Great King? Are you aware that their well-fortified harbour is packed with Persian warships?"

He was interrupted when someone shouted,

"Darius is dead."

"Perhaps, but it may just be rumour. But what I have just said is fact. Fact that was brought here by the leader of our peaceful mission to Aegina, no less a man than the noble Xanthippus who fought on the wing at Marathon."

As with all his speeches Themistocles introduced elements to unsettle his opponents before getting to the real point. This singling out of Xanthippus for praise was particularly effective. Hipparchus rose from his bench, shouting,

"Make your point, son of Neocles, or give way to someone who will."

Themistocles directed his most irritating smile at Hipparchus and playfully wagged his finger before replying.

"Be patient, son of Charmos. I intend to give way far sooner than you'd imagine. My only purpose in speaking to you today is to put some questions to the heroic citizens of a heroic city. When I have asked these questions I can think of no one more fitted to answer them than you, given your kinship with the late but unlamented tyrant Hippias who so recently visited our city with his Persian friends."

This, as Themistocles must have anticipated, provoked violence. Hipparchus attempted to climb onto the dais but had to be restrained by his friends; weapons were drawn and scuffles broke out across the Agora. I was in no position to defend myself so was grateful that we were surrounded by a phalanx of seamen all of them democrats and supporters of Themistocles. Eventually order was restored and he was able to proceed with his questions. Characteristically he threw something else into the mix first.

"My questions concern the island of Aegina where I must tell you these last days a young hero of Marathon was attacked by a pack of thugs set on him by a traitor. Aegina, the island whose leaders almost soiled their robes in their haste to deliver the earth and water demanded by the servants of the Great King."

He paused again, regarding the crowd with the expression of someone wanting to tell a great truth to his friends. This time no one interrupted. What he'd said about Aegina was too near the knuckle and we were at war. So an edgy silence endured until he asked the questions he'd promised.

"Athenians, ask yourselves, how many seaworthy fighting ships have we?"

People shuffled about uncomfortably but no one answered.

"I'm sure I can't be the only one who knows. Well, I'll tell you anyway: depending on how quickly we can effect repairs we have between forty three and forty seven. Now ask yourselves, how many have Aegina?"

Again no answer.

"Our expedition led by Xanthippus counted seventy nine in the harbour and reckon there are at least ten more. That of course does not include the numerous Persian warships. Do you remember what happened last time their fleet raided us?"

There was an outbreak of angry shouting: Themistocles waited till it died down before raising his voice to full pitch and bellowing so loud it felt like an earthquake.

"They burnt Phaleron, the open bay where our defenceless ships were beached. They humiliated us under the angry gaze of our Goddess. And we had more ships back then because we lost good ships fighting besides the Ionian Greeks against the Persians whilst those –"

He stopped and glared, round eyes bulging.

"– Those bastards on Aegina were building ships to use against us. So ask yourselves this: what's going to happen this time round now that the odds are worse?"

A friend near the front told me that as Themistocles was shouting this out he'd been watching the face of Hipparchus and seen its expression change from anger to an incredulous and dawning horror. But it was already too late: Themistocles had arrived at the climax of his peroration.

"But ask yourselves these questions first. Who has been trying to push this city into building a fortified harbour like our enemies have? Who has been trying to persuade the men who lead this city to build a new war fleet so that we won't be at the mercy of those fucking pirates?"

There was an outbreak of shouting from the massed crowd, starting with the sailors but spreading.

"Themistocles, Themistocles."

It built into a chant and seemed as if it would never stop.

But he hadn't quite finished and lifted his hands into the air, palms facing the crowd, and gradually the chanting died away.

"So when you watch their fleet descend onto our few triremes lying unprotected on the shore. When you see the smoke rising from burning ships and buildings. When you hear the cries of your wives and daughters being raped and carried off into slavery. When you are burying your sons killed in a desperate but failed defence. Ask yourselves this. Ask why didn't we build the safe harbour Themistocles wanted? Ask where is the new fleet of triremes he begged our leaders to build, the fleet that would have saved us?"

He paused, leaving us on the edge. I'd seen him do this before, milk every last drop like a good goatherd will. Only then, in a softer but still audible voice, did he deliver the killer blow.

"And to respond to those questions I'll give way to the man most qualified to give you the answers because he more than anyone is responsible for them: Hipparchus, son of Charmos."

He turned his back, stepped down from the dais and walked away from the Agora. Behind him there was an outbreak of shouting as the fighting began.

Chapter Nine

Three days later, just before dawn, Aeschylus walked into our room waking us. He was travel-stained and weary but something else as well. I tried to work out what it was as he talking to Cimon. I'd avoided his gaze: I still felt too much shame. I think he was embarrassed too; these things can hang between men like an invisible curtain. Didn't stop him speaking though.

"If you're capable of feeling shame, Mandrocles, you should feel it now. That poor girl didn't deserve your spite. Treat the ones who love you like that and soon you'll stand alone. Now get out of that bed, I need to sleep."

I got up and headed for the stairs where Cimon was waiting. Aeschylus called after me.

"Wake me in three hours, I've information Themistocles needs. You can come with me if you can manage to forget your own problems for a moment."

Cimon shouted,

"And me, do I come?"

"You make your own decisions, son of Miltiades."

He turned his face to the wall and was asleep in seconds. Cimon and I wandered down to the bar; there were already drinkers in there, no one slept well last night, there'd been skirmishes throughout the hours of darkness as the unstable city prepared for another revolution of the wheel. Then Cimon loped off towards where the Athene Nike was beached and I wandered, with a large honey cake warm from the baker's oven, to a bar near the construction site that Piraeus was turning into. I sat outside with a cup of hot spiced wine letting the rising sun warm my aching bones.

I couldn't shift the blackness from my soul, the Gods had buried it too deep; but I felt the first imperceptible flicker of direction. Above me the sun caught some of the gleaming new marble on the Acropolis. I stared at it, looking for some message that maybe I could be forgiven, but instead tears began to trickle down my cheeks. I rubbed at my eyes with honey smeared fingers. The crying made me feel better; I didn't understand why.

Now, all these years later, I've seen too many brave men break down and weep or sit in silence for years not to understand that it's just the price of courage. You hang on and hang on and later, when there's no need to hang on, you break. So I sat and stared out over the waters watching boats dragged off the beach into the sea until it was time to wake Aeschylus.

Cimon was there before me, they went silent as I entered.

"You've suffered more than I thought, Mandrocles: go to Lyra, talk to her, she will understand."

I didn't answer, however it appeared we'd begun to rebuild our friendship. But we couldn't get anything out of him concerning his whereabouts over the last few days even though we pestered him all the way to the Ceramicus. Themistocles was in great high spirits when we arrived. His brother was there and a number of hangers on who seemed to have attached their fortune to the rise of the Demos.

"Welcome, Athena's greatest poet; tell me, were you successful?"

Aeschylus smiled and gave a typically elliptical answer.

"If you chose to hang about the Piraeus, in a couple of days you'd find out."

Themistocles laughed and clapped him on the shoulders several times before saying,

"You missed a great piece of theatre in your absence: you know, I think you could improve your chances of winning the goat at next year's Dionysia by watching me at work. For instance, no chorus could present surprise and fear better than Hipparchus at my prompting. He's had to go to ground now. Slow as he is he's beginning to learn that there's nothing to be gained by trying violence after defeat in a public meeting. That's where the Demos reigns supreme."

Aeschylus said nothing, just listened wearing a sardonic grin.

"So much so that the lads of the fleet were disappointed: after they'd cracked a few heads Hipparchus's faction disappeared off the streets quicker than snow in spring."

"That's a nice image, remind me to write it down."

"Before you do, tell me about your visit to our friends in Corinth. Are you still held in such high regard in that great city these days?"

"Less since they found out that I'd become your Ambassador."

They both laughed at this, but I hadn't understood a word of this exchange; how could I miss so much and understand so little? Aeschylus changed his posture and suddenly he was the chorus leader imparting the will of the Gods. If he didn't write plays he could have made a decent living as first actor.

"The city fathers of Corinth of the high citadel send their greetings to Themistocles, the Athenian selfless father of the Demos. Out of friendship and respect for our sacrifice at Marathon they are prepared for twenty of their fighting ships to sail out from beneath the high citadel and serve with the Athenians against the Medisers of Aegina."

He dropped the pose and added,

"At terms that can be confirmed later, providing the fighting is quickly concluded."

Themistocles looked relieved; he even let out an exhalation as if he'd been holding his breath while Aeschylus spoke. So his earlier bombast had been an act; well, at least a partial act. With Themistocles it was difficult to know.

"Thank the Gods. That gives us a chance to put up enough resistance to agree peace terms. The real settlement that we'll impose on those bastards will have to wait. But the war will have served its purpose."

He offered us wine.

"Take care how fast you drink, son of Miltiades, too much deprives a man of his judgement and sets other men talking."

It's a measure of the extent that Cimon looked to Themistocles for guidance back then and also a measure of the value of his advice that he drank his cup slowly. There's no acknowledgement of that today: you'll find nothing of it in the scribbles of young Herodotus, only a shadow of it in Aeschylus's great conclusion to his trilogy: Prometheus Fire Bringer. The greatest of all his plays, the finest flowering of all our poetry: something that surpasses anything by the trickster Sophocles or the Euripides boy. But understand this, reader: more than Callias and his money, it was Themistocles who set Cimon on his way.

I never understood why: maybe a promise to Miltiades or guilt over his split with him. Perhaps he saw Cimon as a hedge against the Alkmaionids or had some other use for him. His association with the boy certainly served him well.

But for all that there was a genuine closeness between them back then. Cimon was a wild elemental in his early teens, strong willed and destructive: the fall of his father left him disturbed. Themistocles kept him between the traces and not through fear. Cimon feared no one. No, it was respect – maybe cut with affection, but above all they were both, in their differing ways, consummate politicians. Themistocles saw the path to the future and Cimon wanted to travel it.

Themistocles had one more surprise for us.

"Tomorrow we go to a small symposium where certain matters of great importance concerning the principal of Isonomy will be discussed; somewhere you will find familiar, Mandrocles. Please be here one hour before the lamps are lit."

As we were leaving Themistocles took my arm and whispered.

"The symposium will be a major test for Cimon: you make sure he keeps a clear head, remains sober and passes it."

Next evening's walk to the house of Phrasicles was, for me, impregnated with memories: bitter and sweet. It was here that Miltiades and Themistocles had tested whether they could be allies and almost came to blows as a consequence. It was also where I first met Aeschylus and Lyra; it all seems so long ago.

Cimon, freshly washed with his long hair properly dressed and oiled, wearing one of his father's robes, bubbled with excitement. This was his first real step along the road his father had trod. We walked with Aeschylus behind Themistocles and his brother Agesilaus. In Aeschylus's words it was almost the same cast as last time, before Marathon.

It was dusk when we were admitted into the beautiful courtyard where, years before, the even more beautiful flute girl had cleaned up my tunic after I had disgraced myself in drink. I can still almost taste her sweet breath. Oh, Lyra; if only the Gods would let us back to try again. Forgive me, reader, I ramble.

But any nostalgia was quickly replaced by surprise. There were but ten of us in the andron that night. The other five were Phrasicles, Ajax, a distant Philiad relation of Cimon's two men I didn't know and, on the couch of honour, Xanthippus.

While slaves removed our sandals to wash our feet the tension in the room tightened like an anchor rope. I think that although neither Themistocles nor Xanthippus was surprised to see each other, they realised the stakes. Remember, back then the rules of governing the Demos were being made up from day to day. We picked at the choice dishes of fish and eel on the low tables but without appetite; conversation was desultory. At last the jugs and cups were set up and Phrasicles stood to perform the duties of symposiarch. But this was no ordinary symposium.

"Phrasicles, you are the most honourable of men and an example to all other hosts but I fear even your skills are unequal to stimulating a worthy debate on the principles of Isonomy. We are here for another purpose and one that will not wait."

Xanthippus had spoken well but Phrasicles looked unsure of how to proceed. He mumbled an offer to withdraw but was interrupted by Themistocles.

"No, as host your place is here: all shall remain to listen to what, in the next minutes, could decide the future of the city of the Goddess Athena. There is no place for secrecy or subterfuge in the principle of Isonomy or the rule of the Demos."

I don't know how he managed to say this with a straight face, perhaps at the moment he believed it. Xanthippus couldn't; he tried to look stern and impassive beneath his bulging forehead but then he cracked, trying to stifle a giggle that became an uncontrollable fit of laughter.

"By all the Gods, Son of Neocles, how do you manage it?"

He had to stop and wipe his eyes before gasping out,

"You should let your scribbler take notes; the length of one Chou of wine with you in this form would give him enough material for ten of his satyr plays. How can you get so far up your own arse?"

Then Themistocles laughed; whether it was genuine or not I don't know but it achieved its purpose. We could begin. Only the delicate matter of who would speak first, who would control the agenda needed to be settled. It was then that Cimon, who had been whispering with Aeschylus, took his first step in what we now call politics.

"Was this not the very room in which you, Strategos Themistocles, and my late father began the process that led to Marathon? The battle in which you both fought in the front line."

On the surface it was the question of a callow youth. But the mixture of courtesy and admiration coupled with a memory of the dead hero whose partnership with Themistocles led to the battle settled with great subtlety who would speak first. Themistocles.

"Now shall we speak plainly in front of honourable men who will hold us to account, son of Ariphron?"

Xanthippus looked him in the eye then nodded his massive head. Themistocles began.

"We both know the Persians will be back. We both know they won't make the same mistakes again. There will be no more Marathons."

Xanthippus nodded again.

"The Spartans will never defend our city. Our only chance is the sea. The sea can make us great."

Xanthippus nodded.

"But we don't have a secure harbour and we don't have any ..."

Xanthippus finished the sentence for him.

"Fucking ships. I know, I've heard this speech before. Where does it get us? We can't even fight Aegina at sea and win."

"Yes, and you'd know more about Aegina than most, wouldn't you?"

One of Themistocles's few faults: he couldn't resist a jibe. Xanthippus flushed red.

"Not as well as you know the Great King, son of Neocles."

A deadly insult but Themistocles reply took all of our breath away.

"And not as well as I know his son, young Xerxes. A much better bet for the future, don't you think? Always a good thing to plan ahead because it will be Xerxes we have to deal with."

Xanthippus, adroit as he was, found himself nonplussed so listened as Themistocles spelled out with brutal honesty the reality we faced.

"So we need ships but many of our leading men, particularly your Alkmaionid cousins, don't accept this. One of the reasons they don't accept it is because more ships mean more sailors and more radical trierarchs, which means the Demos grows in strength. And they want to stifle the Demos even though that particular horse left the stable a long time ago and is miles down the road. But you, you, son of Ariphron, are wiser than that. You know the Demos is here to stay which is why you've begun to work with it. No need to look so surprised, you must know that nothing in this Polis escapes me."

He smiled round at all of us like a genial host: he was enjoying himself.

"So, son of Ariphron, here's where we are. I understand the need for a fleet and a harbour and so do you. I understand the Demos is the only way forwards and so do you. Does it make sense for us: the only two men who really grasp this, to fight each other? If we do what happens? You accuse me of secretly dealing with the Great King and I accuse you of leading an expedition to Aegina in order to betray us to our enemies."

Xanthippus blurted out,

"But you wanted me to go, we agreed …"

This time it was Themistocles's turn to interrupt.

"But sadly for you, son of Ariphron, it was you who was stupid enough to go. Everyone in the city's heard me denounce Aegina as a nest of pirates. Just as everyone knows you went there to talk to them and that I tried to have you arraigned for it. No one would believe you. However they would, and with justifiable cause, believe your accusations about me and the Great King."

Xanthippus had regarded him with a look of something like respect as he'd said this. Cimon used the pause to reach for his wine cup. I pushed his hand away: Themistocles hadn't finished.

"And how would that all end? Athens would lose the only two men who can save her."

"And how precisely are we going to save Athens from the Persians without enough ships to even defend ourselves against Aegina?"

"But we do have enough ships. Well almost: enough at least to hold on long enough for a stalemate."

He gestured towards Aeschylus.

"My scribbler, as you call him, has just returned from a trip to Corinth and brought twenty triremes with him."

Xanthippus looked incredulous but it was Aeschylus who spoke.

"I was surprised at the extent of their gratitude towards us over Marathon. They know that after us, but before Sparta, they were on the Great King's list. I saw their defended harbour amongst the lagoons at Lechaion too. Effective but not as strong as the Piraeus could be."

Xanthippus snarled to Themistocles,

"So the scribbler is your agent, your intelligencer?"

"Of course, but you can share the credit for him if you like."

"And why would you offer me that?"

"Because I need you, Xanthippus, Athens needs you if you prefer. It won't last but for now the great families can prevent anything they don't like in this city. It will change but maybe not before we are overwhelmed by the Persians. How will your clever little son, Pericles isn't it, manage to establish a reputation then? When the Persians impose a tyranny over the defeated, smoking ruin of Athens."

Xanthippus didn't reply but it was obvious he was thinking hard over a decision that would change his life. Themistocles sensed this, and he began to push harder.

"And it won't be you, Xanthippus. You're too far from the centre of the clan: scarcely an Athenian in the eyes of some of them. For you and your family to rise you need the Demos and the opportunity to command in war. Let them marginalise me and there's no chance of you having either. Imagine that: a life spent licking the arses of men like Megacles and Kallixenos."

"So what are you proposing?"

But Themistocles was playing a subtle game. He asked Phrasicles for a second crater of wine. Phrasicles clapped his hands and as we waited for it Xanthippus fretted then asked.

"You expect to hatch a plot in company just like that?"

"Of course in the presence of honourable men: I fully trust those who follow me, Cimon trusts his cousin, Ajax. I'm sure you wouldn't have asked Timocrates, son of Timoxenus, or Chrysis, son of Eumachus, to attend today if you didn't fully trust them."

Xanthippus glanced at his friends, who sensibly kept their heads down staring into their wine cups.

"You're taking a great risk, Themistocles."

There was no answer. As the wine arrived Themistocles asked Phrasicles,

"Mix it two to one; suits this old Chian best."

The wine was served and drunk in silence. Themistocles, judging the opportune moment, put his cup down arranged the folds of his mantle and said,

"Yes, but any risk for the safety of our city is worth taking. But I'm not taking much of a risk with you, son of Ariphron: you're a patriot and despite our differences you know I'm right. I'm proposing we work together to prepare our city for war. I'm proposing you command the fleet, including my twenty Corinthian triremes, against Aegina. I'm proposing that together we push the city fathers to finish the fortified harbour at rocky Piraeus. But most of all I'm proposing we build a fleet of three hundred warships."

He gave a soft chuckle and paused before saying almost under his breath,

"But the Gods only know where the money will come from."

Xanthippus stared at him, saying nothing. Themistocles waved his arm indicating the cups should be refilled. I was sweating under my robes; the tension was ratcheting up and the anchor rope taut to the point of snapping. I noticed however that Cimon was quite calm, staring at Themistocles with a look of admiration; learning from the master.

Themistocles looked steadily at Xanthippus across the rim of his cup as he drank then said,

"The city needs you. I can't do this alone."

"And you approach me, the man you called the traitor of Aegina."

"Who better to partner the friend of the Great King?"

It was the timing rather than the chilling implications of this that broke the tension. Made us laugh: Xanthippus the hardest.

"My cousins are right about you. You're more than a showground huckster, you are truly dangerous."

"Yes, I am; and remember no one has greater cause to

know that than the dead Persians lying in their mass grave at Marathon."

"Yes, no one can doubt the part you played in that."

"Nor you."

"No, nor me."

"So?"

Xanthippus was like a man wobbling on the edge of a precipice; which way would he fall?

"All you propose, Themistocles, is that we work together until we achieve those ends that we both know are necessary?"

"Precisely."

He opened his arms and the two men embraced. Not as warmly as I'd seen them embrace on the bloody ground of Marathon at the battle's end, but then the emotion was different. But a pact had been formed. As Phrasicles called for more wine Themistocles smiled and said,

"There might be one little difficulty for you to face though."

Xanthippus, anticipating a joke, asked, ready to laugh at the punch line,

"And what may that be?"

"It will be necessary for some of your Alkmaionid cousins to leave town for a while."

Themistocles wasn't joking.

Chapter Ten

The sea war with Aegina was a scratchy affair: bits and pieces of raids all along our coastline. I played no part, there's no room for injured men on a trireme. Cimon had more of an impact: not through any action but from something he said to Themistocles following the meeting of the board of Strategos convened to confer command of the fleet. I don't know what was said in the meeting but we were there in the Agora when the decision was announced: Xanthippus would command the fleet. So the accord struck up in the andron of Phrasicles's house was working.

After the public meeting Themistocles, in great high spirits, mingled with his supporters, me and Cimon included. We repaired to one of the better wine shops in the Ceramicus, something Themistocles did occasionally to demonstrate his connections with the Demos and the ordinary citizen. The talk was of triremes and strategy, a topic best left to experienced seamen, but Cimon – usually content to listen and assimilate – pitched in.

"My father told me on our escape from the Great King that the only thing preventing fighting ships, like the Athene Nike, from becoming invincible is the lack of room for fighting men on deck."

No one particularly wanted the opinion of a boy but he

commanded respect even back then. So the company heard him out politely then moved on. But it was later apparent that he'd struck a chord in Themistocles, who asked afterwards as we were making our way home,

"So, son of the mighty Miltiades, what exactly did your father have in mind to strengthen the Athene Nike?"

"He said he'd find an experienced shipwright and ask him to examine the possibility of extending the deck between the outriggers so we could double the number of ephibatai. He was sick of being outnumbered by the hoplites on the Persian ships and wanted to be able to carry more himself."

Themistocles didn't bother to reply but I could see he was storing the suggestion up for future consideration. At the public meeting he'd hinted that he had a few surprises in store for Aegina in the war. When we arrived at his house I, at least, understood what they were.

I recognised him as soon as he was shown in. The Aeginian democrat: the bastard who'd knocked me about and broken my ribs. He recognised me too, gave me a mocking smile as Themistocles led him off for a private consultation. I promised myself that if I ever saw him again my dagger would give him an extra rib.

Whatever plan he was hatching didn't work though. When the democrats on Aegina rose up they were beaten, hunted down and killed, their bodies left to rot in the public places of the city. We'd failed to do our part: the Corinthian ships were too late to allow our navy to support the insurrection so my dagger never got its opportunity.

That fiasco more or less summed up the war. They burned Phaleron, burned the boat station at Sounion and raided wherever they wanted. Even with the Corinthians we were outnumbered and couldn't be everywhere at once. When the revolt of the democrats was exterminated we lost our only chance to hit back at them. Without friends on the inside, they were too well defended for our fleet to attack.

It was chance though that levelled things up: a squadron of our ships caught an equal number of theirs returning from raiding our coast and wiped them out. After that they hadn't the strength to raid in force and defend their home waters so the war guttered out and died like an oil lamp before cock crow.

But it gave Themistocles the ammunition he needed to begin his own democratic revolution at home. Before that, though, my own domestic circumstances changed. Cimon and I were asked to visit the house of Agesilaus: Themistocles's brother. You never noticed him when his more famous brother was around, he preferred the shadows, and there was something of the night about him. Ask any man in a wine shop to describe him and no two will give you the same description. I think that's the quality that made him so essential to his brother. Who could suspect a man who wasn't there?

Agesilaus greeted us in his usual unobtrusive manner and escorted us to a small receiving chamber where seated on a couch was a small, stocky, saturnine but richly dressed individual. A sickness clutched at my heart as I knew who he was before Cimon greeted him by name. Callias. This was the man who would enjoy the perfumed nights with Elpinice. I wanted to be sick, but as heartache was a constant companion those days I managed to control myself.

I can't remember much else. Only that the marriage was fixed and the first instalment of the reverse bride dowry paid in the shape of a house. In fact, a house not far from the old family home below the Acropolis; nothing changes, the fates just rearrange the furniture. I've tried to set down the truth in this journal, reader, so I suppose I'd better be fair to

Callias. There has been a great deal of slander aimed at him in order to discredit Cimon and Elpinice. So you may as well hear the real character of the man from someone who has no reason to flatter him, a man who still hates him. Me.

Callias was rich but he was not the same Callias who robbed the bodies of murdered captives after Marathon, because he wasn't there. That man, Callias the Golden, was a snake. Cimon's brother in law stuck to his bargain: he supported Cimon with funds and was kind to his sister. He afforded her more freedom than any other Athenian wife, save for Aspasia, the beloved of the onion head Pericles, enjoys. I suppose that at least is something I grew to be grateful for.

So we moved into our new house where my role was a mixture of steward, mentor and friend. Although they'd not known him for long, many of the old retainers of Stesagoras household drifted back to serve Cimon. Theodorus joined us to fulfil a variety of roles including bodyguard. He towed in his wake some of the Thranitai from the Athene Nike. In this way the household became a comfortable extension of the ship. Cimon was prepared to take advice on most matters but was adamant in his refusal to re-employ his tutor Aristagorus.

Some days after we moved in I was about to set out on an expedition that had long been building in my mind. I would visit Lyra and see if she'd forgive me. I put on my best tunic and dressed my hair in the fashion that I'd seen the young ephebes who surrounded Cimon affect, and was about to set out when Ariston arrived short of breath at our door. It was obvious he had some serious purpose, but despite that couldn't resist a crude joke.

"Got a new job as male pornoi in a brothel have you, Mandrocles? Because if you have you'll have to postpone it, we're needed: the fun's about to start."

He barged past me shouting for Theodorus and the others but was brought up short by Cimon.

"Why all the noise, Ariston?"

"Beg pardon, Master Cimon, but Strategos Themistocles needs all decent democrats in the Agora, particularly them as can fight."

So I never got to see Lyra. I wager you think you know what happened in the Agora that day, reader: well, stick with this and then see if you're so sure. We got there early but the crowd was already sizeable and nasty. There was a large group of men with some wailing women which was unusual. I bet you've not read that anywhere. They were from the coast where the raids had been. The survivors whose homes had been burnt whose kin had been killed, raped or carried off into slavery. Themistocles must have been working through the last two sundials to get them all here. They made for a great but noisy spectacle and because of their suffering and the sympathy of the crowd the Archon's officers made no attempt to move them.

This taught me just how much the power of the Archonate had decreased since Themistocles held it before Marathon. Whatever transpired here today would still have to be passed to the court of the Areopagus but it was clear that the line of power was sharply bending. Most of the early crowd were democrats who made way for Cimon so we passed through the stinking masses to the front, where we were embraced by a great knot of rowers gathered around Agesilaus. He seemed to be enjoying himself: the rowers were. They'd been well provisioned and it was clear the wineskins had been passed round several times.

Aeschylus shouldered his way through us and was greeted with a cheer; he was becoming known as a poet and better known as an active agent of the Demos.

"There ought to be some good material to put into the mouths of Gods and heroes from today's performance, try and remember all you can."

He accepted the proffered wine skin and drank deep. You didn't need eyes to know the crowd was growing, you could hear it and feel the pressure as more and more tried to squeeze into the orchestra. Then the jeering began. It started at the periphery and moved inwards, growing in volume. Catcalls and insults so loud and numerous that any meaning was lost, smoothed out to a single wave of imprecation. Some of this stemmed from anger but most from frustration as the democrats understood where the real power still lay – and it wasn't with us. There was no representation from the rowing benches in the Areopagus.

The jeering grew in intensity as did the jostling; it was difficult to keep one's feet as their minders pushed a way through to the dais for Megacles and his supporters. I noticed with interest that Xanthippus didn't make his entry with them. Then the named Archon – sorry, reader, I can't remember his name, but at least that's an indication of the way the office had declined – tried to open the debate. No one paid any attention and it was left to Themistocles to move forward to assist him.

"Friends, friends, we are all fellow Athenians and all must be heard. It is our way. Please hear your Archon speak."

This was greeted with cheering followed, gradually, by silence. The Archon nervously scuttled forwards and quickly called Aristides son of Lysimachus to speak first. This was unexpected as we were here to listen to Themistocles delivering a denunciation against Megacles's faction.

My first impression of Aristides as a public speaker was surprise: he had a thin and reedy speaking voice and was too concerned with a type of pedantic exactitude to get straight to the point and so tended to lose his audience. In every other respect he was a clever choice: everyone remembered his courage holding the centre together side by side with Themistocles at Marathon.

"Athenians, I fail to understand the need for this meeting: let me enumerate our successes. We have prevailed at sea against Aegina. Since Marathon we are safe from Persia, where I am informed there are grave internal matters occupying the Great King. We must now restore the old principle of Eunomia and put aside foolish talk of harbours and fleets. Do we wish to draw the world's eyes towards us? Do we wish to arouse envy amongst both the Hellenes and the Barbarians? Do we wish to stir up a wasp's nest of discord in our city and overturn the rule of natural law handed to us by the city fathers? Do we —"

Themistocles cut him off.

"The Persians are on Aegina; soon they will be here, Aristides. It pains me to break your flow. You are a dear comrade, at Marathon we stood together, guarded each other's backs, and took each other's wounds. But you have been misled."

This was better. We ceased being restless; the chorus had left the stage and the satyrs were on. Aristides looked perplexed. Whatever he'd expected to be accused of, it certainly wasn't having been misled. The pause this prompted in his peroration was fatal to his argument; Themistocles ploughed on.

"Let me pose some different questions. What would have happened if we'd had the fleet I proposed? Why are the Persians on Aegina? Why is it so easy to ravage our coastline? The very mention of this and the grief of friends, who have lost home and family, move me to tears; forgive me, countrymen."

He paused at this point and made a great show of tears: being able to cry at will like he could is a hard won skill; ask any player. While Aristides tried to reply the crowd broke out in groans and weeping. I wasn't sure the weeping of the sailors was genuine but there again there are none more superstitious or emotional than they are. The communal wailing continued at great volume until Themistocles, having recovered his equanimity as quickly as he lost it to grief, bellowed.

"Athenians, which set of questions do you want the answers to?"

There was a clamour of people shouting, "Yours, yours, Themistocles." He listened, stretching it out, judging his time, then spoke earnestly like a father proffering the advice that will save his son.

"Very well, but you will have to forgive me if I seem to stumble. Remember, I am a simple man unaccustomed to public oratory unlike my friend Aristides or his friends Megacles and Hipparchus, who I see skulking in their seats, simpering."

In fact they were neither skulking nor simpering, they were on their feet screaming abuse at Themistocles. I realised then they'd been played: this wasn't the assembly they'd expected or agreed to. But it was too late and their screams of protest were drowned out until Themistocles continued.

"Perhaps they don't relish the plain speech of a simple man or the assembly of free Athenians. But they'd better listen to this because our future freedom depends on these answers. Well, do you want to hear them, free Athenians?"

There was a roar of yes so coordinated that it seemed to emanate from one gigantic throat.

"Well spoken, citizens. First I'll tell you this: if we'd have had the fleet I've been pushing for, then the poor homeless Athenians here today would still be safe in their farms with their loved ones. They'd be there because that fleet would have stormed into the harbour on Aegina when the Demos on that island rose up. Then we'd have had peace and the

Aeginian fleet lined up with ours against the Great King. Instead, the forces of repression on that island were able to suppress the Demos and butcher their leaders, our friends."

He struck a pose, hands on hips, and pushed his pugnacious chin out far as it would go. Pure Satyr play; and then shouted,

"Who do we blame?"

The name shouted out loudest was Xanthippus.

"Wrong, friends. When he returned from Aegina I thought that too. However secret information has reached me that he was working with the democrats. Xanthippus is an Athenian patriot. Think again while I answer the next question."

I watched Aristides while this was going on; it was clear he had little idea what was coming next and less about how to counter it.

"They were able to devastate our shores because we neglected to defend them. We neglected to replace our old ships and build new ones. We neglected to construct a fortified harbour to keep our triremes safe. Oh Gods, even saying this make me want to weep and scream.

"Think, friends. Think, Athenians, reflect on what would have happened if it had been the Persians instead of Aegina. Every man of you dead, every young woman raped and enslaved, boys gelded, the old cast out to die, the city burnt. Aiee, aiee the grief of what might happen, no, what will happen when the Persians do come."

I saw that Aeschylus was making a mental note of this for future use. I'm sure that you, reader, have noted the similarity to a certain section of his great play, The Persians. Forgive me, I digress.

"For they will come, believe me, and we are unready. Xanthippus has seen them on Aegina, he knows their intentions. For years you have heard my demands to fortify the Piraeus and strengthen our fleet. Why has it not happened,

who is to blame? I demand to know: who is to blame? Who
– Is – To – Blame?"

Several names were thrown back at him: Megacles, Hipparchus, Aristides, and Kallixenos and from the front, round
the Alkmaionid faction, were shouts of Themistocles.

He raised his arms for silence.

"We must be more forensic in our search for the real evil
doer, friends. Think back. Which man has opposed my pro-
posals to make the city safe most vociferously, most consis-
tently? Yes, yes, now you have it, I hear some of you calling
his name and you are right."

He was screaming now, the crowd were worked to a pitch
of fury; he brought them to the orgasm.

"I name him. I denounce him. I denounce Hipparchus. I
call upon the Areopagus for the test of Ostracism. I demand
it, I demand it."

While the crowd screamed assent, Hipparchus fought his
way to the dais bellowing in fury like a goaded bull.

"You worthless lying bastard, I'll pull the beard off your
fucking low born face. Not even Athenian Xenos; fucking
Xenos."

Themistocles re-composed himself into the righteous
upholder of public order.

"See friends, see how he scorns your wisdom, scorns your
love of the city of the Goddess. Do I hear you insist that
we petition the Areopagus to apply the test of Ostracism to
Hipparchus son of Charmos?"

The roar of yes was deafening, Hipparchus was hauled
away out of the crowd to safety by his friends so he probably
missed Themistocles's concluding remarks.

"I suggest, friends, that when the worthy fathers of the
Areopagus convene above the cave on Lykabetos, you gather
outside to help them make the correct decision for the safe
future of the city."

The night following the Areopagus, Aeschylus told me about a party where Lyra would be performing. He suggested that if I waited outside she might allow me to escort her home. As I walked her home through the dark streets we noticed that giant pithoi for the collection of the ostraka had been positioned in their places in the Agora.

Part Two

Chapter Eleven

We were away before the first streaks of rosy fingered dawn caressed the surface of the waters. My feelings were mixed; I'd come close to restoring amicability with Lyra but every time I found myself on the brink of something different we always parted. However my body, if not my mind, had healed and the companionship of the Athene Nike was equally seductive. We'd passed the promontory of Eleusis before Themistocles saw fit to confide our destination to us.

The ship had been prepared in secret at very short notice and as a consequence we were six crew members light. This was partly compensated for by Cimon who, to his delight, Themistocles insisted sail with us. If you believe in omens, and sailors do, then Cimon's boarding of the Athene Nike as a member of its crew rather than a young boy passenger was auspicious. He leapt lightly down onto the deck, scarcely causing the temperamental vessel to vibrate. There was a spontaneous outbreak of cheering from the crew like that which greets a hero. From that first step he was in his element.

Cimon was to serve alongside of me as one of the ephibatai marines and, somehow, Themistocles had managed to procure for him Miltiades's hoplite panoply. It wouldn't serve for long; he was already taller than his father had been. But for him to be able to stand with the other armoured men as Themistocles poured the pre-voyage libation was a coming of age. Lysias was absent.

As Eleusis faded behind us Themistocles beamed at Cimon and announced,

"We're headed for Sparta."

"I've always wondered if Sparta is as bad as everyone says it is."

I gave Cimon a laconic answer that a Spartan would have been proud of and one with the merit of being accurate.

"It is."

That's all I managed to say: of all the places I never wanted to see again Sparta was top of the list. Therefore the shock of hearing our destination tossed out in such an offhand manner robbed me of my equanimity. Not Cimon though, to him it was a jolt of excitement. Themistocles was impervious to either reaction.

"Yes, of course I'd forgotten you were part of Miltiades's foolish and doomed mission to Sparta before Marathon, Mandrocles."

Cimon and I were kneeling on the deck either side of the trierarch's chair occupied by Themistocles, in the stern. The only other man within hearing was Ariston the steersman and he was totally reliable, having presumably already worked out where we were headed. His only comment that morning was aimed at the new trierarch.

"It's too late in the year to be making a voyage like this in a trireme, beggin your pardon, sir. Too close to the storm season."

Themistocles without a shred of concern replied cheerfully,

"Beautiful calm autumn weather: the sun shines and the sea is flat as a fishpond. What could be better?"

"Maybe now, but the sea can change and change quickly."

After that, apart from rapping out the occasional observation concerning rate of stroke or need for sails to Theodorus, he sat slumped and taciturn in his seat. Themistocles seemed quite at home on a trireme; he could turn his hand to most things but from this quiet beginning he transformed our city's relationship with the sea.

Today, though, his mind was on other matters and he was expansive. In this way he resembled Miltiades: men who live a life of subterfuge and sublimation sometimes feel the need to unburden themselves. I think also that he was trying to pass on some of his thinking to Cimon, preparing him. Having brooded on it I asked him,

"Why are we going to Sparta?"

"Why not? No better time and we don't want to repeat the mistakes of the last campaign."

"Because they wouldn't help, because they gave a better hearing to Metiochus than to us, because they never came to Marathon."

"But they did."

"Only after the battle was long over."

"And how did what they saw affect them?"

"I don't know, I wasn't there, we were back in Athens, remember?"

"Well, think about it then. The great Spartan heroes arrive late at a battlefield. They arrive late because they had no intention of taking part in a battle that they believed it was impossible to win. When they arrive they discover that a rag tag citizen army of democrats has beaten the most powerful army the world has ever seen. How do you think that made them feel, Mandrocles?"

I didn't know what to say and anyway Cimon answered for me.

"I think they would have felt ashamed and envious."

"Well done, boy, but Spartans never do anything without full consideration. I think they understood then that the balance was shifting, not only in Greece but in the world. That their farmyard hegemony was open to a little more scrutiny than they'd previously expected. But I think they experienced another most un-Spartan emotion: admiration. They saw what we did and wondered how it could have happened and in that moment they wished it had been them. I think because of those reactions, our reception will be very different from the one they afforded your father."

"But why go there now? After ..."

I left the words hanging, not wanting to seem like I was questioning the judgement of such a great man. I needn't have bothered; he was beyond embarrassment in circumstances like these. He picked up my words and ran with them like an athlete at the great Olympia.

"What better time to go, our Alkmaionid friends have plenty to keep them busy now with Hipparchus out of the city. Even I hadn't anticipated the size of the pile of sherds cast against him. But there can often be a backlash, so where better for the leader of the patriots to be than defending the City of the Goddess on hostile territory? When I return with a pledge of friendship and a treaty to defend the Greek mainland against the Persians, then which true born Athenian will hesitate to cheer?"

Explained like that, it was all so simple, and he hadn't even finished.

"Also, and you mark this well, Cimon, it's sensible for people to get a break from you. It's better to be missed than taken for granted which leads to resentment. That's how they'll be feeling about the Alkmaionids going on and on about the old days and poor old Hipparchus. Better still, by the time we return I'm sure I'll have come up with substantive grounds to begin proceedings for Ostracism against Megacles. Only fair: give poor old Hipparchus a bit of company."

He must have seen the astonishment on our faces, seemed to make him enjoy himself even more.

"You have to be systematic like the Pythagoreans say, so I have all the things that I need to do on a list that I keep in my head. Right now the power has shifted towards the generals elected by tribe, but even so there are too many powerful men who don't want any more change, want to turn back to the old ways. So I have them on a list."

I didn't know what to say and Cimon showed signs of anger; this wasn't his world. Themistocles ploughed on.

"You'll understand this, Mandrocles, it's rather like the way you'd work your way through a list of the flute girls you wanted to fuck or boy acrobats if that's what you prefer. Have one then scratch it off the list. Except my list goes: Hipparchus, Megacles, Xanthippus ..."

This was too much. I interrupted him.

"But you have an agreement, he stood back and withdrew his support from Hipparchus, he helped you win, helped you ostracise his friend."

"Nothing lasts forever, boy."

Cimon asked him coldly,

"Is that why you have kept close links with the Great King?"

"Don't forget about the next Great King, I've links with him too and closer ones."

"Why?"

"Have you ever seen a burrowing animal dig out its new home, son of Miltiades?"

Cimon, nonplussed, nodded his head.

"Well then, you'll have noticed that the first thing it does is excavate a series of alternative exits it can escape through when a predator comes down the main tunnel. Just common sense."

Cimon stared at him; I couldn't tell if he was repelled or fascinated.

"Now let me get back to my list: Xanthippus, Aristides ..."

This was Cimon's breaking point.

"But you stood with Aristides in the centre at Marathon. Rallied the ranks, took blows for each other. It's one of our city's heroic stories, men still sing of it. How could ..."

"This is the Polis, boy, these are the new ways and you need to understand them if you're going to survive. I hope you listened carefully because believe me, this is the best lesson in politics you'll ever get."

The sun was waning; behind us Ariston barked an order and the Athene Nike headed towards the shore. There was no hiding and skulking in caves this trip; we ran the Athene Nike up onto a gently sloping beach of fine shingle. The crew sang as the keel scraped its way up to its sleeping place. This was so different from my last voyage to Sparta. That had been shrouded in secrecy and dread.

Fires were built and fish grilled to supplement our rations and while we waited to eat, wineskins were passed round. Themistocles was the most relaxed I'd ever seen sitting in the centre of a knot of gnarled and weather battered Thranitai. In this way he and Cimon were alike; they both felt most at home amongst the hard men who fought for them.

We finished the wine, licked the salty juices of the fish from our fingers and settled to sleep under the type of star-filled sky that seems almost within touching distance. I lay awake watching the chariots of the Gods streak white and fiery across the heavens, pleased to be free from the company of philosophers who would spout some nonsense about them really being broken off bits of stars.

Looking back over what I have just written, reader, it

came to me that it was on that beach that I began my recovery to a state of equilibrium. From where I sit now the same stars burn high above, unchanging. I wish I could say the same of myself.

The last outriders of the stars still shone faint in the heavens as we pushed off into light surf next morning. The going was fast and easy, the world relaxed and the Gods mellow. I was sitting with Cimon, looking over the stern at a pod of dolphins frisking and tumbling, when he initiated a strange conversation that showed me how our relationship had changed.

"Mandrocles, I know of your love for my sister but you must put that aside; it was doomed anyway, and listen, don't judge, listen."

He didn't know everything about my love for his sister or whatever kind of love she felt for me, but that was for us only, so I said nothing, just listened.

"I've performed my first public act and I'm being judged harshly for it. I know the gossip that for Callias to desire her means that he must have had knowledge of her, to the shame of our family; my shame, in reality."

I began to speak to attempt to reassure him but he waved me to silence.

"I know men say that I've played the bawd and pimped my sister to restore my fortunes. I know about the songs they sing. The stories that she seduced me before I was ten and that she's been fucking me ever since."

He paused, his eyes were red, and he was silently weeping, although out of anger or frustration I couldn't tell, probably both. But I knew now to keep silent. He'd carried this inside for too long; now it had to be leeched.

"The slurs about our poor house being nothing more than a brothel for unnatural acts. Then the final lie that I tired of her because I wanted fresh meat and saw Callias as a means of offloading my sister, to her eternal disgrace, and my profit."

He had to stop and for a time we both pretended a keener interest in dolphins than was the case. Then he was ready to continue.

"For me this is bad enough, it's why I've become the way I have. But for Elpinice ..."

He left the words hanging; there was no need to say more. For her, it was ruin: she was no fit wife for other matrons to entertain. In Athens then there was no way back for a woman like that, if it hadn't been for the marriage and wealth of Callias, there were those who'd have made a case for having her stoned.

I knew what Cimon wanted to say but couldn't. So he moved on to the point he needed to make, the thing that apart from me and perhaps Elpinice – who knows what they said to each other? – he couldn't tell anyone. Couldn't tell anyone because great men don't talk of such things; don't show weakness. Hard, isn't it, when you're still only a boy?

"But I had to let her marry him. What else could I do? It was the only way to restore the family fortune, to restore my father's name and reputation. But now I feel unclean, tainted. I let my sister sacrifice everything for my sake. Those rowers cheered me when I came on board but that was only because my father was their hero. Now they want it to be me. But the real hero in this fucking filthy business is ..."

I knew the answer but I also knew he needed coaxing if he were to purge himself fully.

"Is?"

"Is Elpinice, my sister, your love, the one whose willing sacrifice has restored the fortunes of the Philiads."

We went back to the dolphins and watched in silence until they were just a faint glint on the horizon.

The weather stayed fine as we cruised across the bay of

Argos then followed the rocky spur of the Peloponnese south towards its tip at Hell's Mouth. Sailing these waters you need a sound boat and a skilled crew. Get carried too close to the shore and you splinter on the rocks. The half-humans living along this shore are descended from long forgotten forest dwellers whose ancestors mated with Lapiths and centaurs. A different blood flows sluggish in their veins.

There's no mercy shown to any poor sailor who survives a wreck and struggles to shore in these semi deserted badlands. So we chose our nightfalls carefully. Even so, on the night after we rounded Hell's Mouth and pulled into the bay of Laconia we knew we were watched. We could hear them in the scrub woodland above us. Hear distant chanting and whistles. That night we banked up the fires and doubled the watch.

That same night, after Cimon had settled into his bed roll, Themistocles sought me out and sat with me by the fire, staring into the embers.

"So he got it all out at last, did he?"

I stared at him, surprised.

"Cimon, he unburdened himself?"

I suppose I should have kept quiet but was taken off guard and blurted out,

"Yes, but how did you know?"

He shook his head and laughed softly. He wasn't laughing at me, it was almost affectionate.

"Why do you think you're here, Mandrocles, that was your role. Why did you think I brought you on this trip? Last time in Sparta you tried to kill Miltiades's other son and offended the Ephors."

This time he was laughing at me, but he saw, I think, that I was hurt so added,

"But you performed your allotted role well, and who knows, there may be some further use for you."

I didn't want to answer; I still felt slighted. But then he gave me his gift.

"I have some advice for you. Listen and it will serve you well. Understand the individual and you can handle the crowd. Look inside the individual mind and you will find the levers that drive it. Know that and you know who to trust and when. You can predict them but only if you are genuinely interested in what you find."

I sat glaring at him, but I was learning an important truth.

He concluded the lesson.

"Know what's in men's hearts, Mandrocles, and you control the Demos; and I know what's in that boy's heart. Cimon would only talk to you, and even then only in the right place."

He was right, of course; men have to want to follow you.

As he got up and moved towards his sleeping place I heard him laughing at something he said under his breath. All I caught of it was,

"You like dolphins."

Next day we would arrive at the Spartan port of Gytheion and anyone who hadn't known that would have soon picked it up. As the sun rose we were joined by a flotilla of Spartan triremes that shadowed us all the way to the dock. It was clear we were expected. It was only then that the first stage of fear gripped us. The Spartan triremes blocked the harbour mouth behind us.

Lined up on the harbour mole, red cloaked and helmeted, was a phalanx of armed men.

Chapter Twelve

Gytheion is cheerless and dispiriting so it sets the mood for visiting Sparta perfectly. There was no singing or gleeful anticipation as we moored the Athene Nike to her allocated position. The Spartan red cloaks on the quay affected not to have noticed our presence. But we'd more than noticed theirs, why were they here? Had some of Themistocles's political enemies tipped them off? An air of unease permeated the ship, even affecting Themistocles, although he bustled about attempting a great show of confidence.

Only Cimon seemed pleased to be here but when he and Themistocles prepared to disembark, the commander of the Spartans curtly ordered them back on board. So we waited uneasily as the sun climbed the heavens. Then there was the clatter of hoofs. A group of horsemen burst out from the dingy alleyway leading up to the town that seemed to serve as a main street. Their leader reined in on the quay above us and pushed back his hood, eliciting a peal of joy from Cimon: it was Brasidas.

"What brings a crew of Athenian bandits to Sparta?"

It was as unfunny as it was unusual but what can you expect from a Spartan? Humour is bred out of them except jests concerning cruelty: that they seem to like well enough. However Brasidas was making an effort so we laughed, but mainly from relief at seeing him and for our appreciation of a Spartan joke's rarity value.

After the greeting as he was talking to Themistocles and Cimon I took the opportunity to look at him. The years since Marathon hadn't been kind, the skin seemed stretched tight like papyrus across the prominent bone structure of his face and he'd lost weight. He looked like a man who'd taken at least one wound too many, one which wouldn't heal: a legacy from Marathon, I suspected. In my short life I'd had the misfortune to see that look on too many men: few of them lasted long and none prospered.

Arrangements had been to billet the crew in Gytheion while a small party of us rode to the city. Very different from my last visit, when we'd arrived in secrecy and darkness forced to bypass Gytheion and avoid the highway. Also this time we would ride; Brasidas had brought us horses.

It didn't take long to get clear of the port and again I was surprised at the rugged beauty of the land, and more surprised by the absence of farmers and workers and sellers of produce along the highway. But then, the peasants who farmed this land for their Spartan masters weren't free. They were held in bond, like slaves, and kept in order by fear. As we approached the city of Sparta the land increased in fertility, sheltered by the wild range of the Taygetos Mountains. Ruled by a better state, it could have been an Arcadia fit for the Gods.

For the last section of the ride to the city we were tired and strung out along the road. I was on the left of Brasidas and we were remembering our days with Miltiades. He flinched in the middle of a tale about how the General had tricked the assembly and I saw all the colour had drained from his face; it was dead white. He brushed at his leg with his hand and I saw the spread of blood from above the knee. He noticed my glance.

"A gift from the Medes on the beach at Marathon, never healed properly, too much exercise and it opens."

I asked,

"Then why send you to fetch us?"

"Can you name another Spartan you'd trust?"

That's all I can remember of the ride. I've no recollection of arriving in Sparta and yet that little exchange with Brasidas is clear as day. I remember that we didn't have to eat black broth in the mess tent however and for that, at least, I was grateful. Themistocles had got it right about our welcome. This time was very different: we were housed in one of the few civic buildings, the one they used to house embassies from friendly states, and although shabby it was a great step up from my previous experience. Themistocles was treated as the guest friend of King Leotychidas who was, in theory, the senior of the two kings. Although you can never be sure, as nothing is the way it appears in Sparta.

Let me tell you about these two kings, reader; it's worth your attention. Few outside the ranks of the Spartiates get to come even remotely close to a Spartan king yet I've known four of them. Yes you did read that correctly, known four – although you'll have to wait a while to hear about the fourth. Poor mad Cleomenes was the first, Miltiades's guest friend who died cutting off the flesh from his own legs with a small blunt knife. Neither of the current crop – Leotychidas and the world's hero, Leonidas – came close to him for leadership and skill, at least while he was still sane.

Leotychidas was cunning and cautious but, as are all Spartans, susceptible to flattery; they're like little children in that respect. You could see the pleasure in his little piggy eyes when Themistocles ostentatiously deferred to him, lavishing praise on his sagacity and talent.

Anyone who really wants to understand how we managed to supplant them as leaders of the united Greek fleet needs to look at how Themistocles established a relationship with him. A relationship that enabled him to burrow into the jealousies and insecurities that underpinned his kingship. After that, Themistocles could exploit these weaknesses and manipulate them at will.

As for Leonidas: well, he was driven and fanatical, but also different. Different enough from other Spartans for them to be uncomfortable in his presence. He was a complicated, mixed up man. Remember Cleomenes was his brother and he'd betrayed him, probably been responsible for his death. He'd benefitted from those hideous death agonies and succeeded him as king. Not many people warm to that in a man and in that respect Spartans are no different.

He married Gorgo, Cleomenes's daughter and heir. What type of man would do that after the way he'd acted? She'd been a strange little girl and had grown up to be an intense young woman who was touched either by the Gods or madness. Put together, they magnified each other's extremes and fanaticism; it was a volatile mix for a king and queen.

Anyone who spent time with Leonidas, anywhere except on the battlefield, felt disconcerted by him. You looked into his strangely unfocussed eyes and saw he wasn't there. I think he was made for death and lusted after it and maybe that's why the powers in Sparta were happy when it took him early at the Hot Gates. For all its welcome, Sparta seemed less at ease with itself and more unstable than during the final days of the reign of poor, mad Cleomenes.

Not all of this was down to the strain of upholding the grip of terror over their Messanian helots, although slave would be a better description than helot. Our victory at Marathon had been a blow to Spartan prestige and judgement and it was a signal to their helot bondsmen that the old order could be broken. No wonder they feared the spirit of the Demos as much as the might of the Persians. All of this was very evident from the first day of our visit. Evident to everyone but Cimon, that is.

He'd always entertained a strong and totally misplaced admiration for Sparta. And remember, reader, in the end it was his loyalty to those treacherous preening bastards that brought him down. Perversely it was the best of the Spartans, Brasidas, who was most to blame for that misplaced loyalty. I was there. I watched it develop.

On our second day in Sparta when Themistocles was ensconced with the kings, Brasidas turned up early at our quarters.

"Unless this is too early for gentle Athenian city folk, come out and I'll show you how Spartans live."

Outside there were three horses and some rangy underfed dogs.

"Come on, mount up and follow me."

We rode out of the cluster of houses where our party was accommodated, past an ancient simple shrine and into the fields. Sparta was more like a series of loosely attached farmsteads or hamlets than a city. There were no walls or defensive structures but that was all part of the myth: for who would attack a settlement defended by the mighty Spartan army?

But it was good to have some time for ourselves, even though our first destination was the last thing I wanted to see. Sparta straggles across several low hills protruding like pimples and we rode across a number of these towards the river Eurotas. I had a pretty good idea right from the start where we were going, because there aren't many places worth visiting.

So I wasn't surprised when we joined a winding track with a plain temple at the end. Lying just beyond it was the older sanctuary of Artemis Orthia, whose roots stretch back into the mists of time. I suppose that they positioned this monstrosity so far from the centre indicates that even the

Spartans might have had some hidden reservations about it.

It is a grim place and well suited to its purpose which, despite all Brasidas's justification, is cruelty. Here, for reasons which in barbarian lands would include sexual perversity, they whipped and abused young boys. Some of whom died in the process. This they regarded as in some way designed to add character to them as they grew to be men. To an intelligent Athenian, it is obvious that in reality it is just another of the things that render them unable to enjoy normal social relationships with themselves, their women or anyone else.

After leaving that dark and sinister chamber it was almost a relief to arrive at the exercise fields. Here Spartan men and youths competed and honed their military skills; women are meant to compete here naked but I've never seen any. Nor to be honest would I want to if they were to be drawn from the ranks of the Spartan matrons who attend our lodgings. The only exception being Gorgo but it would be a rash and brave man who bedded her. Something of the night hangs over that intense and strange young woman: something that I think goes partway to explaining the unsettled and searching look in the eyes of her husband.

Cimon threw himself into the exercise of arms on the field with enthusiasm. Brasidas and I stayed at the periphery and practised at a more sedate pace, because my body was recovering and his wasn't. When we took a break he asked between deep breaths,

"How do you find Sparta this time, Mandrocles?"

"Better than last: at least no one's tried to kill us."

"That's because you Athenians have become surprisingly popular since Marathon."

"You're good at hiding it then."

"That's our way, but Marathon came as a shock here,

most Spartans never thought you'd fight and the ones who did bet on you to lose."

"So you must be feted then, being the only Spartan there?"

"It's not our way to fete anybody, I thought you knew that. Anyway, as you can see, Marathon's been the cause of death for me. Even if it's a death that's very slow in coming."

He smiled, there was no trace of self-pity in what he said and now it was in the open.

"There's no hope."

"No, the wound's too far gone, all I can hope for is too hang around long enough for one last chance to help redeem Sparta's honour."

He was as good as his word.

Cimon returned from the exercise in high spirits, flushed and carrying a collection of slight wounds and bruises. To my surprise I too felt the benefits: I was fit enough to fight which, bearing in mind what was headed in our direction, was fortunate. We bathed in a clear cold stream that gushed down from the mountains. The season was turning and the leaves on the scrub oaks turning brown and falling. Too late in the year to be sailing a trireme. As we climbed back onto our mounts Brasidas said,

"Tonight there is a supper being held in the honour of your delegation hosted by both kings and you will attend."

It was the most un-Spartan affair I've ever seen and although it doesn't appear in any of the heroic stories that are told of the coming war, it did as much as anything to decide the outcome. The supper was held in the house of Leonidas, which had more of the atmosphere of a shrine than a dwelling.

The bewitching Gorgo made an appearance to welcome us. I don't know if it's possible to be both exotic and modest but that's how she seemed, more like a priestess than a queen.

But the place was tainted and the scandal of how this daughter and brother of Cleomenes had benefitted from his death through their unholy alliance seemed to pollute the very pillars of the house. You could sense the ghost of the mad king lurking in the shadows.

We ate in a dimly lit hall but were kept waiting by the late arrival of Leotychidas. Themistocles, full of confidence, affected not to notice; he was like a man on the brink of achieving something great.

Eventually Leotychidas swept in and the glance he exchanged with his fellow king revealed the lack of any love or trust between the two. In that sense it was a typically Spartan arrangement and exactly the type of situation the Ephors liked. With each king keeping a suspicious eye on the other, they could divide and rule. At Leotychidas's entrance Gorgo did everything except arch her back and spit before withdrawing to her own quarters.

The food was poor but better than expected, as was the wine, which also had the virtue of being less watered than usual. The conversation was dull and repetitive until the tables were cleared, the slaves withdrew and a last crater was mixed. Then it happened.

It started badly and, to me, it seemed disaster confronted us. Leotychidas was speaking at length, putting a Spartan gloss on Marathon. He'd just reached the concluding point.

"You Athenians fought well. We respect that: but of course you had to, because in the Persian ranks there was an Athenian traitor ..."

He hadn't finished but Themistocles interrupted him with a statement that not only ran counter to all rules of guest friendship but was also a direct insult to our hosts.

"Just as there is now a Spartan one."

A few words, but I've seen draggers drawn and blood

spilled over less. Leotychidas was speechless but Leonidas, flushed and furious rasped,

"That is a lie which you will retract."

This was a man whose favoured response was physical rather than intellectual. Themistocles shrugged his shoulders with the palms of his hands outwards in an expression of puzzled resignation. He smiled then spoke, but it wasn't the apology Leonidas was expecting.

"I meant no offence; I had wrongly assumed that the whereabouts of the recently deposed King Demaratus of Sparta would be as well known here as they are in every other polis in Greece."

Leotychidas and Leonidas exchanged glances, firmly on the same side now. Leotychidas made as if to speak but Themistocles hadn't finished. The room, the earth and the stars stopped in their tracks as we waited for what would come next.

We didn't have long: Themistocles smiled affably at each king in turn then began one of the speeches that would change the world. Whether it would be for good or evil hung in the balance. It was only short and I remember every word so I'll recount it here. It is worth your attention, reader, and after you've read it you will be among the select band who understand the truth.

"Forgive me, generous hosts and allies. I am a simple man, plain of speech which can sometimes unintentionally offend. All I intended was to lay a platform of understanding upon which we can build. You Spartans are reputed to respect plain speaking?"

He phrased this as a question, looking at each in turn. Neither responded in any way and he took this as assent to continue. I could feel the hairs rising on the back of my neck. I glanced at Cimon, two emotions chased each other across his face: anger at Themistocles's betrayal of guest friendship, and anticipation of what was coming.

"You are correct about the traitor Hippias as I am about Demaratus: in this way we sit in the same trireme. You are also correct that we fought well at Marathon. Marathon changed the world in many ways. Two of these are of particular interest to Sparta."

The chamber continued to hold its breath and he continued to speak into the cold silence.

"The first is that Persian defeat at Marathon means that no King can safely rule the Persian Empire unchallenged until that defeat is avenged. So it has become inevitable that the Persians will return with a far greater force, and this time you will have to fight or be destroyed. We Athenians will not be capable of another Marathon against far greater odds. Do we agree?"

The two kings nodded. Their mood altered, they were hooked.

"The second is a direct consequence of your failure to fight with us that day. You know as well as any that Greeks wonder why you, defenders of the mainland and leaders of Greece, were not present. They now look towards Athens with different eyes. So this is your dilemma. You will have to fight, but –"

He paused on this word 'but', left it hanging in the air. We knew that the kill was seconds away.

"But things have changed: your hegemony over the Greeks is no longer unquestioned. There are many who would rather be led by us and, even worse for you, there are some who would love to see you weakened, fighting alone against the Persians. I speak of your slave population, the Messanian Helots, who would rise against you."

At this, I expected both kings to leap at him. But they

didn't: maybe Spartans really do appreciate plain speaking. They nodded for him to continue but I sensed if he misjudged this next bit disaster would follow.

"So your position has weakened since Marathon whilst ours has strengthened. And not only in terms of reputation."

He paused, not only for effect; I think he was truly relishing the moment and wanted to draw it out. What he said next astonished everyone in the chamber, Spartan and Athenian alike.

"When the Persians return they will face a fleet of three hundred new and specially modified Athenian triremes."

I almost fell off the bench at this lie but managed to control myself; Cimon was staring at him now with undiluted admiration.

"The coming war will be fought as much at sea as on land. But mark this well: it is only at sea where it can be won."

He paused again, giving time for this to sink in.

"The Great King will have to supply a large army on hostile ground. For this he will have to control the sea routes and the Greek coastline. We can prevent this. Athens now has, if not the biggest - that will still be the Great King's - the most effective and deadly fleet the world has seen."

Then he finished, shrugged again and looked from one king to the other.

For a moment there was silence as the kings exchanged glances and Themistocles beamed benevolently at them. Leotychidas nodded and Leonidas asked tersely,

"So what are you proposing?"

Themistocles replied with the slightly hurt demeanour of one whose charity has been rejected.

"Offering, not proposing."

He was enjoying this. Leonidas controlled himself sufficiently to snap back.

"Offering, then?"

"I'm offering you leadership of a Greek alliance, including command of the mighty Greek fleet."

The two kings silently interrogated each other for a few seconds and then, to my astonishment, they began to clap.

Chapter Thirteen

The first glimpse of danger was just a tiny speck on the horizon. You needed good eyes to see anything. So nobody got too excited, except perhaps Ariston; his mood changed and he became gradually more subdued. This we did notice because he hated Sparta and had been in high spirits from the moment we rounded Hell's Mouth and set off back north down the Peninsula towards Athens and freedom.

Everyone except Cimon was happy to be away: there's a feeling of tension and unease hanging over Sparta. Maybe they've got used to it, but it's no place for Athenians. Themistocles put on a great act while we were there, good enough for any of our dramatists to want him on their cast. I remember Aeschylus once saying that when Themistocles decided to devote his life to the polis it was a bad day for the drama festivals.

But once we were away from that place of dread and cruelty, whose atmosphere you inhale daily alongside air, he visibly relaxed and wanted to talk. Thus he indulged himself and educated Cimon and the rest of us in the stern as we rattled down the coast driven by a strengthening breeze. It was useful having Cimon because he was sufficiently proud of his birthright to be any man's equal and artless enough to ask any question that came to him.

"When did you manage to procure three hundred new triremes, son of Neocles?"

Maybe it wasn't artless; perhaps he was teasing. Whichever, it didn't bother Themistocles in the least, and he boomed with laughter.

"You know the answer to that as well as I do, son of Miltiades. I haven't got any of them, I made it up on the spot; the Gods inspired me."

He beamed back at the puzzled faces staring at him, and then answered more seriously.

"But if they don't exist now then they'll soon have to, and not just because I promised them to those twin boobies who rule Sparta."

Cimon started to ask,

"But how ...?"

"Doesn't matter how. We have to find a way of building those ships because without them Athens will die and the new ways of the Demos will be finished. So when we get back, that's what we'll turn our hands to."

The breeze continued to strengthen and the day was dying so Ariston turned our prow towards a sheltered cove with a gently sloping shingle beach. That night Themistocles broached a jar of decent quality wine he'd brought along for this moment. We sat round the fires drinking and talking as the breeze dropped and the moon rose. Tomorrow would be a good day for voyaging. Any thoughts concerning the distant speck on the horizon were forgotten.

Next day we got away slightly later than usual; the festival mood of the night relaxed our vigilance. It was a mistake. As we pulled out of the bay to resume our course northwards we saw them. Still some distance off, but lying across the course we had to steer. Not just a tiny speck on the horizon: two ships with a third lagging some way behind. Theodorus sent one of the Thranitai scuttling up the mast for a better view.

"Two ships, like us low in the water and another so far behind it must be in trouble. They're too far off to be sure, but I'll wager they're triremes."

Ariston shouted up,

"What course?"

"Can't tell, but if it's what we saw yesterday then they must be after us cos they're getting closer on a course to intercept us."

Ariston turned back towards Themistocles.

"What course do you want: we can either meet them or run?"

"Depends on if it's two or three."

Ariston shouted back up the mast.

"How far behind is the third one lagging?"

"Hard to say: two, maybe three hours."

"How long till we hit the other two?"

"If we take it nice and slow, sometime after noon."

Ariston looked at Themistocles; he didn't need to say anything, everyone on the Athene Nike had heard the shouted interchange. Themistocles said nothing, just stood staring out to sea. He was going to have to make the decision on which all our lives depended. A decision that had nothing to do with the Polis and his experience. He'd never commanded at sea, knew nothing about sea fights. He was at a crossroads and managed nothing more than,

"Where could we run to?"

I don't think he wanted an answer: he was playing for time. Time which Ariston gave him by asking me,

"What about you, Mandrocles? You'll have to lead the hoplites if it comes to a fight."

I hadn't considered that, but looking round I saw he was right; there wasn't much leadership to be had from the other seven or the four archers and Cimon was too precious to risk. I didn't know what to say. Theodorus had joined us in the stern and prompted me.

"You fought against two ships on the escape from Samos."

It gave Themistocles the space he needed.

"Helmsman, rowing master, is the ship up to it?"

Ariston, who wouldn't have gone back to Sparta for anything, nodded then Theodorus said,

"The Athene Nike's the equal of any two ships. Just need to do what we did last time: get between 'em then pull out the Diekplous."

"Diekplous?"

"Means we get between 'em like, sir, then veer left and ram one of the bastards."

Ariston grunted while Themistocles asked,

"What about you, Captain of the Marines?"

It took some seconds before I realised he was talking to me, then I managed to grunt,

"It worked last time."

And that's how it was settled.

In that way I assumed my first command. But it would be a long time before I'd need to do anything and the agonising period of watch and wait that precedes any fight at sea began its slow unravelling. It doesn't take long to check your gear's in order: the armour straps aren't too slack or tight, and that the edge of your sword and spear are sharp.

Then it's just sit and wait, trying not to fidget or run off at the mouth. Cimon helped fill in those unforgiving hours. Once he'd equipped himself in the parts of his father's panoply that fitted comfortably enough, he carried on with the questions he'd been asking.

"So, how will you persuade the best men to support your plans?"

"Once we've replaced Aristo-Kratia with Demo-Kratia then I won't need to."

I recognised an evasive answer when I heard one and so, apparently, did Cimon.

"But for now the assembly just listen and shout, it's the five hundred who make the decisions and most of them don't want your ships or dreams of the sea."

"It won't always be that way, but for the moment you're right so I'll have to find a way of convincing them."

They went on like this for some time and we were glad of the diversion. Thinking back over it I realise that Cimon, even when so young, had a good sense of how to turn the wheels of power. Themistocles was proved right of course about the coming of demokratia but it came too late for him. The system that you are so familiar with, reader, and which onion head manipulates with such skill is precisely what Themistocles envisaged.

By the time the sun shone directly overhead we could see clearly what we were up against. Two triremes from Aegina were powering their way towards us, obviously anxious we wouldn't escape. They were coming on to us at considerable speed. Fortunately the third must have been severely inca-pacitated and had fallen further behind. Whatever was to happen, this ship would be in no position to play a hand.

We'd been betrayed, but by whom? There was no time to speculate; we had too much else on our minds. Our tactics puzzled Cimon and Themistocles at first, both of them being novices at sea. Themistocles had shrewdly left the running of the boat to Ariston and Theodorus. In those hours waiting for contact I believe I missed the presence of Lysias as much as I've missed anyone in my life. If he were there he'd have taken command and judged when to turn and ram. As it was, it would be down to the helmsman and bosun to manoeuvre and to the fighting man in command to give the orders. That man was now me.

Cimon asked the question for the both of them.

"Why are we going so slowly when they're racing at us?"

Ariston shrugged.

"We're not the ones who want this. Let them tire themselves out: see where that gets them."

All the same our pace was increasing and as the tension ratcheted up, the leisurely manner aboard the Athene Nike was replaced by sweaty-handed fear. Skins of watered wine were passed round, along with food for those who could stomach it. There are men whose appetite is sharpened by the approach of battle, but I think that most are like me and their guts shrivel up with apprehension. Everyone drinks, though.

Waiting is a lonely time and you never get used to it but I found, to my surprise, that responsibility helps. Here, for the first time, I had others to think of and even if I hadn't been thinking about them, Themistocles had.

"Whatever happens in the next couple of hours, Mandrocles, keep this thought in your head: Cimon and I must be saved."

I stared back at him blankly. Cimon yes, but I thought Themistocles would fight in the front rank like Miltiades, and like he had at Marathon.

"Come on, don't be stupid, Mandrocles. Athens can't afford to lose me in some no-account skirmish at the arse end of a pointless war with Aegina. Likewise, think what the reaction back home would be to Cimon falling here as a youth."

I wasn't too slow to realise that this latter blow would be as much about his reputation being the man who led the son of Miltiades to his death as the actual loss to Athens of a teenage boy. Though looking back at what Cimon subsequently achieved for the city, maybe I was too harsh.

He was fiddling with the strapping of his shoulder guards while watching the two black hulls with their murderous rams cutting through the water, approaching at speed. Such sights I've found either focus a man's mind or shroud it in a fog of panic and confusion: Themistocles's mind was clear.

"You and these two in the front rank with me and the boy behind. If we grapple and they board us, hold them back until the sailors cut us free."

If only reality was so simple. I'd had one experience of a deck fight and I knew it was unpredictable. If you managed to control your fears you dealt only with what was directly in front of you. If you lost control you were killed.

The archers tested their bow strings and notched the first arrows. We only carried four archers this trip; like most, they were Scythians who kept themselves to themselves and communicated in some barbaric tongue that didn't even sound like words. Most of them didn't speak Greek so they and our crew didn't have much to do with each other. In fact, you only really noticed them when they were needed. They were needed now.

The only other fighting men were the four in partial hoplite gear at the prow. Like my two grizzled companions, they weren't of the best quality. If things got really bad the Thranitai would fight, but if it ever got to that stage it was only because hope of escape was lost.

Behind me I could hear Ariston shouting directions to Theodorus and Theodorus setting the tempo for the rowers. At least we were going into this with a well led and experienced crew. I prayed they wouldn't board us. I'd adjusted my fighting gear, no heavy bronze body armour for me, I'd a horror of going over the side and being dragged swiftly down into the depths by the weight. I'd fight as I did at Marathon: crouched behind my shield, wearing only shoulder guards over a padded linen corselet.

Themistocles was swearing and grumbling a stream of oaths and complaints but, as is the way of things at such times of heightened emotion, one fragment lodged in my mind.

"Last time I take risks: this could stop everything. If I get back, Oh Father Poseidon Earth Shaker, I swear I'll proceed straight away in having that bastard Megacles ostracised."

Cimon was next to him behind Miltiades's shield so I couldn't see if he was wearing full armour. I smiled at him, intending reassurance. I couldn't speak, my mouth was dry and I needed to piss. Strange how it's always that way. He smiled back, well in control of himself.

We were nearly set: in minutes they'd be within range of the archers. Their two triremes were well handled: they'd kept pace and maintained their distance. At the opportune time they'd split and come at us from different directions. One would ram and the other board unless they just wanted us sunk, in which case it would all come down to their sharply serrated rams.

Our only chance was to get between them and try the Diekplous: something that only triremes that had engaged with the Persian navy knew. Our best chance lay in them not expecting it. Only a few lengths now. A first exploratory arrow came whistling across with sufficient force to stick in the deck. I heard a shout.

"Mandrocles."

I looked round at Ariston red faced veins in his neck bulging. What did he want?

"Mandrocles, do your fucking job."

Then I remembered why I was in front at the centre. My mouth had dried completely and I had to work at getting some saliva before shouting,

"Archers fire at range."

As I shouted arrows were already outbound; like the crew, these lads knew their jobs. After the stately slow motion dance stretching out to eternity that had led us here, everything speeded up. The rowers picked up the stroke and the deck hummed under our feet as the Athene Nike leapt across the water.

Men were praying under their breaths but other than that and the creaking of timber and the regular plash of the oars there was only one sound. The beat and shout with which Theodorus set the pace. Calculating the correct pace was everything. Well, almost everything. The decisive factor in whether we lived or died was the timing of Ariston's orders. Sailing under Miltiades, Ariston told him when and what to shout. Now he'd have to do it all himself, although I'd shout it with him.

So no one spoke; we waited for his command. I motioned to the marines to crouch and brace then pulled my helmet down over my face and disappeared into the claustrophobic and isolated world of the partially sighted. Athene Nike flew at full pelt across the narrow gap of water separating them from us, her old timbers and ropes creaking with the strain.

From somewhere below came the stench of fear loosened bowels. Almost in slow motion arrows were flying across us. I sensed one miss my face and sink into a target further back. The prow seemed to lift with its speed across the waves as, with our killer ram foremost, we flew at them.

On the ships facing us, the decks were no longer packed with an undifferentiated mass but with distinct and recognisable men. Within minutes, maybe less, either they or we would be dead.

So it begins.

Chapter Fourteen

Then it happens: you watch and see before your mind understands. Like in a dream, but one you can't wake from however hard you try. I've seen men cover their heads with their cloaks before the death stroke takes them, as if they thought that if they couldn't see it then it wasn't real. Nothing helps: you fight or you die; nowhere to run to at sea.

Heading towards each other seems to more than double the speed, makes every movement your ship takes slow and clumsy. What happens next and what happened last get confused, all you can do is try to react in time. So it's no wonder a complicated manoeuvre like Diekplous so often goes wrong. The two triremes headed straight at us; until they split we couldn't make our move. Perhaps they knew that, knew what was coming and threw the lucky dice.

I watched Ariston's face as he waited to shout the order. Saw the wave of confusion and uncertainty cloud it as it hit him that maybe they wouldn't split. That they'd ram us together then pull back and watch us sink because they had no intention of boarding.

I could tell from his face that he had no other plan and that if they came on we were finished. He thought we were finished. A screech and frisson of pain made me blink; an arrow skittered off my shield rim and sheered off past my right cheekbone, a splinter from the barb hit me under my jaw. I pulled my head back in behind the shield, gasping with shock. That must be when they split.

I heard him shout,

"Diekplous!"

We lurched to the left as the rowers on that side drew in their oars. It was too late; there wasn't time or space for it to work. I could see their helmsman clearly: he was laughing, head thrown back in triumph; he knew they'd timed it right. But everything at sea is chancy, nothing's in the wineskin for certain. I was staring, fixated at the great red bearded face of their grinning helmsman. Then I felt what he felt and saw the cocky grin vanish as he was thrown out of his seat.

We'd missed the manoeuvre, couldn't turn quick enough to ram as close to ninety degrees as possible. Instead we careered at nearer forty five down their side so our heavy ram smashed and splintered its way through their three banks of oars.

Nothing but screaming and squeals: blood splashing in gouts out through their oar holes. The worst that can befall a trireme, as a heavy ram moving at speed makes splinters out of ninety oars. Smashing the chests, arms and hips of the benched in rowers. Changing them from hard muscled men into slippery, mangled torsos.

Their deck became a bloody froth of confusion and screaming as they lurched off course, directionless, now only capable of rowing in a circle. The agonised squealing must have carried all the way back to Aegina.

It had happened in the blink of an eye as I crouched behind my shield. Ariston was shouting to Theodorus, not to reverse as expected but to carry on clear then turn to face the other ship. This was only feet away but backing water not wanting to plough into its crippled companion.

So now it was down to who could turn quickest. I was

sweating inside the helmet, watching the limited patch of water visible through the eye slits of my helmet glistening in the fierce sun. Looking round I saw we'd taken some hits from arrows and that the archers on the stricken ship were still firing. There were screams below deck on the Athene Nike too: I guessed this must be from some of the lower deck rowers, less experienced men who hadn't drawn their oars in quickly enough.

But there wasn't time for worrying about any of that; just three banks of rowers backing water and the other three pulling straight ahead for all they were worth. As we turned I tried to orientate myself so I'd know how to position my men for what came next. As we turned, I could only see the other trireme by looking over my shoulder. Suddenly it lurched into view.

It happened in a blur: we were going head on at each other. Something no trireme should do, hit head on at ramming speed and both ships are fucked. So we both blinked at the last minute: both swerved but Ariston and his counterpart from Aegina had both held their nerve for too long and we left it too late.

The Athene Nike careered down the side of their boat. I could see its name, 'The Flying Dolphin', and I remember a foolish thought rattling through my mind that it was a fitter name for a pleasure boat than a weapon of war.

The screeching and tearing of wood was horrendous, even though most of our rowers and theirs managed to pull their oars back in time to avoid splintering and mutilation. The impact turned the prow of our ship toward their stern, there was the crash, a further impact, and I was thrown to the deck.

Both triremes slithered to a halt, locked in fatal congress. Now it was about which crew would recover quickest to win the deck war. For us it was worse: we had more men down and knew if this lasted long enough then their other broken up ship would reorganise its surviving oarsmen sufficiently to pull alongside its sister craft and cross its deck to board us. For us, we were in no hurry to leave the deck of Athene Nike. Our only chance was to hold them back long enough for our crew to disentangle us from them and push off.

There's nothing clear about it, see? It's all confusion, chance and blood rage. Our prow was clear of their stern so all our fighting men gathered in our stern section in two rough ranks of three, masking Ariston with Cimon and Themistocles at the rear. Our other man stayed in the prow with an arrow in his throat.

Then they were spilling over the side and at us.

There's a simple procedure for defending a deck. Simple, that is, to understand, but not to execute, and it all depends on keeping your balance. Lock your shield with the shield of the man next to you then crouch behind it and keep your elbows in, your head down and your weight low. Try anything fancy and you're a dead man.

Normally the crew boarding are doing it from a position of strength so you only get one chance to beat them because you only hold one advantage. They're shifting from one moving deck onto another so by comparison you're well balanced and stable. Use that and hit them with your shields as they land.

There was a breeze, I remember, and a slight swell. They came over the side on a roll and as a consequence the drop onto our deck was extended. I shouted something and we moved forwards into them, our rank leading the three behind, pushing. Being hit by an armoured man in balance as you jump down onto his deck is close to a death sentence.

We used the roll to rock into them, shoulders behind our shields. Once you clash they stumble and when that happens, whatever guard they have disappears. That's when you stab out with swords between the shields. The first on board are dead men, staggering between you and the ones jostling them from behind. The ones who hit our deck were no different. The man facing me lost his footing and was twisted round. So when I crashed into him he wasn't even facing me as I killed him. The pressure of the men behind us gave us ballast, the pressure behind them just destabilised.

If you get it right, then the first on deck stagger back into their comrades as you cut them down. The comrades can't get their arms free to ply their weapons so if you've maintained your balance and you're up close, you can use the point of the short sword to good effect. We had the momentum with us: the first comers went down, impeded the next wave who we fell on, killing them too. Behind us Themistocles and Cimon were jabbing with long spears over our shoulders into our opponents.

The first seconds went as well as they could have, but at this point you run out of advantage. Momentum has carried you to the side. The deck's slippery with blood and you're standing on dead and dying men. There's no chance of another charge because there's no more ground. And this is where their numbers begin to tell, because your initial success has lured you onto a killing floor.

Seems so clear and logical when you read it, doesn't it reader? Like a ball game with rules. Not when you're there. Not when you're in the belly of it. Mired in its entrails you're either raging and out of your wits or terrified and unable to think. Strangely it's the only time when being in charge helps. Helps because you have to think about more than just your own survival. You have to think about your men and what comes next.

So we came to a halt where our deck met theirs, winded and breathing heavy. For a second we stood near enough to touch them, waiting for the next move. It didn't come from either us or them. It came from the ship. The deck heaved and we swayed out of balance.

Their faces weren't so near; there was a gap between the decks. Then the deck jagged backwards, my right wingman, Thestochius, a farmer from out toward Sounion I think, lurched forwards and over the side into the narrow gap between the two ships. Didn't make a sound; slid smoothly into the water and was dragged straight down to the depths by the heavy and expensive armour which had been the pride of his life.

"Don't just stand, help us push off."

The voice was Theodorus. He was wielding an axe, cutting the ropes they'd thrown to bind our ship to theirs. The crew were using their oars to push the ships apart. A crazed youth from the Flying Dolphin leapt across the widening gap to our deck. Perhaps he thought it would bring him glory. He fell short and was swallowed by the man-killing sea to join Thestochius and the fishes. A couple of ragged pulls on the oars and we were moving. I saw their rowers push out their oars to begin the chase.

But Poseidon Earth Shaker was with us that day. Their ship moved but in a different direction than intended. We'd smashed one of the steering rudders as we bumped our way along her so the ship couldn't heed the helmsman's direction. Their archers fired salvos into us until we were out of range. It was all they could do now, with one ship crippled and the other unable to steer a course.

Once we were out of range, or they'd run out of shafts or lost interest I took off my helmet and rejoined the world of men. We had eight dead and about twice that broken. But worse, we were damaged and on open water.

Triremes are good fast fighting platforms but hard to handle and precarious in anything other than smooth waters. We'd been hit twice: sections of the hull had buckled and we were taking water. The deck was offset and there were gashes in the timbers. So if they'd been able to pursue there's no chance we could have got away. But what might just be a setback on land is often a mortal blow at sea. Things were about to get worse and if I'd studied Ariston's face more carefully I'd have been aware of our predicament earlier.

We made slower going than Themistocles wanted: he worried about the third ship and the possibilities of the other two patching themselves up. So there was no chance of pulling the Athene Nike up to a beach for repairs. We couldn't afford to be caught. So that night we anchored just inside the mouth of a sheltered inlet. No fire, no hot food and no sleep. Well, not until the early morning by when it was too late.

The first watches of that black night were disturbed by the howling of one of the worst broken up third row oarsmen. He carried on for hours until his mates must have done what was necessary to ease his passage. After that it was quieter; I think the example had an effect on the other wounded. Themistocles didn't sleep at all: I think for him this was a night of self-doubt and creeping fear.

I woke before first light, thinking I'd not slept. I was filthy with the coagulated blood of whoever it was I'd killed and smelled rank; we were short of fresh water. The dawn was stained an unnatural livid shade of yellowy orange. The sailors didn't like it. And it was calm even then at dawn when there should be a breeze. Still and close, more like midday.

Ariston, with Theodorus to back him up, suggested that we stay put for the day but Themistocles refused.

"Why, it's a calm day? That must be good for the ship."

"Calm now, Sir, but it's later I'm worried about."

"Stay close to shore then, any sign of a storm and we can shelter."

"Beg pardon, Sir, but that's not as easy as it sounds. Get caught on a lee shore and ..."

"I don't care about that. Whatever the danger, it's less than them catching up with us."

"But they're seamen too, they won't want to sail any more than we do."

"Even better, help us get away. Now get this ship moving."

Ariston turned back to the helm and Theodorus to his position between the rowing benches. I could see they were agitated and this troubled me. If experienced men like them, the best in the fleet, were scared to sail then we were taking a big risk. It wasn't just me troubled: the mood across the Athene Nike was the same, tense and brooding.

It didn't get any better as the day grew increasingly oppressive and the men sweated over their oars. Not a trace of breeze to fill the sails, which remained furled. High above, the sun shimmered opaquely red behind a dense haze and below the wine dark sea lay sullen, black and still. Those of us with no particular duties sweltered on the deck taking advantage of whatever scant shade there was. During the morning, another smashed up oarsman died and went over the side.

So it went on, that nightmare day: so oppressive you could feel the flaccid air compressing your skin. The shoreline we sailed along lurked under the heat haze and seemed to shift about like a mirage. I developed a sick headache, even Cimon's high spirits evaporated; slumped and sullen, he gazed down into the water.

No one looked at Themistocles, who sat silent in the trierarch's chair. The crew knew something bad was coming and they blamed him. Even drinking the limited ration of watered wine brought no relief: as soon as it was swallowed it oozed out of the sweat pores in a sickly slime.

The light was so strange it distorted distance; at times I

was certain I saw black ships close up following, at others it seemed we alone existed, sailing forever on a sea of horror. But there was some relief: sometime in the afternoon Ariston called across.

"We're sailing our own coastline now, just negotiate this next headland and we're almost home."

There was a ragged cheer from those close enough to hear, which as the news spread was taken up on the lower benches. As we rounded the point I realised we were sailing round some type of island, we had to sail clear of the rocks then steer a course for the mainland. The late afternoon light was a bruised mix of colour: black, purple and red.

Then, out of this preternatural silence, there was a deafening clap of thunder straight overhead and the sea which had been a turbid listless mass began to heave.

I've never seen a storm like that one, conjured up out of nothing by the Gods. From nowhere a strong wind was blowing and the figurehead of the Athene Nike began to toss like a spooked stallion. A jagged streak of forked lightning hit the sea about half a stade away and suddenly everything aboard was noise and commotion. Orders were screeched as Ariston tried to wrestle the twin rudders to point us at the shore.

Holding on to the side of the trierarch's seat, I watched in horror as the flat surface was transformed into a watery mountain range. We balanced about fifteen spear lengths above a foaming trough, then – like some lever had been pressed releasing us – we tumbled down into the foam tossed abyss. We were underwater, the deck swamped by a universe of water. I held on for dear life, others weren't so fortunate. When we came up there were spaces on the rowing bench. Rope, smashed oars and other debris were strewn across the normally immaculately neat deck.

Then we were climbing another mountain of water, and I

saw Ariston's face: it was a mask of terror. He had no control and we were lost. The boat was coming to pieces, there was a great crack running up the mast, it began to vibrate violently. We were thrown about the sea like we were a child's plaything and turned right round.

I could see land ahead; we must be being blown back towards the island. With a splintering of wood, the mast fell across the rowing benches and down into the sea. It was still attached and began to act as a type of counter rudder. All was screaming, cracking timber, thunder and howling wind. I covered my head with my cloak and waited for death.

The crash, when it finally came, drove all the breath out of me. I wondered for a moment if I was dead because the sickening movement had reduced to a rolling of the hull. Someone grabbed me, shouting,

"Get to the prow, help pull her out."

I got up and stumbled for'ard: the prow was a mess, the figurehead gone. Down below men were standing in the water. At first I didn't understand.

"Get down and help them, damn you."

I jumped, landed on shingle, was knocked over by a wave; someone helped me to my feet. It came to me that we'd been thrown up onto shore. The Gods were saving us for another day.

We couldn't save the Athene Nike though. She broke up on that shore. My link with Samos, my most loyal friend, pounded to pieces. Next morning we still sat on that beach, those of us who survived, that is. We were in an inlet staring across at the Attic mainland, gathered round the salvaged figurehead of the Athene Nike. Between us and the mainland there was a deep water channel which fishing boats were sailing out to sea blown by an early morning breeze.

Ariston had been weeping for his ship.

"The barky, the lovely barky, my ship. Gone, my ship."

Themistocles, who was fully recovered now back on land, tried to comfort the man whose advice he'd refused.

"She'll rise again helmsman, soon you'll sail her successor."

The words had no effect so, after watching the fishing boats a while, he changed tack.

"Tell me is there a breeze blowing down this channel every morning?"

"Far as I know there is."

"What is this bay?"

"That's Salamis, sir, it's the bay of Salamis."

Chapter Fifteen

Themistocles was good as his word regarding his promise to the Gods. He began his prosecution of Megacles as soon as we got back. So by Spring festival the following year, the council of five hundred were gathered to rule on another Ostracism. This one didn't go quite as smoothly. I was eating honey cakes and drinking hot spiced wine with Aeschylus and Lyra when the summons came. Aeschylus was excitable; there was talk that his trilogy for this year's Dionysia might win the prize goat and the celebrity that would follow.

He'd been watching over Lyra since she'd been hurt at an entertainment in a merchant's house that had spun out of control. A rich Thracian trader had taken her to a private chamber and used her beyond the limits of her role. Taken her by force, brutally, as if it was her agony he enjoyed rather than the act itself.

Demetrius, the girls' guard, had been drinking elsewhere in the house and therefore arrived too late to intervene. The only positive consequence of his tardiness was to ensure that it will be a long time before the Thracian can use his generative equipment again without considerable pain.

For Lyra, though, healing would take longer. She looked wasted and feverish: round her eyes there remained visible signs of bruising, although the real scarring was internal.

The owner of the flute girls' stable had demanded a hefty sum for the damage, most of which he kept for himself.

I'd been trying to persuade her to move on, but with no success.

"Move on to what, Mandrocles? What else is there for women like me in Athens? The mistress of a rich man for a while perhaps, but that never lasts."

She was right: what else was there? But she'd obviously been thinking about it more deeply.

"Anyway, I'll have to give it up soon, I'll be too old and then what?"

We didn't need to answer; we'd both seen enough of ex-flute girls grown too old plying their trade in the Ceramicus amongst the tombs.

"So now we've something else in common, Mandrocles: life has damaged us both."

She looked hurt too, no brave face this time, too much suffering. I think if there was ever a moment when I came near to saying something real to her, maybe even offering her an alternative, that was it. But Aeschylus was there and I've never been good at talking in front of others. Even without him there wouldn't have been time, as Demetrius hammered at the door.

"Themistocles bids you attend him at his house by the ..."

"We know where his house is."

Aeschylus answered for us, cutting off Demetrius in mid flow, to his chagrin. He enjoyed any opportunity to extend his role from the routine thuggish tasks to something more elevated. Although, to be fair to him, he tried to take good care of the girls without attempting to sample any of the merchandise.

The house was crowded: all the great man's clients were there and a surprising cross section of the Athenian Polis: men who you would both expect and not expect to find in the house of Themistocles; Xanthippus, for one. The atmosphere was febrile and rumour stalked the corridors and whispered in quiet corners. This was more than just the machinations of the Athenian Polis: there was a fast ship just moored in the Piraeus that had brought news from Persia.

Darius was at last dead, it seemed, but that's all that could be agreed upon. There was a school of thought that believed him to have been dead for some time, the news having been kept a secret to prevent turmoil. Others asserted he'd been toppled in a palace coup and then killed after being blinded and gelded. There was no clear evidence for either of these propositions but then most people love to complicate a simple truth.

Conspiracy and plot are ever seductive, particularly with those either too lazy or lacking the intellect to apply the rigours of logic. I'm surprised to find myself writing these words: it would appear that the influence of the parasite philosophers who clutter up the city's public places and who I've always detested must have found a chink in my armour.

What everyone was agreed upon however was that this must have imposed a state of stasis on the empire and that whatever its intentions for us had been we would now be granted a respite. We believed this until Themistocles, whose face shone with an unnatural sheen of excitement, shouted us to quiet and said,

"Why behave like children? Start to think. There is a succession in the empire, Xerxes will succeed: at this very moment he occupies the throne of gold and ivory. Mardonius is his man and what satrap can any of you name who can withstand those two and survive?"

This was said with absolute certainty and later I came to wonder how he was in a position to be so certain. Later still I understood but back then, like everyone else, I just waited, silent, to hear what would come next.

"But."

He paused, milking the moment keeping us in suspense.

"But, and it's a considerable but: he won't rest secure until he proves himself."

He cast his eyes across us as we waited, silent, even Xanthippus. I saw Aeschylus studying him in fascination and if you care and know where to look you will find much of the manner of Themistocles in his plays. Even down to his last ones: the spell Themistocles cast over him was never broken. In the silence I think we were all starting to anticipate what was coming next.

"He can never think the crown and diadem are truly his until he asserts his authority, and we all know the only way he can do that, don't we?"

Well, we were beginning to at least suspect.

"And not only he but every Persian who slunk back home in shame with his tail between his legs from our glory at Marathon. Every Persian from ambitious young Mardonius and the proud satraps who shat themselves with fear as they ran from us that day to the badly led common soldiers and the grieving mothers, wives and daughters they'd left at home. Since that day no one in the empire is at ease with themselves, from the Great King to the slave who empties his piss pot. They itch with shame and there's only one way to scratch that itch."

One of Themistocles's few weaknesses was that he obviously enjoyed holding men in the palm of his hand too much. He was certainly enjoying himself now.

"Well, isn't there, Athenians?"

No one answered; we knew we weren't meant to.

"Because you know what the itch is, don't you?"

Still silence: all Athenians know and enjoy the rhetorical question.

"Well, you should do, because it's us; we're the itch and until he's scratched us good and proper he can never really be the Great King. So don't go dreaming that the death of Darius is good news and it delays the inevitable because it doesn't. It's the exact opposite. The death of Darius has brought the war nearer to us, almost near enough to touch."

This wasn't good news and standing there in his house we didn't know how to react. After Marathon, despite his warnings, we'd convinced ourselves we were safe and it would never come; or if it did, it would be far in the future. Some men let out involuntary groans of anguish.

"Near enough to touch a city that's not ready. A city that's done nothing but ignore the frightening reality since Marathon. Where is our fleet? Where is the Greek Alliance? Where is the pledge of support from Sparta?"

Now we were scared, particularly those of us who'd stood and fought at Marathon.

"And why are we in this state of pathetic unreadiness? You know, you know, don't you?"

We knew he was going to tell us. And now, as with all great orators his mood had changed: thunder replacing sarcasm. He face red suffused with blood anger.

"Well, I'll tell you this. We're unready because those fucking great men, those aristos, those good men have been too busy greasing their own palms. Too busy greasing their sticky palms to look out for the safety of the city of the Goddess."

I don't know how he could keep a straight face considering his was the reputation for palm greasing. But I think that one of the traits of a powerful speaker is the ability to, for the moment, believe every word he is saying. Themistocles certainly seemed to and thundered on.

"Those same Alkmaionids who didn't want to face the enemy last time, who even tried to betray us by signalling to their Persian friends on the field of Marathon. They are the ones who've opposed every measure of mine to prepare us for war."

He paused again, but this time he was forced to. I'd been watching Xanthippus while Themistocles spoke and from his face it was clear that whatever their agreement had been, this went well beyond it. At first he'd looked amused, then surprised. At the mention of his clan his face changed; he seemed to be on the point of interrupting. Instead he gestured to those around him and walked out. About half a dozen followed him.

"There! See there, friends! We have proof: as soon as the voice of truth is heard the aristo flinches and leaves the house. Only the Demos understands. Understands that if we are to fight the Persians there is another battle we have to win first."

We understood this, before our very eyes the battle lines had been redrawn – and not in Themistocles's favour, it would appear. Most of what he did seemed to make sense only in retrospect but it seemed particularly rash to reduce his support so publically. If he sensed this himself he didn't show it.

"The five hundred meet tomorrow in the Agora and they need to understand what the city of the Goddess thinks, so burn the midnight oil and rouse up our support. All the friends of the Demos need to be gathered before the rostra for tomorrow's meeting. This city needs to know what the death of Darius really means to us."

We were thus sent on our way and a long night it proved to be. Especially for me, as I was not to go with my friends and the others. Part of Themistocles's genius was his ability to back up his vision with an understanding of the importance of detail. He knew that no plan, however brilliantly conceived, was worth anything unless it was buttressed with thorough organisation. He understood the connections, the way things would unravel if all the ends weren't tied up.

"Mandrocles, you go home, stay with Cimon; this isn't a night for him and his hot-headed aristo friends to be out on the streets getting in the way and making trouble. Make sure he keeps out of the way."

He must have seen the look of disappointment on my face.

"It's only one night boy, over these next months you'll get more excitement than you can handle."

So I sloped off back to the house, back to a night far worse than I'd envisaged: Callias was there, he'd come for his bride. Nothing about this travesty marriage was less than under-hand and his presence, against all tradition, in the house that night was no exception. He was in the andron drinking with Cimon and I saw from their expressions neither man was comfortable with their position.

It seemed that Cimon had no intention of going out that night and my attendance was pointless. But I had my orders, so I slunk away to my cell where I sat disconsolate. Close by, in terms of measurement, but a continent away in terms of possibility were the women's quarters. Somewhere in there Elpinice was spending her last hours of freedom. I don't know whether she wept. I know that I did.

After the house was asleep and the shameful comings and goings ended, I could stand it no more. Cimon had retired for the night and my obligation to Themistocles had been fulfilled. I tucked a sharp dagger into my belt and left the house. I had some vague idea of joining up with the others and hoped for a brawl where I could vent my rage and frus-tration in the blood of some enemy of the Demos. But again I was out of luck.

Whatever business had been conducted in the streets and bars of the polis was long over; even the whores in the Ceramicus were finishing for the night. It was a clear night;

the earlier rain had washed away the clouds and the stars were out over the acropolis. There was a gentle breeze and it carried with it a promise of summer.

I found myself outside the house where Lyra and her fellow flute girls were housed: through a crack in the exterior courtyard wall I could see a glimmer of yellow lamp light. I scratched at the door and to my surprise heard the bolts being drawn back and the door opened. I found myself looking into the scarred face of Demetrius.

"I wondered when you'd show up again: she's still awake, you can go in."

As I walked past, he grabbed my shoulder and hissed into my face so close that I caught the full weight of his wine and onion breath.

"Hurt her in any way and I'll break every little bone in your body."

I knew he would, but in a strange way liked him for the sentiment. I placed my hand on the door to her room prior to knocking and it swung open. By the light of the one dim lamp on the table I could make out a small shape huddled on the bed.

"Lyra?"

There was no reply but I sensed she was awake and stood for a moment hovering at the threshold. I wasn't sure quite what I'd come expecting, but whatever it was I suspected that I wasn't going to get it. A man shouldn't have to hover at the door of a flute girl's room and I was about to leave when:

"Mandrocles."

Spoken weakly, barely audible; I pushed the door closed behind me and walked across to the bed. The smell of the room was a cross between a sick room and a rich man's brothel: fetid and cloyingly sweet. The room was too hot and she was covered in a sweat drenched sheet, hair plastered to the sides of her head.

She'd lost weight, the confident beauty transformed to a wasted fever-wracked waif. It came to me that this was the fate that awaited her and all girls like her in this trade, and I was surprised at the thought. Not at its accuracy but that a man like me should be bothered by such a consideration: whatever happened to flute girls was part of the natural order.

I sat at the foot of the bed, inches away from her feet. Neither of us spoke or moved. I don't know what she felt but I felt foolish. What was I doing here when it was obvious the shop was closed and wasn't going to open? And even if it did, I didn't want the merchandise in this condition. The fetor of the room was affecting me: I began to sweat.

Then she began to speak, faltering and broken.

"Mandrocles, he hurt me so I still feel it. Why, all I tried to do was play well, give pleasure. The other wasn't part of the contract but when he forced me I didn't fight, just waited for it to end. So why did he do it, use that thing? It hurts."

In this moment, as Callias was enjoying the aristo charms of Elpinice and salivating over what would follow the marriage vows, I was perched on the edge of the bed of a ruined flute girl.

"Mandrocles? Are you still there?"

Where else was there for me to go? I moved up the bed and took the sweat-soaked, sheet-shrouded bundle in my arms. Her head flopped into my chest and she began to cry: softly at first then with greater energy as all the shit that the Gods load on us began to pour out of her, first as a trickle then a flood.

I said nothing, just pushed the damp hair back from her forehead and gathered it into a mass behind her head and ran my fingers through it as she wept.

I don't know why, or perhaps I do. There is a blackness the Gods visit on us. I know I still carry some of it. She didn't deserve it any more than Elpinice deserved to be pinned down under the grunting weight of Callias whenever he wanted her. I think maybe that just sitting there, stroking her hair, saying nothing, was the best I could do for her. I hope so because it was all I could come up with.

After a while, just before the lamp guttered and died, she began to babble. A stream of words in no particular order. Gradually out of them the picture of a life emerged: struggle and disappointment mainly.

But a discernible pattern – pure logos, as our philosophers would deem it if it were coming from one of themselves. Sometime before dawn, she cried herself out and drifted into sleep. She was cooler I think; maybe the flow of emotion carried some of the fever away with it.

I settled her down and turned the sheet so the sweat-stained end was over her feet. My shoulders and back ached from supporting her in the same position. Strangely, inside my soul I felt better. I don't know why; it makes no sense. I'd felt no lust there on the bed with her, I'd felt something but didn't know what it was.

I disentangled myself as gently as possible; she moaned softly, like a child, but didn't wake. I readjusted the sheet and left the room, pulling the door closed gently behind me. Right outside the door I was surprised to see Demetrius.

"Here, take these."

He handed me a cup of warm spiced wine and a honey cake.

"You'll need these if you're going to spend the day howling for Themistocles with all the rest of his Demos riffraff."

He walked away and I sat in a chair on the porch as the light increased and the day began, dipping pieces of the honey cake in the wine. I could hear movement outside, footsteps and voices. Themistocles's mobilisation was underway so there'd be no time for me to go home to sleep. When

I finished there was no sign of Demetrius; maybe he was ashamed of his act of kindness. I dipped my head in a water butt and slipped out of the gate into the flow of grim-faced men heading for the Agora.

Chapter Sixteen

I've just had the boy Ephialties read that last bit back to me. It seemed to move him. To such an extent that for a moment I thought he was about to pass some comment. If he was, he thought the better of it and walked away. His reading surprised me too, did I really write that? Sometimes it feels it must have been written by someone else, but then the memory still feels genuine.

I'll bet it surprised you too, reader: not what you expect from my memoirs. All I can say is life changes you inside even more than it alters your appearance and behaviour. All of you, believe me, will often do one thing but intend another. Do it often enough and your life is pushed so far off course that it can never get back. Now I have time to think, I can weep with the best of them and Lyra, Lyra …

No, that's not for this parchment, not for you. You can make your own mistakes: which, believe me, you will.

Anyway, back then the council didn't convene in their present chamber. Back then, before the Persians razed our city to the ground, they gathered in the orchestra in the Agora the way the Gods intended. Themistocles's timing was perfect: with the Spring Dionysia just around the corner the city of the Goddess was packed and expectation of excitement after a hard winter was high. The warm caress of early summer on that spring day was just good luck.

But it wasn't only timing that delivered for him that day, it was a stunt worthy of the Dionysia itself. The meeting of the five hundred was in many ways an artificial affair, much affected by the crowd, which grew as the day lengthened. Although always outnumbered by his opponents in every sacred council of the polis, it had been conceded by his enemies that in public gatherings his supporters would dominate.

They had no constitutional role to play in affairs of the council but their presence couldn't be ignored: fear speaks with its own language. Themistocles had spoken fear to his supporters and they now shouted well-orchestrated fear at the council.

That there would be Ostracism was beyond doubt, but who would go? When the debate of the council eventually got started most of the opinions from the delegates, when collated, formed a panegyric to the character and leadership of Megacles. Themistocles barely rated a mention, but behind that silence lay the fact that he was the man to be ostracised in the view of the aristos.

The case for Megacles was his birth and his family's ancient roots. Themistocles's questionable antecedents weren't debated but they hovered in the ether above every compliment paid to Megacles.

Themistocles himself was mute and made no attempt to influence proceedings, much to the dismay of his thousands of supporters who grew strangely silent. As the meeting drew towards closure, those of us watching became downcast: we'd long since ceased shouting insults at Megacles and his friends. We'd had nothing to cheer and become too dispirited to jeer. The mass of a crowd is like that: its mood can swing from one emotion to another rapidly. That's why leading the Demos is so difficult: the democratic leader faces difficulties unknown to an oligarch.

The crowd was showing signs of drifting away and that's when Themistocles made his move. He asked to speak: address both the five hundred and the mass of the Demos. Such a request at this juncture of course fell outside the etiquette that regulated the five hundred in those days. But it would have taken a foolishly brave archon to veto the request. As the world knows, that day the Archon was neither of those things and later proved to be close to Themistocles.

So he got his chance to turn the day around. Out of the crowd a block was produced as if from nowhere. He climbed on to it: the only man who'd thought of bringing his own rostrum. Towering above other men, he pushed back the folds of his robe, revealing his brawny arms complete with scars. This unaristocratic gesture brought him the first roar of approval before he'd even opened his mouth. I wasn't too far off and swear I saw him choke back a grin. Then, fixing a look of dignity mixed with anger on his face, he began.

"Worthy Athenian friends, men of the Demos who stood in the front line at Marathon and who will soon have to stand in the line again to defend the city of the Goddess against the Empire of the Great King."

Another great cheer: that's the way to manipulate the Demos, make it think it's better than it is. But it takes a leader touched by the Gods to do it, although Pericles, onion head, is possessed of the same ability. We settled back awaiting the denunciation of Megacles. It didn't come, at least not in the way we expected.

"Men of the Demos, I thank you for the love you have shown for the city of the Goddess in the sacrifice you have made in giving up a day's work to stand and listen to the five hundred, knowing that while you stood, your women and children went hungry."

He employed a simple code in his appeals to the masses in which certain words attained an emotional significance beyond their ordinary meaning. Stand was one of the most frequent of these. In the Themistoclean logos, men stood in the front line so it always had a heroic connotation. The fact that being in the crowd meant you had to stand in no way diminished this. We were heroes, even the majority of us who'd been nowhere near Marathon.

"Let me first congratulate the five hundred on the decision to proceed with the Ostracism. Let me agree with what they said about Megacles, son of Alcmaeon: it is true he is a high born aristocrat tied to his family and the old ways. I could say more, but that would be outside the spirit of this meeting."

We hadn't expected that. Where was this going, men began to murmur.

"No, I have something very different to tell you something that will determine the future of our polis. Something that would also benefit the gracious son of Alcmaeon and his noble friends. But I'm afraid I will have to keep you waiting a few days out of respect for the great Dionysia. You are aware that one of the heroes of Marathon, the poet Aeschylus is presenting a trilogy this year and I have the honour to be choregus.

"But the morning after the Dionysian rites are concluded, I invite you to attend the Piraeus at sunrise. I promise to show you something to gladden your hearts and still your fears."

He jumped down from the block and, magus-like, disappeared. We milled around awhile, dissatisfied. This was his genius: whatever had been debated now meant nothing to what was to come. Those of us who thought about the nature of things, however, spread the message that we thought best read the entrails of his utterance: seek a message in the plays of Aeschylus and bring it with you to Piraeus.

I found myself at the Piraeus next day for another reason. Back at the house there was no sign of Cimon; it was suggested he was revisiting the old estate at Brauron which it was rumoured Callias had bought and presented as a portion of Elpinice's bride price. I was hurt that he had not taken me with him. So when Ariston suggested that as we had no duties we go fishing, I agreed.

Rowing out into the bay, once passed the limit of where the great drain Eridanos dumps its human waste into the sea the waters were clear. The great rock of the Acropolis was sunlit above the city and there was silence on the breeze. We caught little and spoke less. Ariston was still mourning the Athene Nike whose crew were now drifting away to farms, workshops and for the lucky few onto other boats.

"This'll be as close as I come to the sea from now on, pissing about in a little row boat. Theodorus has a mind to try Syracuse; he thinks there's demand for good seaman there."

"Will you go with him?"

"Me? No, too old for that now, anyway who'd want an unlucky helmsman who broke his ship up on the Salamis shore?"

I hadn't any comfort to offer him and wondered if I should give Syracuse a try. Ariston swore as a fish wriggled away from the line and concluded conversation for the day.

"So tomorrow at your poet friend's play may be the last time the old crew get together."

We pulled back into Piraeus as darkness slipped its black cloak over the divided city.

Next day we got to the play early; this was the first year the festival moved from the Agora to a site on the side of the great rock where some work had been done to expand a natural space. Some rude benches of natural stone were fashioned, which were supplemented by the planking seats of the old unstable scaffolding. Despite its thrown together appearance, the place held a type of magic.

You don't need me to tell of the significance of his trilogy that year: the first where he revolutionised the nature of the festival by introducing a second actor. You, like me, will know by heart the lines of his great ground-breaking play Ixion.

But you won't have been there to see and feel it. Feel the terrible shiver as the chorus burst through the entrance chanting and stamping in the rhythmic dance to the shrill of flute and reed. That day the Goddess spoke through him and spoke to us. You know the terrible fate great Zeus, cruel father of the Gods, inflicted on Ixion, binding him to a wheel on which he whirls in an eternity of torment.

But in this play there was concealed another coded message: a message to the polis, a message to us who sat there spellbound in the presence of the Gods.

Ixion spoke with the voice of Megacles; the actor had his mannerisms and speech pattern so well that it was hard to believe that Ixion wasn't Megacles. So the impiety of Ixion was Megacles's impiety.

You don't need me to remind you that Ixion was first punished for failing to provide what the Gods required: well, in the play, the parallel between that and Megacles's opposition to the building of the fleet that Themistocles demanded was made clear. Sitting there hearing the very messenger of Zeus speaking from the stage straight to us, we saw this all too clearly.

"Shafts of the ship building pine ablaze with fire
Never the wine dark sea to touch
Promise to Heaven's thunder reneged
Doom to the land. Doom to the line of Ixion

Who would escape his sacred obligation.
Through suffering comes learning
You did not learn
Learn now Athens
Look to the sea
For time, as time grows older, teaches all."

We never knew where his plays would take us: you could start on Olympus with the laws of stern unbending Zeus and end in the Athenian council chamber. But after this play, we knew where we would be going next day. We'd be at Piraeus by dawn and look to the sea.

Dawn wasn't what we expected: there was a thick sea fret so the massed Demos picked its way gingerly through the huge mason's yard that Piraeus was in those days. The bay had changed beyond recognition in the previous years and Themistocles's dream of a protected harbour was close to becoming a reality. So we gathered in the miasma of the sea cloud and the unwashed stink of the Demos. As we waited, the stench and crowd grew. I can't remember how long we stood muttering. But I do remember the moment the sun burnt through.

The fret dispersed in an instant to reveal Themistocles in the middle of his supporters standing like a magician on the quayside. There was some cheering; above us the temples on the acropolis, hitherto invisible, were struck by the sun and sparkled. Themistocles raised his arms then lowered them, demanding silence which gradually settled over us. I saw his brother, Lysias, and to my surprise Cimon, amongst those around him.

But the greatest surprise and certainly the most shocking for any Alkmaionids present must have been the sight of the man standing at Themistocles's right hand. Cleinias!

Yes, the very same: the man who you will probably only remember today as the father of that uncontrollable whelp Alciabiades who onion head adopted and couldn't keep in order.

Back then he was infamous for being married to the untameable minx Deinomache, which of course made him the son in law of Megacles! How in Hades Themistocles had got him there was a mystery no one could work out and you could hear different attempts at answers all round Piraeus. Cleinias had the good manners to look embarrassed while Themistocles radiated delight. He let us drink in the drama of this alliance for a while, then again raised his arms for silence.

When the harbour was quiet he made a signal to some men behind him in response to which there was the harsh blare of horns. Then as the discordant noise dissipated he gestured seawards and a number of men scattered about the harbour, obviously planted by Themistocles, shouted.

"Athenians, look towards the sea, for there lies your deliverance."

It was as if the Dionysia had become reality and we were all players. We looked to the sea. At first nothing. It wasn't easy as scattered patches of haze still hung above the waters. Then someone shouted and, still obscured but just visible, there were two pinpricks. The sun rose, the sea cleared and we saw pulling hard towards us two triremes.

As they drew closer it seemed to those of us amongst the crowd who'd crewed on triremes that there was something strange about these two, but we couldn't agree on what.

Until, until they were no more than fifty lengths away. Then we knew: the outrigger through which the Thranitai rowed had been pushed out to accommodate extra deck space. These new sleek killing machines could carry a larger complement of hoplites. What Themistocles had learned from our skirmish off the Peloponnese he'd put into practice. Within seconds the seamen in the crowd were explaining benefits of this new weapon and soon we were all cheering.

But for a select few of us there was something way beyond this, so much so that whatever Themistocles was shouting out into the crowd we didn't hear. We had eyes for one thing only: resurrection. Gleaming from the prow of the leading trireme, flashing in the son was a gleaming figure we knew and loved.

Athene Nike. The Athene Nike reborn and coming for us. Even now, this memory fills my eyes with stinging tears. But let me tell you my tears were nothing compared to those of Ariston, Theodorus and other veterans. From wherever we stood in the crowd we forced ourselves through the mass of cheering Athenians until we came together on the quayside to receive our lady Goddess.

This was something Themistocles had not anticipated; the press of sailors swarming round the triremes as they moored up disturbed his pitch, which was approaching its climax. But, as ever, he adapted.

"And see, fellow Athenians, here are the men who will sail and fight from these ships."

We milled about him as he spoke so I was able to catch every word; they've stayed with me and I report this accurately: mark it well.

"These are the means by which Athens will grow great; these are the ships that no others can match: the first of a new breed. You must know, Athenians, that we have to thank noble Cleinias and a certain other who wishes to remain hidden for them. Men of the polis who put the city of the Goddess above the wealth in their purses."

This news took us all by surprise; you could hear the gasps of surprise all around the harbour. Today it still surprises me.

Not only that Cleinias should bear the huge cost of building a trireme but that he should stand shoulder to shoulder with Themistocles as they were presented to the people. It defies logic, and yet most of what we achieved in those days of glory defeats objective reasoning. Best to surmise that we were touched by the Gods. Cleinias spoke a few words: I can't recall any of them, then Themistocles concluded.

"Great ships, but there are only two. Give us two hundred and no Persian invasion will ever succeed. Give us three hundred and Athens will be queen of the seas."

Simple and clear, see: no faction or mention of the Ostracism, no mention of himself. He was careful to say us, not me. He spoke for the city and an Alkmaionid stood with him. Megacles might as well have packed his bags there and then: in those moments he'd lost the contest before a single ostraka was cast into the pot.

"Now return to your daily lives and think how you can help the city pay for three hundred such ships. Let our leaders know your views."

With a final cheer the crowd began to drift away; they'd had more than their money's worth. The skeleton crew who brought the ships across from Corinth, where they'd been built, climbed down onto the dock ready to be paid off. They mingled with Athenian sailors on the quay and talk about how to handle the new triremes spread like wildfire.

The other trireme, 'High Citadel', came first: Cleinias climbed aboard and made his way to the trierarch's seat followed by his followers. He was an Alkmaionid but his act that day was touched by greatness and he commanded the ship with distinction in the coming wars.

That left the Athene Nike awaiting her family. Themistocles gestured to Cimon.

"Son of Miltiades, the Athene Nike was your hero father's

flagship, yours is the honour of boarding first."

Then Cimon gave us an indication of his greatness as leader.

"Thanks, noble son of Neocles, for the honour you do my father's memory. I will be honoured enough simply to fight from her deck. Let the heart of the ship enter first: the men who sailed and fought her under him."

He indicated to Lysias that he should board first, followed by Ariston. They moved towards the gang plank but this strange ritual had one more surprise in store. Ariston, eyes wet with tears, grunted.

"Beg pardon, trierarch, but luck's a powerful important thing."

Lysias stared at him blankly but others understood; Themistocles threw back his head and laughed.

"Well, go on, you won't be asked twice, Mandrocles."

Cimon grabbed my arm and steered me towards the ship. I reached up to touch the statue of the Goddess in the prow: it felt warm, as if alive. Then I moved along the gang plank onto the deck and stood while each man touched me for luck as he boarded. In that way, I returned to my home.

Chapter Seventeen

Megacles lost the Ostracism but the victory came at a high price. He created a myth concerning what divided the city. A division that haunts us still today. He changed the nature of the struggle, or at least cast it into sharp and simple relief. To us, those who followed Themistocles, the issue was between those who knew the Persians would return and those who preferred to bury their heads in the sand. We wanted ships to defend the city; they would betray it.

This wasn't the analysis Megacles spouted: let me give you a flavour of his thesis. He didn't speak the words; that was done for him by Aristides.

"Athenians, remember your roots in the land, remember what makes the city sacred: our land. The land we tend and water, the land our blood defends; the sacred land soaked in the blood of our hoplites stretching back to the time of heroes. That is our tradition: men of worth who can afford the panoply of hoplite armour and defend the city are those who decide how we govern the city. Their blood nourishes the earth, which nourishes us. Leave the siren calls of the sea, of the fleet crewed by men of no account, landless men, violent men who envy your virtue."

Get the picture? Recognise it? He established the battle lines within the city: traditional hoplite against feckless sailor, tradition and stability against anarchy and the Demos, land versus sea. Powerful, isn't it? And it's causing as much trouble for Pericles today as it did back then for Themistocles.

Powerful because it appealed to small landowners scratching a living from the stony soil of their poor farms. Men struggling to fulfil their obligation to defend the city in their hoplite armour. Farmers tend to follow the traditional lead; their lives are too hard to think of anything fanciful that draws them off the land.

So we had another schism: struggling hoplite landholders scattered around Attica raged against the city dwellers, tradesmen, sailors, artisans and the growing mass living any way they could. The former supporting Megacles, and us who wanted him gone. Not the best of ways for a city to prepare for war.

We got the first real intimation of how this was going to work that night. Obedient to Themistocles's request and buoyed up by the new triremes, we were roaming the city in bands shouting our demands that Megacles be the one exiled. The re-united crew of the Athene Nike being particularly vociferous: we strayed from our natural stamping grounds around the Ceramicus and were entering the Agora when it happened.

I was near the head of our group talking to Theodorus; we'd had a few drinks and were in boisterous spirits, some of the lads were singing. We turned onto the Panathenia through the small square opposite the old fountain house when our way was blocked. They were strung out across the road, a group of about thirty wearing long homespun cloaks. We laughed at first; Theodorus shouted.

"Hey onion breaths, you're too late, the festival is over."

That's when we found out why they were wearing cloaks. They pushed them back off their shoulders to reveal

elements of hoplite war gear: shoulder guards, padded jer-
kins, even chest armour. All hefted swords and some carried shields, but I didn't hang around long enough to look
closely. They pitched into us and we broke and scattered.
Drunk as we were, we still had the sense for that: sailors
with knives and clubs against armed men with swords. It
wasn't a contest and those of us who'd fought as hoplites at
Marathon ran first.

We kept running till we reached the Ceramicus but they'd
probably given up chasing long before then.

All the city laws, of course, forbade them from parading
in the city in their armour but as they were acting in defence
of the men who made and maintained those laws, there was
little chance of those laws being upheld. So in the couple
of nights before the test of the ostraka, the city was more
peaceful than might have been expected.

Peaceful but split as we stuck to our areas: Ceramicus,
Piraeus and the poorer areas by the ancient walls while
the state buildings and area of richer housing flanking the
Acropolis were guarded by this new militia. We weren't too
worried for as Themistocles said,

"Farmers have to return to their farms. We live here."

He was right; it was unsustainable. The day of the contest
dawned and the atmosphere in the city of the Goddess was
febrile. As a Xenos I had no right to cast a sherd but I wasn't
going to miss out on a day that would provide excitement
and entertainment. Don't believe that back in those days,
the casting of the ostraka was carried out like some solemn
religious duty where men behaved like priests and acted
with dispassion.

Every man went prepared for violence and women were
even more strictly restricted within the precincts of the
household than was usual. Remember Ostracism, before its

extended use by Themistocles, was rare and it brought all the animosity and rancour in the city out into the open and legitimised it.

Cimon was too young to participate but he led the household contingent to our allocated collection point. Not only the household but all his father's men who'd kept allegiance, and that included the men of the Athene Nike.

Like his father, he knew how to do things in style. We gathered at dawn in the courtyard and, as the loyal gathered, soon spilled out of it. Household servants and slaves threaded their way through the throng with platters of flat bread, cheese, honeyed cakes and pitchers of spiced wine.

Almost half of us there weren't eligible to cast a sherd but we joined the boisterous circle round the ancient family Herme, set into the wall facing out at the street. Not one of the mass-produced copies that the new potters of the Piraeus churn out these days. This was a work of art produced by one of the old masters for a great sum. Its beard and erect cock aggressively jutting, but its eyes knowing and unsettling.

Cimon placed a fresh garland of laurel on its head and after speaking the ancient prayer, most of the meaning of which is lost, he turned and headed downhill towards the Agora. We followed shouting and cheering in his wake. The sun rose; it would be the first truly hot day of the year.

By the time we'd reached the outskirts of the Agora we'd already broken and scattered a hostile group who tried to dispute our passage. Cimon felled their leader, a bearded drunk, with one swift vicious blow. Still a youth, but halfway to becoming the ruthless instrument of death of his mature years.

In the Agora things were calmer: at opposite ends were a group led by Themistocles's brother and, at the end we entered, a group led by Xanthippus and Aristides. It appeared neither wanted things to deteriorate into a bloodbath. As we passed Aristides shouted,

"How would your father react to the shame of you leading his clients to cast their sherds in favour of the enemies of his blood, son of Miltiades?"

I could see Cimon was stung by this: his face coloured but he walked on by, keeping his silence. Aristides shouted after him,

"Casting sherds in order to destroy the sacred principles of Eunomia and pass the city of the Goddess into the hands of those no better than barbarians."

Cimon became a loyal, generous and open handed leader but never one who could dissemble: his emotions always lurked just beneath the surface. In this way he was like his father. This parting jibe was too much for his self-control. He turned and shouted back his own challenge and for a moment, two heroes out of the Trojan stories confronted each other.

"You dare say that, Aristides? Standing beside the man who traduced my father in court and brought him down when he was too badly hurt to defend himself."

I could see from Aristides's face he regretted this, but not as much as Xanthippus who could see where Cimon's ire was directed. This wasn't just about the governance of the polis; this was blood feud. Like his father's, Cimon's anger once roused was slow to cool.

"Betrayed my father while he was fighting our city's enemies, you worthless piece of Alkmaionid shit."

His hands reached for the dagger at his belt and in the madness of that moment I think he would have killed Xanthippus – and bearing in mind where Xanthippus's son has taken our city, maybe that would have been for the best. But of course, not being able to see the future, back then we didn't know that.

Those of us who loved him best restrained him while

Aristides and others led Xanthippus away. That must have been no easier, for Xanthippus had listened to an insufferable insult hurled at him, in public, by a youth. Had Cimon not had the self-control to keep walking at the first jibe then this exchange at close quarters would have ended in a death and the story of Athens would have been very different. All the same, a mark had been put down.

There is a question that is asked in our courts of law: "Who benefits?" The answer that day was clear to everyone: Themistocles. Cimon should have been a natural sympathiser for the views of Aristides and his clique. Now, despite the differences, for the time he was bound to their enemy. No bad thing either that day. Those of us eligible collected their ostraka. Those who could scratch the name of Megacles by themselves took pride in choosing pristine sherds. Some of the more literary amplified his name with a pithy phrase such as 'lover of Datis', referring to the Persian satrap liberal with money, or 'Persian friend'.

For those unable to write at all there was a range of sherds waiting with Megacles's name already scratched on them. Once a man had his ostrakon, he entered into a large square penned off area in the centre of the Agora. This pen had ten entrances: one for each tribe, and officials checked each man as he came to throw his sherd with its scribbled name into the giant pithoi. This was done to make sure that no one could vote more than once.

Friends who cast their sherds in this way said that looking into the giant pithoi in which the ostraka were then thrown they could see hundreds of versions of Megacles's name. We weren't meant to know until the official count and announcement stating who would be leaving the city for an exile of ten years, but by nightfall it was clear.

Then came the news that Megacles was that evening hosting a farewell dinner for his friends and would leave the city next day, crossing the Megarid, headed for Corinth. So there was no need to wait to hold our own celebrations.

Themistocles processed through the areas where his support was strongest. But his message wasn't one of victory; he read the omens far too shrewdly for that and was never one to look back, only forwards. As night was falling, he addressed us by the light of flickering and greasy tapers from under the shadow of the Hangman's Gate. A huge crowd of us, composed largely of the poor of Athens, eager for change and simmering with excitement, had gathered. We were in the mood for celebration but in that we were to be disappointed.

"Friends, today you served the City and its Goddess well, but there's no cause for celebration."

This wasn't what we expected; even the drunks amongst us were stilled. There was silence for a while after which someone, probably planted with the question in advance, shouted,

"Why's it not a cause to celebrate when an aristo traitor is ostracised, Father of the Demos?"

Despite what he liked to think, no one called him that so it must have been one of his servants, but it gave him the chance to tell us what he'd intended to all along.

"It is never a cause for celebration when Athenian bites Athenian and it's even less cause when there's more biting to come."

This was so cryptic that he didn't need to rely on a crony to ask any questions; several of us including Ariston were shouting.

"What do you mean more to come?"

"I'll tell you, give an answer that will turn even a man like you, Ariston, who's steered a trireme into battle and who stood in the front line at Marathon, pale at the thought."

Ariston forgot his question at this and just stood there beaming with pride, which made him look a bit simple.

"I'll give a full answer, no less than a man like you deserves to hear and I'll deliver it in the plain language that we of the Demos speak, not the flowery rhetoric of the five hundred."

If anyone was an expert in flowery rhetoric it was him, but, as usual, he got away with it.

"Today we rid the rat's nest of one aristo, agreed?"

We all shouted our agreement, this was more like it. But it didn't last.

"But what do we know about rats, Athenians? Yes, you have it, they hunt in packs. Now we've stirred up the Alkmaionid nest. It's not about driving one of them out of Athens; that only leaves the others to do his dirty work for him. And that's why we have no cause for celebration."

He'd reached the difficult bit and the more astute of us were on the brink of reaching it with him.

"Yes friends, that means against our desire, for the sake of the city, we are compelled as good Athenians to deal with the two most dangerous."

He paused as if he could not bring himself to use the word rats, and then continued his voice shaky with emotion. I'd watched him operating at close quarters and saw through the act but most of my friends swallowed it.

"Yes, it means for the sake of the city we must exile two men who stood with us at Marathon."

He put his hands over his eyes as if to hide tears, some in the crowd groaned; I suspect men who fought in the regiments of Aristides and Xanthippus on that day.

"I feel your grief; no one could grieve over this more than I do."

He stopped and performed a splendid piece of theatre, ripping the neck and sleeves of his tunic to display scars that looked even from a distance deep red. A much deeper red than they'd been when I last saw them.

"I took these wounds fighting beside my brother in arms, Aristides, and he took scars for me. Those of you fighting in a less desperate part of the field will have taken wounds alongside Xanthippus. But you must be brave and dig deep into your reserves, fellow Marathoni, for if I can sacrifice my love for these two men on the altar Of the Goddess for the sake of our city, then …"

He had to pause, overcome by a prolonged and noisy show of weeping, and it was only when his brother ostentatiously placed an arm round his shoulder to lead him away that he shrugged him off and continued.

"No, I will finish. If the goddess condemns me to sacrifice myself for the sake of the city by driving out Aristides and Xanthippus, then I must steel myself to do it. For if they stay then the fleet of ships that I designed and the noble Alkmaionid Cleinias financed will never be built. So I will sacrifice myself as, friends, I know you will."

A clever touch that, because for many Athenians the opportunity to drive out powerful men in the belief that it's themselves making the sacrifice doesn't come very often. But not everyone was fully behind this and there were murmurings within the crowd. He'd obviously anticipated this.

"But friends, today you have done well. Today you were strong and as I have explained, you will have further need of courage. So you will find that in all the bars where friends of the Demos gather tonight there will be no charge for the drinks. That is the least I can do."

That got the loudest cheer of the day and consciences were forgotten. He accepted the cheer and concluded.

"But freedom-loving Athenians, you will have to excuse me as my heart is too sick with grief for me to drink."

He staggered and was helped away by his brother having covered his head with the cowl of his mantle and wailing in a piteous manner.

I was so astounded by the performance I didn't even laugh, just thought back to sitting on deck with him on the return from Sparta and listening as he'd explained exactly this strategy.

Much later, when the earthen floor of 'The Bald Man's Tavern' was slippery with wine and vomit, I did get round to laughing. We'd been there for some time and finished three chous of thinly cut, alleged Samian, when Aeschylus walked in with some of the girls from Lyra's stable of flute girls. It seemed that night was a holiday for everyone. Lyra came in last; Aeschylus put an arm round her shoulder and led her over to me.

So with her sitting on my lap, I watched Aeschylus mimic Themistocles's performance complete with painted wounds and tears. Comic theatre lost a performer of genius when his saturnine disposition inclined him towards tragedy. Most of our table wept for the second time that day, on this occasion with tears of laughter. Another free chou of wine accompanied by some sausage and bread had disappeared by the time he finished to roars of applause and beating on the table.

Aeschylus slipped away and my sailor friends had reached the stage of drink when, according to inclination, they started to shout out bawdy songs or started to touch up the girls. The place was too full and the acrid smoke from the cheap grease lamps was beginning to sting my eyes. Lyra was still, her head on my shoulder. I thought she was asleep but she whispered,

"Can we go home, Mandrocles, perhaps if you were gentle we could …"

Chapter Eighteen

The next months are a blur; perhaps not much happened or perhaps it did and I've forgotten. All I recall are a few scattered images: serving Cimon and helping him maintain a household commensurate with his status. I remember time with Lyra and I know that it was then early, too early, in her marriage to Callias that Elpinice miscarried. But it's all mixed up.

What came next is clear, vivid like it were yesterday; a harsh stony landscape, no softness or colour, no trees or grass, just pitted rock and waste heaps. All of it wind-blasted and scorched by the pitiless gaze of the sun. And of course the smell: a foul mixture of human misery and smoke from the furnaces.

We were visiting the state owned silver mines at Laurium, a few stades south of the city by the coast not far from Sounion. I didn't even know such a place existed but despite that, one night just before the time of lighting the lamps, a messenger from Themistocles had arrived at the house. Cimon was just back from hunting and had called for wine. When I showed him the message he forgot about that.

"To Cimon, son of Miltiades, from Themistocles, son of Neocles.

There are things I need to show you; meet me the hour

before dawn at Piraeus by the Athene Nike. Bring Mandrocles, tell no one else."

No one loved a mystery like Themistocles but a message liked this indicated a serious purpose, so we were there on time. The ship was fully crewed, including some from the household like Ariston, so they obviously knew in advance. We climbed onboard, savouring the scents of recently dried out timber and resin. Themistocles was in the trierarch's chair in great good humour but excited. Behind him Ariston knuckled his forehead in respectful greeting to Cimon, who started to ask,

"What's all this for, son of Ne ...?"

Themistocles cut him off.

"Ssh, not till we're well clear of land and eavesdroppers."

So we watched in silence as the ropes were cast off and the Athene Nike slipped across the smooth water of the harbour and through the new fortifications at the port's mouth. Only when we were well clear of land round the bay did he deign to give any sort of an answer.

"An agent of mine arrived yesterday with some interesting news he'd ridden hard to bring. News that I'm rather keen to check out for myself; I thought it would interest you."

This told us nothing, but it's all he'd say. We passed Sounion with its temple to Earth Shaker Poseidon gleaming in the sun. Theodorus was explaining the differences of the new Athene Nike.

"Pushing the outrigger further out gives more room to carry soldiers, but it's more difficult for the Thranitai who have to row through it. The angle of the oars to the waters changed, see? So we're not as fast as the old Athene, bless her, but we can modify that with a bit of work. But she turns quicker so once we get the hang of her she'll be the equal of any other barky afloat."

I was more interested in this and watching how she handled so our destination crept up on me unexpectedly. A dismal dirty dockside with timber hoists and cranes and a row of deep bottomed hulks only fit for shoreline crawling. The smell was unexpected though; not a sea smell at all and despite the wind blowing in from the sea, the odour seeped out from the land. Stronger even than the fumes from the furnaces. Slaves.

The docks were crude and filthy but compared to what lay just inland they were the enchanted glades of Arcadia. Broken rock pitted with manmade fissures and tunnels. A warren of them part-obscured by greasy smoke. If it weren't for the wretched men women and children swarming all over, it might as well have been the surface of the moon.

The sight seemed to cheer Themistocles.

"You're looking at the wealth of the city, son of Miltiades. At the wealth that's going to build us the best fleet of fighting ships the world's ever seen."

Cimon made no reply. I could tell he still didn't understand.

"Silver, lad! These are the mines of Laurium, owned by the city and franchised out to merchants to be worked for us. They take a percentage and the city gets the rest. Today there's something special we've come to see."

He set off following a track across the broken landscape, led by a black bearded man with a face weathered to the complexion of a walnut, wearing a filthy stained cloak. We joined the track in his wake, stumbling on the pitted and crumbling crust of the earth. We wound between great spoil heaps, detouring round crude furnaces fed by slaves pushing barrows heaped with ore while others raked out the clinker and ash.

The track forked several times with tributaries ending in deep chasms gouged into the rock. We kept to the main path, Themistocles explaining to Cimon. Walking behind them I could catch fragments of what he said. Not all of it, even though I followed close behind: the din of the place was too great for that.

"Around twenty thousand slaves live here and work the mines----- --- Deep tunnel, follow the vein--some passages so small, only children ..."

Then we came to a stop. We were covered in dust, ash and sweat. The sun seemed determined to burn this place; outside the hell of the shafts there was no shelter and heat bounced back off the scorched rock in waves. I felt sick. The Gods know how the slaves lived. These weren't like house slaves or farm slaves. These were filthy and dwarfed, skins ingrained with soot, clad in rags, eyes devoid of hope.

You've come to know me pretty well by now, reader. You know I've lived hard and can deal the blows that steal a man's life with the best of them. But standing there with my eyes stinging from the smoke and grit in the air, I thanked the Gods that this was a life I didn't know. Those poor wretches, malformed and twisted. They didn't last long, which was clear from the rag-covered bundles scattered across the site waiting to be tipped into a pit or burnt.

"Are you coming, Mandrocles?"

Cimon's voice. Whatever he was suggesting I'd no idea, but he set off after Themistocles down a narrow path leading into a newer looking shaft so I followed. After a few paces we passed into the mine under a crude wooden lintel. Then we were forced to crouch to follow the track. The way led sharply down and in an instant all trace of daylight had vanished. The only light came from guttering tallows set in niches in the rock. They cast off as much greasy smoke as light.

Cimon stopped ahead and I barged into him. I hate enclosed spaces. We'd reached a pit that descended vertically down: the bottom of this shaft was lost in darkness; the tip of a crudely hewn ladder extended a few inches above its lip.

By the light of a lamp the guide was holding I could see Themistocles's face. He was grinning; in that light his chipped discoloured teeth seemed to gleam white.

"Well, this is what we've come to see. What's the problem, Mandrocles? Not got the stomach for it?"

He laughed then climbed onto the ladder and began his descent, following the guide into the bowels of the earth. I followed Cimon onto the ladder: it was like descending into an unusually deep grave. The air was fetid and grew warmer as we got further down. The guttering light from the lamps flickered and faded. They missed the surface air as much as I did.

Then we were at the base of the shaft on a crumbling path of grit. I shuffled after the others, my shoulders brushing the walls on both sides, my head bowed to avoid the rock roof. Cimon stopped and I stumbled into him. Down there, in that Hades, I found it more difficult to control my fear and my breathing than I do before battle.

We were in an open space with a series of dark passages running off it, some so small that they could only be worked by young children. The whole of the earth piled above us and down here only darkness. I began to worry that the lamps would die. I wanted to scream. After a brief pause, the guide set off down the largest galley. It settled down into a narrow passage low enough to force all of us to stoop. The passage changed direction a couple of times; I'd no idea which way we were facing. Ahead of us now there was noise, like the demons of Hades were tending their forge.

It grew louder, the walls fell away and we found ourselves in a long narrow cavern. I hadn't been wrong about the demons. The right hand wall was lined with filthy unkempt figures, some naked, some in loincloths. They were hammering and picking at the rock face, which glowed a dirty grey colour. Behind them groups of boys carried what they excavated and sorted it into heaps. Despite the desperate state of the pathetic workforce, Themistocles threw back his head and crowed with delight.

"Look the great seam, the mother lode: see, it stretches on beyond sight. This is the future of Athens. This is ships and the defeat of the Great King. This is no longer having to fear Sparta. This is the triumph of the Demos. This is the miracle."

It didn't look much like a miracle to me; all I wanted was to get out. Cimon was impressed though, it seemed he was unaffected by this sojourn in Hades. He asked,

"How much is there?"

"Enough for the merchants who run this place to take their profit and for a public dole to be given to each Athenian citizen."

Cimon saw through this dissembling answer.

"But that's not why you've brought us here, is it?"

"No, of course not. What do you take me for?"

"So why are we down here choking on these fumes? You'd better tell us quickly, Mandrocles doesn't look like he can take much more of this!"

Themistocles looked at me as if just noticing I was with them. He grinned and said,

"What's wrong with you, Luck Bringer, your face has gone green, don't you like it down here in the city's main treasury? Lucky you weren't born a slave then or you might have to live here. "

He paused before adding, as if to himself,

"Not that it would be a particularly long life."

As if on cue one of the slaves working at the seam collapsed in a faint. He was pulled to his feet and slapped by an overseer. His mates ignored him as he tottered back to his place; he didn't look like he'd last much longer. The overseer looked towards Themistocles, which made me think that if we hadn't been here the slave would have got a worse beating. Themistocles took the hint saying,

"Take one last look at what these poor wretches are hacking out of the earth, because before too long you'll have reason to be thankful to them."

He signalled to the guide to lead us out. I don't think I've ever been so glad to get out of anywhere in my life. I can't remember much about the scramble up and out of the mine, only that the surface atmosphere which had seemed so toxic before we'd descended now seemed pure and ethereal. We sat on timbers scattered amongst the waste heaps and a wineskin was produced. Themistocles had it passed to me first: I could have emptied it in one swallow. Then I sat in a trance until a kick from Cimon disturbed me.

"Are you not interested in why we came here, Mandrocles?"

For me it was good enough just to be out of the place, but I nodded in feigned interest. It shouldn't have been feigned because what Themistocles was about to tell us bordered on the fringe of madness – but to look at him casually reclining back against a rock while he spoke, you'd have thought it was the most natural thing in the world.

"That silver lode is going to build my fleet: the fleet that will transform Athens into the most powerful city in the world."

He grinned, then modified that incredible statement.

"Well, if we have luck on our side that is."

There wasn't need to prompt him further.

"That's the largest vein these mines have produced, and no one knows about it but our guide and the wealthy man whose section of Laurium this is, and he's a friend of mine. Oh, and a few hundred slaves but they're not about to go anywhere and spread the news. We know it and knowledge is power as your Samian philosopher keeps telling us, Mandrocles."

He was certainly right about the slaves; a grubby disco-loured rag shroud covering a pathetic bundle a few paces away showed us the only way they escaped from this hellish inferno. I saw him follow my gaze; he stood up and said,

"Perhaps better if I tell you how we'll do it back on board the Athene Nike."

I needed no second invitation.

Maybe it was just my imagination but we were well out of sight of Laurium before the stink of the place was out of my nostrils. Themistocles must have been thinking something similar; he said,

"Strange, isn't it, that the wealthy estate of our aristo friend Aristides lies just over there between Sounion and Laurium, and I'd wager that's where his difficult slaves end up. Serve as a good example to the others."

Cimon, who always liked a sense of balance asked,

"But what about his reputation as a just man?"

Themistocles laughed.

"You have to be rich to afford a reputation as a just man. Not that they matter but I'd guess that not many of his slaves refer to him as Aristides the Just."

The Athene Nike was cutting a fast track through the wine dark waters, turning our wake to churning froth: the crew were using the opportunity to put her through her paces. Apart from Ariston and the three of us, the stern deck was empty, so that's where I learnt of the plan, the real plan, reader, not whatever jumble of misunderstanding you've heard. An appropriate place too, on the deck of the first of the new breed which would change the world.

Themistocles was sprawled in the trierarch's chair; we sat on the deck either side of him. I'm not sure but I think he'd put the flesh on the bones of his plan as we'd pulled away from Laurium. So to borrow the new meaning young Herodotus has applied to the old word, we were present as history was being made.

"We either let that fortune be wasted by doling it out to be dribbled away into buying goats or roof tiles or whores or wine, or –"

He paused, spinning the moment out, or perhaps not because his eyes were bulging and the veins on his bull-like neck swelled out. It may have been a type of possession and that while we saw his body he was in another place walking with the Gods.

"Or we do what fate dictates we should, we roll it all up into one pithos and build two, no three, hundred triremes like this one once we've modified and smoothed out the faults. The Gods have put this into my hands."

I was about to warn him of the dangers of hubris, having already spat on the deck to avert evil influence, but it was Cimon who spoke first: cool and confident and for the first time I caught the cadence of his father.

"And how, son of Neocles, will you manage to pull that off?"

"By suggesting we act for the city of the Goddess and sacrifice the individual for the good of all."

"Just like that?"

Now Cimon was sounding like Themistocles at his most provoking. Only he wasn't provoked.

"Not quite just like that, young man. I'll supply other good reasons."

"But your supporters are the very men most in need of the money."

"I'll point to the growth in jobs building and crewing the ships, there's more money to be had that way."

"But not cash in hand and for doing nothing."

"Then I'll scare them into it."

"What, with the Persians? That'll scare them off the ships; they'll think it will just bring the war closer."

"Then I'll scare them with something a little less frightening, son of Miltiades. You can't expect all the details at once. But don't worry, I can be very persuasive when I have to."

"With your own I've no doubt, son of Neocles; but with your enemies and the farmer hoplites who hate the sea? Think of what their leaders will say to them."

For a moment I had a flash of what the future might be like if these two were to become enemies. But that thought was dispelled by a greater surprise.

"They too will be dealt with, son of Miltiades."

"And do you have the details to hand for how you will achieve this dealing?"

"For that? Oh yes I think I do, young man."

I think Cimon had an inclination he was being tested, played with now, so he said nothing; just stared at Themistocles waiting for him to finish. Which he immediately proceeded to do.

"There will have to be an internal war amongst the men who govern the Polis. Those who stand for the past will have to be removed and that, I admit, will prove difficult."

He smiled at Cimon, who continued to stare at him until at last he asked the question that Themistocles expected.

"How and when will you achieve this, Themistocles?"

"By starting tomorrow with Xanthippus, Cimon."

Cimon's face was a mask of astonishment mixed with admiration. The sun dipped then fell behind the Acropolis, gleaming silver in the distance.

Chapter Nineteen

"See, Mandrocles, see how they play with us the Gods: I'm not even sure they notice or care."

He spat the olive stone onto the floor.

"I've been thinking of Prometheus, how he tried to help humanity with the gift of fire, a generous gesture towards us primitives, and what was his reward? To be chained to a rock so an eagle could swoop down and eat his liver while he lived. Not just once but condemned to have it happen every day. I've been thinking about it ever since the affair with Xanthippus."

It was Aeschylus speaking, but you already knew that, didn't you reader? No one else speaks like him, not then nor ever since. It had gone easily, even easier than Themistocles had hoped. I didn't care much; ever since the trip to Aegina I'd carried no love for Xanthippus, not after what he'd led me into. This wasn't Aeschylus's opinion.

"He stood with us at Marathon so don't feel happy about what's happened; no one's safe now. He never thought it would happen to him, just like Prometheus."

He finished off the dregs in his cup before adding,

"You know I'll use this for a play one day."

He filled our wine cups. We were in his late brother's bar

<hr/>

a couple of days after Xanthippus's departure to join the growing number of his friends and family in exile. It had hardly been a contest: he was an aristo who lost his traditional support due to his favour of growing the city's power at sea. But there was only room for one leader of the sea searching Demos and it wasn't him.

Still, despite the fact that it cleared the decks for Themistocles, he got little joy from it. I think he'd liked Xanthippus and he'd been a useful dupe at times. Now it was a straight fight for who would pack their bags next between Themistocles and the undisputed leader of the aristos: Aristides. Before they went for each other, though, they needed to try and restore order in the city. Behind the legitimate process of Ostracism the city was wearing a darker face: blood shed, scores settled. Two nights of skirmishing, running fights in all the public places in the city.

It was stirred up by young aristo hotheads, some of them friends of Cimon, who were trying to make their mark on public life. They'd copied the example of the poor farmer hoplites and carried their weapons into the sacred precincts of the city. However you couldn't mistake them for dirt pushers, with their carefully barbered and perfumed long locks.

At first, following the advice of Themistocles and his minion, the first archon Nicodemus, we'd ignored them, but each morning the mutilated bodies of honest artisans and sailors were found murdered in the streets. It's not in the nature of Athenians to ignore such provocation.

When one of the morning bodies turned out to be the elder brother of Gylippus, one of the most respected Thranitai of the Athene Nike, it became personal. The man had been touched by the Gods at birth; he was simple but friendly, like a child and earned bits of change doing odd jobs and carrying messages. Having not exposed him to die at birth his family had invested care and love in him and to the crew he'd been like a pet dog: they wanted revenge.

Ariston had asked Cimon for permission to join a little expedition the following night. Cimon agreed; he understood the demands of honour. As Ariston was leaving the room he looked at me, then Cimon and asked,

"And Mandrocles, skipper, can he come?"

Cimon nodded and said a curt,

"Of course."

Neither bothered to ask me. I didn't want to go, had no taste for street fighting but it seemed it wasn't my decision. So that night a large band of us went hunting and this time we went properly armed; like the farmers, we concealed our weapons beneath cloaks and blankets.

We roamed the city, hearing sounds of shouting and clashes, but found nothing. Near midnight we'd had enough and wanted to call it off. Ariston and Theodorus managed to persuade Gylippus, who was still blood crazed, that we might just as well go for a drink. We knocked the Bald Man up: made him open the tavern and mix us a couple of chous of wine, and that's where it would all have ended if the Gods hadn't wanted some sport.

We were almost finished when a couple of men I recognised but couldn't put a name to came crashing into the bar. They were flushed, angry and clearly not here by chance and as soon as they saw us shouted,

"They're in Piraeus, a group of the bastards, messing with the ships."

It was a fair distance, maybe near half an hour at a jog, but we were fuelled by wine. Before they finished their garbled message we were legging it downhill, headed for Piraeus. Others joined us and by the time we were at the outskirts of the new square by Zea Harbour we had the whole story. A group of aristo youths from the oldest families holding the most traditional views had decided for a game to come onto our patch. The cream of their jest had been to piss into the triremes.

Sounds ridiculous, doesn't it, reader; just a stupid boyish prank. But remember we were after revenge and drunk. The Gods got their entertainment that night: we had no trouble finding them. They were coming into the square from the direction of the ship sheds as we came in from the city. Both groups came to a halt; we could see they were young Cimon's age, short of full manhood.

I think it still could have been resolved this side of bloodshed if the opening exchanges had been handled sensibly, but that goes for every tragedy, doesn't it? Their leader was a youth called Mikon, a relative of Callimachus, the hero martyr of Marathon. We knew him; he'd a reputation for wildness and arrogance, a spoilt loudmouthed brat.

For a second we pulled up and both groups stood facing each other, the future hanging on a knife edge. Ariston was near the front of our group and I could tell he was about to prevent what was going to happen. You know with men, solid men like him. He never got the chance; Mikon lived up to his reputation. He must have been drunk like us. He crowed across at us,

"Slum dwellers, make way for your betters unless you want to be found in the morning with the refuse."

It wasn't only the words, it was the voice, pitched in the fashionable aristo lisp calculated to give offence to working men. I can still see the sneering grin on his face as he turned for the applause from his friends.

Then it all happened in a flash. Gylippus went up to him, I don't think he was going to hurt him much, just shake and abuse him. I don't even think that Mikon's reference to rubbish meant dead democrats, including Gylippus's brother, although I'm sure Gylippus thought it did.

I saw the look on Mikon's face as Gylippus reached out to catch hold of him; it was fear, so I think what he did next he may have done in self-defence. He shrunk back from Gylippus's clutch and reaching into his cloak, pulled out the weapon he'd customised and carried: a cut down hoplite lunging spear.

He must have spent the better part of the day honing it to get a point like that: it slid into Gylippus's breast like a knife through soft whey cheese. So easily that the bloodied point pushed its messy head out of the back of his sweaty tunic. I think Gylippus still hadn't realised what had happened as he slumped to the ground and his soul fled, wailing, for the Elysian Fields. But we knew, we'd seen, we understood and we'd have our revenge.

I remember the look on the face of the youth immediately behind Mikon, a mix of surprise and shock. A look that he took to the grave with him as Theodorus jerked the long perfumed locks of his hair to pull his head back and thrust his sword between the open lips, smashing through the well-kept teeth up through the roof of his mouth and into the soft pulpy interior of the head. He was the first to go down; Mikon, surprisingly, was still standing no one had touched him yet.

Those at the back turned and ran with a pack of sailors chasing them, slashing at their backs; they were the lucky ones. The remaining three had no chance; one tried to run and was spitted. One dropped his weapon in terror and was smashed to the ground and Mikon, who looked dazed, was pushed up against a stone pillar. Theodorus had his face pushed up against Mikon's; he was screaming at him, lost in blood lust. Strange how we value that in battle, because there on the streets of Athens it was howling madness.

I had no appetite for this: since I'd killed the youth on the boat at Marathon I never wanted to do it again. But when you're with your mates, what can you do? I was trying to hang back when I saw that Ariston was trying to stop it. He was shouting.

"Leave them; this'll take you to the gallows, stop, it's gone too far!"

You know the type of thing people shout in a brawl. He grabbed me.

"Mandrocles, help me stop them."

I made a move towards Theodorus and Mikon. He grabbed me again.

"No chance there, the other one, save the other one."

He was right; no one could have saved Mikon from Theodorus any more than they could have saved Hector from Achilles. The other one was on his knees, face bloodied, he'd pissed himself and was crying as they slapped him around prior to killing him, or buggering him then killing him. Ariston waded into them and the ones he unsteadied I pulled away. He was roaring at them like he did on the ship.

"Stop it, you fools, stop: do you want to hang? I order you, stop it; fucking stop it."

I think it was as much naval discipline as regaining their senses that did it. They didn't so much stop as lose interest, allowing Ariston to get to the kid and pull him to his feet. He was blubbering and hung onto Ariston as if he were his dad. He's a member of the Areopagus now; then he was an inch from death. Ariston held the kid's face between his two hands and spoke slowly and clearly to him.

"Listen, we'll not harm you but remember this. Your friend struck the first blow."

Behind him there was a dying gasp from Mikon, presumably a consequence of Theodorus striking the last blow; the kid's head jerked back, his eyes rolling.

"Easy, easy now boy, you're safe we'll get you home; but remember, you started this."

Human emotion is meant to be something individual but in that moment it was collective: something visible and visceral. I could feel the men coming to their senses, realising what they'd done and what it would bring down on them. I was aware of Theodorus, bloody handed behind me: Ariston diverted his attention from the boy long enough to direct one sentence at his friend.

"Go to the harbour, get the first fucking boat out and disappear."

The big man looked stunned – it can be like that after the blood rage – then he shook his head as if trying to clear his thoughts and, without a word, turned and loped off into the night towards the docks. The men stood in a semicircle, looking at Ariston for direction.

"Round up the others, get home, clean up and lie low. You was never here, get it? Go on, what are you waiting for? Me and Mandrocles will see this kid home."

They didn't need a second invitation and within seconds the three of us were alone with the corpses of the youths and Gylippus, whose mother had lost two sons in forty eight hours.

"What's your name, boy?"

"Myron, sir."

"Well Myron, thank the Gods that we were there to save you."

Myron began to snuffle his thanks but Ariston hadn't reached the point of his speech.

"Now understand this. You have a responsibility to the Gods and the city to tell this how it really happened or there'll be more blood."

He nodded dumbly, looking like a young calf being led to

slaughter; we began to walk him home. After we'd left him close to the district where he lived and we were heading back to Cimon's house, I asked,

"Do you think he'll do what you asked, will this be the end of it?"

"I doubt it: we'll probably hang."

But we didn't: the next day Themistocles and Aristides got together and brokered some type of amnesty. They were both good Athenians and neither wanted the impending trial by Ostraka to be conducted against a backdrop of civil war. As Themistocles said, after he'd tongue-lashed us for our part in the skirmish and Cimon for letting us go,

"Somewhere out there just beyond your home island of Samos, Mandrocles, the Great King is preparing the most powerful army the world has ever seen. While we few Athenians in our pathetic little city are murdering each other."

There was nothing to say after that. But the world is full of troubles and my share for the day was still to come. Sometime after the lamps were lit I was sitting in my room staring at the wall when Cimon appeared in the doorway. I knew something had happened, otherwise he'd have sent the steward to fetch me. He said curtly,

"There's someone who needs to see you. I should forbid it as my father would have, but ..."

His voice trailed off; he was struggling with this, and I could see both anger and sorrow in his eyes. I watched him closely and thought 'so this is what the man will look like'. I suppose I'd always seen the boy: this was different, this was the man's outline and the essentials for the future were all in place, ready to be weathered by the burden of experience. In that moment the nature of our relationship changed. He said,

"I should, as head of the family, veto this, but these are

strange times. We were close during the escape from the Chersonese and it's you she wants. So this time, and this time only, she can have it. You'll find her in the andron."

When I got there I understood what had shocked him into this betrayal of propriety. She was thin, draped in black, but the trappings of grief were nothing compared with the dark cloud of desolation that the Gods hung over her. I think a madness was afflicting her because when I entered she ignored me, just stared into the corner. I'd never seen Elpinice like this; I think it frightened me. After some moments that seemed an eternity she turned towards me and shrieked.

"I lost the child, it's gone, I'm punished, even Callias shrinks from me."

She began to howl, like a dog at the moon. I watched, she didn't stop. I tried to touch her to comfort her.

"Keep away from me, I'm defiled."

She shook me off. Tears ran down her face; she pushed back the veil and began to tear at her hair. I'd seen it in the tragedies, never in real life. In real life it's worse: she clawed at her face, raking the lovely gaunt cheeks with sharp fingernails. Still scratching as the blood began to flow. I tried to stop her, but before I could she stopped herself and said,

"There, it's done, it's over, that is my childhood and youth gone, gone with the stillborn. Hardly formed, unrecognisable, just a slight thing in a bloody puddle when it was lost."

There was something so chilling in the image that the thought stopped her in mid flow. She took several deep breaths and then finished her message.

"Now it's gone and the girl you knew has gone with it, tracking it on its wailing course to Hades. I'm no longer that girl, Mandrocles, I'm something else."

She looked at me, an intense stare, but something else:

pleading? Longing? I didn't know, didn't know then anyway. Now looking back I think I should have known; I think I did know. I know something was expected, something I ... such grief.

Chapter Twenty

In the end it was all decided by our crazy system like Themistocles had predicted. Not in the Agora, either, but up on the ridge of the Pnyx hill, about a fifteen minute uphill walk to the South West. The assembly used to meet there in the days of Cleisthenes but ever since I'd been in Athens it was closed for repairs. Now it was to host the most important meeting the city had held since the decision to fight at Marathon.

Let me describe what it was like back then for you, reader, used as you are to the new Athens. It was a large, vaguely semicircular area with a slight downward slope towards the Agora, ending in a retaining wall with a space for the five hundred members of the Boule. It was dominated by a small speaker's platform so whoever was speaking could do so from an elevated position.

There was some rough stone building: accommodation for officials thrown up in a higgledy-piggledy manner. This was where Cleisthenes had envisaged that the Demos could gather to give assent to the legislation that their betters in the Boule deemed right for the city of the Goddess.

As a place to meet and take decisions it had some advantages: being elevated there was often a breeze up there, and from the upper levels there was a view down across the Agora and out to sea. It was possible to watch our ships heading out for Sounion, Salamis or to where the carbuncle of Aegina lurked beneath the heat haze. This was particularly useful during dull meetings of the assembly.

The disadvantage was more significant though. It was far too small for the big life and death meetings when the Demos was mobilised to oppose the Boule or agitate for an alternative strategy. It could hold about eight thousand in some semblance of comfort: ten thousand at a pinch. Hardly the full mass of the Demos. Maybe that's why Cleisthenes chose it and radicals from Themistocles onwards preferred the Agora. There were more than ten thousand of us squeezed in and sweating that day.

The whisperers had done their work well. I know you don't need whisperers today, reader, now that there are laws that regulate everything, but back then if you needed your people to turn out, whisperers were essential. Themistocles had set them whispering before the news of the silver lode was made public. A clever ploy because from the first there was a sense that the wealth discovered at Laurium was in some way down to Themistocles.

Like in the tragedies, the whispering had two voices: one whispered the danger of Aegina and the size of its fleet. Every Athenian knew someone who had seen the Aeginian pirates swarming ashore on our Attic coast to steal our wealth, rape our women and kill our men. So this fear-spreading whisper was particularly contagious.

The second voice spoke of the wealth in trade and the demand for highly paid seamen there would be if we could build a fleet large enough to finish Aegina once and for all. With a fleet we'd have their wealth, kill men and take their women. There was no whispering about the threat of Persia because fear breeds conservatism.

They'd whispered well, because when I arrived early that

morning with Ariston and some of the lads the place was already heaving. Packed, rank and sweaty.

We pushed our way as close to the front as we could, treading on toes, using our elbows, exchanging jokes, blows and insults. We collected wine, olives, onions, cheese pies and honey cakes from the vendors we passed and eventually found a spot near where the entertainer Hermaphroditus had established his pitch. I think the name was just part of his act. His trick was to fart popular songs, allegedly from two orifices. I've always found that brand of act overrated but my companions loved it. He did good business that day.

The press of the crowd got thicker and tempers began to rise with the temperature. Scuffles broke out, Hermaphroditus judge the mood, collected his props and takings and scuttled off with his two orifices still intact.

Maybe it would be a good idea to forbid drink from the assembly but, of course, no one would obey the ban. At last the trumpets sounded and the named Archon, Nicodemus, led the representatives of the Boule onto the podium and after fulfilling his sacred duties to the Gods and the Polis he invited Themistocles to climb onto the speaker's platform and outline his proposition.

Thus it begins.

"Athenian friends, behind me befouling our pure wine dark sea lies the pirate island of Aegina. Recently we had an opportunity to change it, guide it. We failed."

He folded his arms and stared out at us as if it contemplating whether he should continue. This was one of his better tricks and I knew then the act would be worth watching. There was isolated heckling; he ignored it, shrugged his shoulders and started again.

"We failed because we lacked the ships. They didn't lack ships so they raided our shores. Some nights ago the Goddess of Athens and wisdom came to me in a dream. She came as a ship, a trireme sailing towards Laurium. When I woke I knew what I must do. No man can stand against the wish of the Gods."

He paused again and for some moments gave a silent impression of a man communing with the Gods.

"When I woke, I followed the Goddess to Laurium where I found the silver that Mother Athene had placed there for us. Placed there for one purpose, and not to be doled out to each Athenian and pissed away on wine or boys or roof tiles or goats."

He smiled patronisingly at the obscene suggestions hurled at him from the landed factions in the crowd, replying only to one jibe with,

"Well as a farmer, Timachus, you'll be well acquainted with the versatile hindquarters of goats."

This drew applause and whistles from us. Then, at last, he got down to business.

"Whose head do we see on our silver Athenian coins? Yes, the Goddess Athene, and now she wants these coins used for their true purpose. Shipbuilding. We will use that silver to build the fastest, deadliest fleet of triremes in the world. Those ships will bring down Aegina and free us from fear. With those ships we will control the seas. I won't try to win you over, friends, by pointing out the demand for rowers and Athenian craftsmen that building these ships will bring. I won't detail the high wages or the chance of gaining increased status through becoming a Thranitai on an Athenian trireme. I know that you honest Athenians are not standing here through self-interest. So I appeal to your love of your city. Your desire to see Athens become great."

He gave us space to let this sink in; then,

"I offer you the chance to make Athens great and to become great yourselves. I speak to you the same words that noble Miltiades spoke to the hero Callimachus that day at Marathon. He said: right here, right now you have the choice to settle this matter, Callimachus. Only you, only you right now."

He raised his hands to the heavens, another favourite ploy, waiting for the crowd to settle and when they did,

"So today, Athenians, each of you has the chance to become Callimachus, become a hero. Refuse the dole that is your right: make the city great, build a fleet. Right here, right now, you can do this, you can do this."

Without waiting for a response he jumped down from the platform and settled next to his political allies on the front bench. There was no real applause; we were too busy thinking. So preoccupied, in fact, that when Nicodemus rose to announce the next speaker, Aristides of the deme of Alopeke, hardly anybody bothered to shout out the traditional jibe, "Foxy bastard," stemming from the similarity of the pronunciation of the deme name to fox.

So Aristides got a less raucous reception than he might have expected. It was obvious to us that he hadn't expected Themistocles to speak the way he had, and equally obvious he was confident that his proposition would be accepted.

"Athenians, the son of Neocles was right to invoke the Goddess Athena: the Goddess of wisdom and tradition. Tradition that dictates that the city's share of the silver be distributed amongst us. Distributed in the form of the city's silver coins stamped with the sacred head of the Goddess. He may scorn these amounts, but remember: roof tiles build a roof, goats make a farm. Citizens, today you can leave here richer men and that wealth flowing through your honest hands will enrich the city and please the Goddess."

It was a good speech, simple and to the point and Aristides might have left it there. But he felt Themistocles had laid some sort of trap, which the sight of Themistocles sitting with a broad smirk on his face encouraged. So he laid down his own challenge.

"And Athenians, I wonder how the son of Neocles would attempt to make his crazy idea work. How would you magic up a hundred ships, Themistocles?"

"Would you like me to elucidate, son of Lysimachus?"

Themistocles smiled as he spoke and I saw indecision cross Aristides's face but it was too late: he'd offered the challenge.

"I think we'd all be fascinated to hear what you came up with, son of Neocles."

"Then I'll fascinate you."

Aristides stood down and Themistocles mounted the platform looking like a man whose dogs pissed honey.

"A hundred triremes would need seventeen thousand men to row them. Those men are you, my friends, most of you men with the low status of thetes. Men with few rights and privileges in this city of tradition. Once you claim your place on the rowing bench of your new trireme, your status changes and the city changes with you. The son of Lysimachus and his friends, the men of tradition, don't want that but I have a challenge for them."

I was watching Aristides as Themistocles said this. His face shone with the realisation he'd walked into a trap. Themistocles moved to spring that trap.

"Listen: this is how we'll get the ships. You aristos, you pampered elite, you men of wealth. You, yes you will build them."

Where was this going? We didn't know and it was clear that they didn't either. Themistocles beamed.

"Again, friends, we are in debt to the Goddess who planted this seed in my mind as I lay in a slumber induced by the Gods. Now I will plant it in yours. From our share of the silver we will take one hundred talents. To the hundred richest men we will give one talent each."

For a moment there was uproar. Themistocles stood there smiling until Nicodemus managed to restore order.

"You, the richest men who employ craftsmen, own land and slaves, will take that talent and turn it into a trireme. Just one each, easy. Oh, just one thing: if you don't do it properly we'll take the talent back and fine you another one."

There were roars of protest but now Themistocles was shouting above them.

"Not possible, you say: well I'll tell you this. Your aristo friend Cleinias managed it twice. Not once, twice, understand? One of your own; but a real patriot and servant of the city blessed by the Goddess. I think we can assume that what he did twice you can manage once?"

Shouting and scuffling chaos disorder, but a chant starting.

"We demand a vote, we demand a vote."

Nicodemus mounted the platform and gradually we calmed down but before he could speak Aristides used the calm to shout,

"A vote yes, but the traditional vote. I demand that the proposition put before us be my proposal: do we accept the Boule's proposal of a ten drachma dole to each citizen."

Themistocles nodded assent and Nicodemus called for a show of hands. His tellers looked out at us, then conferred with Nicodemus who announced,

"There is no need for a head count; the decision is clear. The proposition is defeated."

Screaming, fighting, chaos: pure Athens. But we could see Themistocles shouting so we shut up and shut our friends up and so at last could hear him.

"The Goddess requires a decision; we must move to the alternative proposition. I demand in the name of the Goddess who speaks through me a vote on the ships."

It took them about an hour to agree on a proposal which

requested that a hundred men be given a talent of silver to undertake a project that would benefit the city of the Goddess by supplying her with a trireme. By the time the vote was taken, many of the proposition's opponents had drifted away. Didn't matter really; it was passed by a huge majority.

That evening in the tavern of the Bald Man we celebrated. Aeschylus, who didn't normally pay much attention to the business of the Polis, said a couple of things that made me see what we'd done. I remembered enough to scratch it down the next day.

"He's made the men who fear the fleet, and fear equally the sweepings of the Demos like you lads who crew them, build a monster to destroy themselves. But don't think any of this is about Aegina. This is about the Great King and what you've voted for today will change this city more than any of you idiots can imagine."

He was right about that as well. It was a time of change in my life too. Elpinice disappeared: it was rumoured that her wits had been dislocated by the Gods and she'd been spirited away to one of the many country estates owned by Callias. What a tragic waste of one of the greatest spirits in Athens. But as Aeschylus has written,

"The Gods throw things at us in order to see who becomes stronger and who crumbles into dust."

I think Cimon was more affected by the plight of his sister than he cared to show; the guilt of her sacrifice for his future burdened him and he departed for the Brauron estate. Of course, the scurrilous rumour and gossip of the city claimed that consumed by unnatural lust for his sister, he'd followed her. Rumours also, as you would expect, reader, attributed fatherhood of the stillborn child to him.

Athens seethed with change and rumour: the rumour I'll come to later but the change! Once the vote had been taken it became clear that the city precincts of Athens were not extensive enough to accommodate both Themistocles and Aristides. But for reasons none of us could have foreseen the clash was delayed. Themistocles was stricken.

I think his success in persuading the assembly to act in the common good rather than in self-interest surprised him. He certainly didn't celebrate, he took to his bed, didn't speak to anyone for days. His brother said a black cloud had settled over him after the vote and turned away all visitors. It was this that told us how serious a malady it must be that affected him. He couldn't sleep, couldn't settle to anything, and stopped eating. He'd tried almost single-handedly to change the city and I think the burden was too great.

Strangely Aristides didn't choose to take advantage of this; so maybe his self-serving and self-circulated title for himself of 'The Just' had some merit to it after all. Instead he worked as hard as he could to delay and obfuscate the ship building project.

For me, though, the new ships opened a great future. There was a shortage of seamen and rowers but an even greater shortage of men who knew how to fight from the deck of a trireme. There were less who'd actually done so, but I had twice. So I slipped from Mandrocles the youth blessed by luck to Mandrocles the experienced sea fighter. As such, over the next months I had my work cut out training others.

One more thing as I straighten out my personal life for you, reader. Some weeks after the vote, Lyra left the city to visit family in the Megarid. She didn't tell me, just left a note with Demetrius. We'd been getting on well as lovers and friends, so why did she go? I couldn't understand why the owner of the flute girl stable let her go, despite her duties now being restricted to playing and looking pretty; she was still the greatest asset.

I was bitter and unhappy and when I asked Aeschylus

why she'd gone, he said nothing; just looked at me as if he couldn't believe I'd asked the question and didn't know.

But all of this was about to be eclipsed by a rumour that cast all our private lives into the deepest shadow.

A secret messenger from the exiled Spartan king Demaratus, now established in the court of the Great King, slipped out of the city of Suza at night and sped towards Sparta.

Part Three

Chapter Twenty-One

Scents, it's the scents I remember most clearly from that last spring before the war: piles of fresh cut timber everywhere and caulking to waterproof the hulls, sweat from men learning the back breaking art of working an oar all day. The spume of sea spray thrown up as the new triremes rolled and tossed through the swell. But above everything else, hanging over Athens like a pall of storm cloud: the smell of fear.

We were late with the triremes, of course: no one can accuse the Demos of being straightforward or efficient. Every procedural trick to slow down the shipbuilding programme was pulled out of the Alkmaionid bag. Successfully too, much to the frustration of Themistocles, whose black mood kept him from the councils of the city.

So when it arrived, the news everyone dreaded supplied him with the shock of energy he required. The news, which the Spartans had damagingly kept quiet, finally reached Athens by way of a direct and secret message from the kings to Themistocles. Once he read it he had no choice but to rise from his sick bed.

The first I heard of it was a message waiting for me at the dockside when the Athene Nike pulled in to her mooring. I'd been drilling some men in the skill needed to fight from a trireme deck; it was like teaching mules to dance: when they weren't rolling and swaying they were throwing up. The new rowers interspersed amongst the veterans weren't any better and Alexis, the replacement for Theodorus, did his best but without his predecessor's skill and authority.

By the time we reached the dock side we'd exhausted every oath in our vocabularies to little effect and gained an inkling of how difficult it was going to be training up landsmen to crew a war fleet. Building the ships was the easy bit and we were way behind schedule with that. One of Themistocles's runners was waiting with a command to go directly to his house.

I arrived late: the house was crowded and the session nearing its end. It wasn't difficult to catch up on the news; the room was alive with it. The Persians were coming, their mobilisation well underway and their campaign strategy formulated. There was a further problem though: the motive of the warning.

The Spartan Ephors had received two blank wax writing tablets from the exiled king Demaratus, now resident at the Great King's court of Suza. It made no sense until Queen Gorgo suggested they scrape away the wax. This they did and found the message scratched into the wood. Being Spartan, they decided to keep the information to themselves. The information that meant life and death to free-living Greeks.

I suppose they had some fair reason for this. Could they trust it? Was it genuine or an attempt to scare them? Whatever the motive, even they couldn't sit on something of this magnitude and after a period of subterfuge and in-fighting the kings, remembering Themistocles's promise of a fleet, decided to inform him.

I'd managed to pick up on this when Themistocles came to the point of the gathering.

"We have, if we're lucky, about eighteen months, maybe two years before they're here burning our city. We need the rest of the ships or at least another hundred."

He paused and looked at us, packed, sweating in his courtyard and corridors. He looked tired, drawn and old. He let us digest his message. It was simple: we'd never be ready in time; there were delays and excuses at every turn. One faction in the city was striving to build and train a fleet, the other half was trying to prevent it, while across the sea beyond my home on Samos, the most powerful army the world had ever seen was preparing to cross the seas and crush us.

"We can't afford the luxury of opposition any longer. Aristides must be ostracised along with anyone else who gets in the way. They need to understand that it is life or death with us now."

For the first time listening to him speak in public, I could discern no rhetoric or dissembling manipulation. These were words driven by desperation; a stark truth forced out by crushing reality. I found this very frightening.

You know what happened next: the Ostracism of Aristides was the last engagement in the internal war of the polis before the arrival of the Persians. It was hard fought and bitter but left surprisingly few scars. When the sherds were counted and Aristides left to join his friends in exile there was no celebration or triumph. Particularly from Themistocles.

Afterwards, when the noise had died away, he gathered his chief supporters together. I was there with Cimon and his manner surprised both of us. He didn't speak for long and ended with these words, which I'm sure will surprise you too, reader.

"And that's an end to it. Soon we'll need them back from exile, need them standing with us keeping their supporters loyal to the city. Without them, how will we recapture the spirit of Marathon?"

The next day the council granted money from the silver

at Laurium sufficient for the building of another hundred triremes. Representatives of the Athenian Demos carried this silver to any part of Greece where good seasoned timber could be acquired and skilled shipwrights employed. The speed of shipbuilding increased. For men like me and the crew of the Athene Nike, every day became the same: we trained and bullied landsmen into sailors.

For their part the exiled Alkmaionids made no attempt to stir up trouble or impede progress: for all their faults it appeared the grace of their stand at Marathon outweighed their hatred of the Demos. At least until after we either beat or succumbed to the Persians. Strange also that in many ways, his Ostracism was the making of Aristides. I know, reader, that you will be familiar with the legend of his probity during the actual Ostracism.

You know, the story put about that some illiterate half-wit from the countryside with a blank sherd of pot was wandering around trying to find someone to write a name on it for him. He stumbled into Aristides and, not knowing him, asked for help. Aristides asked him who he wanted ostracised and the countryman said:

"Aristides."

So Aristides scratches his own name on the sherd and throws it into the pithoi for counting. Then as an afterthought he asks,

"Tell me, friend, why do you want to ostracise Aristides? What has Aristides ever done to hurt you?"

The man replies,

"Nothing, I don't even know him."

So Aristides asks,

"So why condemn him to leave his homeland?"

To which the man responds,

"Cos it pisses me off always hearing him calling himself

'The Just'. If he thinks he's that much better than the rest of us he can fuck off out."

Unlike the other invented stories about themselves that the Alkmaionids like to circulate, I'm half inclined to believe this one. Mainly because it was later used by Themistocles's supporters as an example of political stupidity rather than moral rectitude like the Alkmaionids asserted.

Strangely, once he'd gone and with him the opposition to building the fleet, the city seemed a much lonelier place. Lonelier and more frightening. Whoever it was who said as soon as you conquer one problem you hit the next was right.

Except it wasn't one problem it was a whole pithoi full of them. This became apparent a couple of days after Aristides left and was started by a rumour: an advance squadron of the Persian fleet had been sighted off the coast of Delos heading for Athens.

Anyone with any sense knew this was wrong; problem is you don't need sense or information to state an opinion, and within hours the Agora and the bars were packed with men working themselves up into a lather of panic. It was like the tense months before Marathon lived all over again.

My first taste of it came a couple of days later. The Athene Nike was in dry dock for modification so I had some spare time on my hands. Spare time and nothing to do: Cimon was still playing the role of country squire at Brauron and Lyra hiding away somewhere in the Megarid. So having no other plans, I strolled through Athens.

It was the first warm day after several of skirmishing rain, I remember. The same skirmishing rain that had fallen throughout the period of spring at Dionysia, soaking both the actors and crowd. I wandered the back streets, where in those days patches of dense poor dwellings would suddenly open out onto cultivated fields and goats replace people. The city wasn't so crowded back then: the waves of immigration that followed the wealth created by our empire hadn't really started rolling in.

I was passing a bar near where Phrynichus used to rehearse his players when I heard shouting and laughter from within. I was bored, I was thirsty I, went in.

Through the door I joined strange company: a type of society of the theatre. They were well gone in wine and roaring. Strange that presiding at the centre of several plank tables pushed together were the most bitter rivals of the day: Phrynichus himself and Aeschylus.

Maybe not so strange though: the Dionysia was ended for a year and rivalry could be temporarily set aside, ideas and alliances for the next year talked through and the failings of the choregii who sponsored the plays bitched about. A smooth faced ambiguous looking man sitting across from Aeschylus was in full spate.

"Would you believe the mess Themistocles has got himself into, dears? Doesn't know whether he should be in Sparta, trolling round Greece trying to form an alliance or back here in Athens supervising his little ships. Poor dear, so confused: sees an amphora and doesn't know whether to piss or drink."

This was going down well; had the players in fits of laughter as they spluttered over their wine.

"And dears, he's not helped by his little friends of the Demos, is he? Some of them want to leave the city, some want to make peace with the Medes while some want to fortify the Acropolis. I rather fancy he's beginning to miss Aristides and all the others away enjoying an extended holiday."

I bet you think, reader, that this affected manner of speech was invented by the current generation of aristocratic youths to enrage their fathers. Well, let me tell you, they always minced about like this in theatrical circles. Wouldn't have been a good idea to mock men like Kalamis, whose name

I'd just remembered: he was very handy with a dagger and enjoyed using it.

Aeschylus had seen me and waved me across to join them. Kalamis paused, rolled his eyes and made an obscene gesture before lisping,

"Ooo look, Aeschylus, your special friend has come to, shall we say, join you; welcome, Mandrocles the beautiful."

I smiled at him and squeezed into the space on the bench Aeschylus had made for me.

"I give you thanks, Kalamis: I'm not often called the beautiful these days."

I was passed a cup of wine and the conversation moved on. But even here, beneath the surface of mockery and laughter, fear was the undercurrent. They were discussing the recent drama festival knowing that, depending on the speed of the Persian mobilisation, it may have been the last. Aeschylus enquired,

"Will you write about our current dangers for next year?"

Phrynichus shook his head: he'd won the prize this year with a trilogy based on the labours of Hercules. It had been a good, if safe, choice. He wasn't aging well but was still the most respected poet in the city.

"I don't think so: the scars of my last literary flirtation with modernity are yet to heal. Anyway, I wouldn't tell you if I were. What about you?"

"Next year; no I don't think so, maybe someday. I was thinking of the fall of the house of Atreus following the Trojan War, but in the current circumstances I'm not sure that would be appropriate and anyway –"

He came to a halt, undecided whether to continue. Then said,

"Anyway, who knows if there'll be a Dionysia next year? Who knows if there'll even be an Athens?"

"This has all become too gloomy for me, my dears."

Kalamis got up from the table, made a mock bow to Phrynichus and left. Several of the others drifted off after him. Those of us remaining moved closer together and the atmosphere became increasingly morose. When the last jar of wine was empty, no one ordered another and we dispersed. As we were pissing against the back wall of the bar Aeschylus said,

"Walk with me up to the Acropolis, Mandrocles."

We picked our way uphill, avoiding the pools of stagnant water scattered along the track. The city was unusually quiet and empty; people were either skulking indoors or out practising with the growing fleet. We didn't speak on the way.

We paused at the top of the ramp to leave an offering at the shrine of Athena and I remembered being taken here by Theodorus and Ariston on my first day in Athens. The day I first glimpsed Lyra. Dusk was falling over the city, a pall of fire smoke hung above the houses. We wandered through the forest of steles, plinths and statues of the Gods. Apart from the keepers of shrines it was deserted.

Away through the gloom we could see the fleet bobbing on the water at Piraeus, where the harbour was dwarfed by the army of newly thrown up boat sheds. The preparations looked to be years off being completed. Was this what we'd torn the city apart to achieve? It looked frighteningly fragile. I think Aeschylus was thinking the same; instead he said,

"Yesterday we received information from the court of the Great King."

I knew what was coming wasn't going to be good. I was right.

"He's so sure of victory that he doesn't feel the need to conceal his plans from us."

I waited; I've learnt from experience that poets tell you things in their own time.

"In fact, so confident that he wants us to know and understand them."

This seemed against all sense. I asked,

"How can you know that?"

"Because he sent a messenger with them directly to Themistocles."

An owl hooted from somewhere in a small grove surrounding a shrine. Despite it being the servant of the Goddess, it made me shiver.

"His army is ready to move and this time he's not leaving anything to chance: the whole empire's mobilised."

"But he can only ship so many troops at a time, we beat them last time, remember Marathon?"

Aeschylus looked at me, smiled, and for a moment I thought he was going to ruffle my hair like I was still a boy.

"This won't be like Marathon; listen, Mandrocles. This time he doesn't need ships to march his army over to Greece. While we've been fighting ourselves, he's fought and won a war with the ocean."

My expression must have told him I'd no idea what he was talking about. He explained.

"He's bridged the Hellespont. He's built a raft of boats across the sea: a bridge wide enough for three chariots to ride side by side. He's turned the sea into land and he's going to march the biggest army the world's ever seen across it. Back at Marathon we faced an expeditionary force sent to punish us. This is an invasion, this time he intends to wipe us out. While his fleet blockades us, his army will march across Greece through the Hot Gates to wipe us, and anyone stupid enough to stand with us, from the face of the earth."

The owl hooted again, a message from the underworld.

"Every spot we've set foot on today, Mandrocles, will be destroyed, every building pulled down, everything that can burn will burn. My plays on Prometheus, the House Of Atreus and all the others will never be written. Democracy will cease to exist."

I'd never seen him like this, even when drunk. Today he'd been drinking but wasn't drunk; he was lucid. Lucid and terrifying. I tried to encourage him.

"Go to Themistocles; talk to him, he'll have anticipated this, he'll have a plan."

"Well there's a slight problem with that, Mandrocles."

I waited for it, waited for the lightning strike.

"No one knows where he is. He's left the city."

The owl broke cover and swept into the night searching for prey.

Chapter Twenty-Two

By the next day it was all round the city, embellished by a lavish covering of rumour. The Gods were punishing us by allowing the Persians to walk on water and Themistocles was at the court of the Great King, advising his generals. Sounds ridiculous, doesn't it, but then you have the advantage of hindsight, don't you, reader? Back then, even if you were smart enough to allow for exaggeration it was still terrifying.

The Alkmaionid view propagated by their whisperers was that Themistocles had purged the true leadership of the city so that the Persians could walk in unopposed and install Themistocles as tyrant.

In a sense this was true. Without Themistocles there was no leader. Nothing put this in sharper relief than the efforts of Nicodemus and his other democratic supporters to reassure the city. Without Themistocles they were nothing and their efforts were pitiful and made matters worse. Fear and suspicion grew, neighbour feared neighbour and those with enough money or interests elsewhere made plans to leave Athens.

So it was a relief when the Athene Nike was back in the water and we could resume our training of potential oarsmen. Now, when the city has such a large standing fleet spread across the empire and to row as a free man in the fleet is a mark of pride and citizenship, there's a large pool of skilled rowers in reserve. Back then it was very different. And it wasn't just the lack of bodies: it was the class of men.

Throughout our history it had been the hoplite class that fought our wars. Local wars in the main, with set times of year for fighting, a pretty good understanding of the rules and conventions on both sides and limited engagements with few casualties. The hoplites were landowning citizens who would turn out when required but not for too long and never during harvest.

Marathon changed all that; now we faced total war, the kind not seen since the fight at Troy. A war which destroyed both the Greeks and the Trojans. Like the Greek heroes of old we would go to war in ships, but unlike them we'd also fight from them. Fight against the largest and most experienced navy the world has ever seen.

We lacked men with experience and this was exacerbated by the fact that most of the men crewing the triremes came from a class of men previously not trusted to fight. Our situation was desperate. The experienced rowers were spread throughout the fleet to train the new men so no ship performed well: a fact that particularly rankled with the perfectionist Ariston.

"Thank the Gods Theodorus isn't here to see these donkeys fucking up the strokes. Lucky for them, too."

He broke off to curse Praxiteles, a clumsy landsman who had the added misfortune to be rowing from the Thranitai benches in the outrigger and so was particularly visible.

"Why don't you grab a lump of bronze and jump over the fucking side; do us all a favour. You're meant to be stroking the water, not trying to spoon it up so we can all fucking drink it."

He shouted to the most experienced of the Thranitai on board.

"Sophilos: show him one more time how it's done and if he still can't, pitch him overboard. The Gods help us, what are we meant to do with the likes of these?"

It didn't help that we were soaked most of the time by the spray occasioned by the clumsy splashing of the oars. But that wasn't the worst part: triremes are delicately balanced fighting ships and unless handled steadily, highly unstable. We'd already heard of two that had overturned during training exercises. Not quite the way the preparation for war is told in the heroic stories, is it?

But for me it wasn't so bad: I was one of the few men regarded as an experienced sea fighter and men respected me. Privately I'd begun to entertain the idea that one day, if I wasn't killed first, I might become a trierarch. We all need to dream, and me especially, because reality was grindingly harsh. Almost everyone I loved I'd lost. The light began to fail, Ariston leaned on the joint tillers and we turned for port.

Aeschylus was waiting for me on the dockside. He didn't look like a man bringing good news.

"Mandrocles, I think it's time you paid a visit on your young master."

He turned and walked away; it was clear he wasn't going to speak further in a place where it was so easy to be overheard. I followed him towards his dead brother's bar above the port. The bar was empty but there was the sound of someone moving about in the upper chambers. He poured some wine straight from the pot into two clay cups and handed me one. I was glad of the drink; my skin prickled with the salt from sea spray and my mouth was dry and stale. I only had time for a quick gulp.

"Stay here tonight: tomorrow you go to see Cimon at Brauron."

I suppose it's some weakness that the Gods placed into my soul but there are people in my life who, when they command, I obey. It seemed that Aeschylus had joined that select group: I didn't question him. I was about to ask him if he had news of Lyra but it seemed his mind was running along a similar track.

"I'm trying a play about war, the testing ground of men, yet every time I write the scroll fills with women. Strange, don't you think, when everything in our lives is filled with the preparation for killing?"

"Not too strange, I've been thinking about Lyra."

"I'm not thinking about anyone we know, about individual women, Mandrocles. I'm thinking about how their feelings penetrate the city and affect us."

He'd lost me; I said nothing, just drank my wine and listened.

"They play no part in the affairs of the polis, in the affairs of men, in the decisions of life and death or war and peace. Respectable, they cover their faces, keep to the women's quarters or if not respectable they service us."

I didn't know where this was going but I clearly wasn't going to find out anything about Lyra.

"Yet they haunt my plays. They stare into them from the margins. Then when I least expect it they are centre of the stage. They assume a place denied them in real life: In front of the chorus they make things happen, change the action. Change it in a way I'd not imagined, never mind intended."

I poured myself another cup, this wouldn't be over quickly: he'd caught me like this before, used me like a potential audience. Looking back I think I was lucky to have listened to the inner daemon of the greatest poet ever born.

"I write of how the Gods play with us, I write of fate and men. How we believe we think and act for ourselves, control our own destinies but it's all a cruel joke. Yet now, when I grapple with the return of Agamemnon from Troy, it's not he or Orestes the words drag me towards."

He took a drink, stared into the rafters: for the moment I didn't exist, he'd gone towards the words the God gave him.

"It's not the men or their actions the words drag me to: it's the murderess Clytemnestra, possessed Electra, cursed and helpless Cassandra. Even Our Goddess the great Lady Athena decides the outcome. The words teem with women. The men are lacking all conviction and are directionless, driven by madness. The women are unnatural, filled with a passionate intensity and their strange voices shred the soul."

He threw his cup across the room; it shattered on the far wall and the dregs and lees trickled down the new plaster-work, leaving a dark stain. This was a trick I'd seen before, there was no point reacting: we sat in silence for a while then he got up and fetched a fresh cup from the counter, filled it, topped up mine and picked up where he'd left off.

"Doesn't matter what I'm driven to write about, they're there: If I choose Hector, Andromache worms her way inside, if I write about Thebes there's Antigone. Even in my work on Prometheus, which as you know I've been told to keep for safer times, my speaking voice the chorus are women. I can't silence their voices; Why? Phrynichus doesn't have this problem, neither does anyone else."

I wish he were still alive now, I'd be able to tell him that Pericles's pet poet Sophocles and, it is rumoured, the school-boy Euripides share the same problem. But back then Sophocles hadn't started writing and Euripides's parents hadn't even met, so all I could find to say was,

"Write about war and courage in the face of the Gods."

It was this innocent statement that led him to the strangest of his musings.

"You think that's the only form of courage, Mandrocles?"

He didn't want an answer; at least, he didn't wait for one.

"What about Andromache watching Hector from the walls of Troy, seeing her son killed yet surviving slavery to end in dignity?"

I knew the answer to this one.

"She had no choice, that's not courage, all she did was endure."

"What about a woman prepared to sell herself to protect her family honour?"

I knew he meant Elpinice: this hurt and stung but before I could tell him he said something; something which at the time I didn't understand. Something so close to me and my life. Something I was ignorant of, that I didn't even suspect.

"What if a woman keeps a secret which destroys her life because she doesn't want to compromise her man?"

I didn't know what he was talking about, and anyway I'd become bored with the topic. I didn't reply, just yawned. We finished our wine and began to talk about my trip to visit Cimon at Brauron. I knew there was more to it than just that, but whatever it was, he wasn't going to tell me. Whatever the purpose I was ready for a change.

By now the lamps were lit and it was dark. A group of men with blistered hands and wind burnt faces were sharing a chou of wine after a hard day learning to work their oars. I knew them, or rather, they recognised me and called me over to drink with them. When they left I helped Aeschylus close up the bar before we went to bed. As we went up to our pallets he said, as if our earlier talk hadn't finished,

"Compare the voice of the women in my plays to the voice of women in the city."

I replied,

"They have no voice in the affairs of the city."

"Yes, they do, but we don't hear it."

"How would you know?"

"Because it's there. I write about it because it's there."

The next day I was up early and rode out of the Piraeus before the sun had reared its head from below the waters. Passing through the mass of shacks that now formed a substantial shanty town beyond the gates, I realised that like ten years earlier, refugees fleeing from the might of the Persian Empire were flocking towards Athens for safety.

The city was growing beyond its capacity. The same applied to the fields beyond the city limits and the mountain foothills: every spare plot that was capable of growing anything was under some type of cultivation.

Our city was changing rapidly; soon, the nucleus of the original sacred precinct with its temples and dwellings would be overwhelmed by a tent city of the dispossessed, destroying that which they desired. The day was pleasantly warm: summer was on the breeze and once into the routine of the ride I settled into that beatific state of trance that such days bring with them.

Once over the mountain pass, that almost ten years earlier I'd marched across to Marathon to fight for freedom, I took a slight diversion through the grove of Heracles to the great mound: the mound on the beach which covered our dead.

I stood for a moment in its shadow looking up towards the pennants and trophies decorating its summit. Inside were the bones of some of the best men to whom Athens ever gave birth. I said a particular prayer to the goddess of victory for the brother of Aeschylus, who had bled to death on the beach during the skirmish round the Persian ships. Turned to the sea and invoked the forgiveness of the Persian boy who I needlessly killed and whose shade still haunts my dreams.

The blood-soaked salt marshes, dead lands before Marathon but now ghost-filled, lay forbidding in the dying sun. In that place of victory and death you could feel the living presence of the sly and malign God Pan.

Wandering through the groves that house his shrine,

where we camped before the battle, I felt the presence of the dead more than the living. Here in this home of the God of sudden fear, I knelt and wept for the shade of Miltiades. His story would have ended well if he'd died here at the site of his triumph. He would have lain in honour next to his friends and not had his dishonoured bones tossed out for the dogs.

Strange how emotion is deferred, how we understand and feel our lives backwards. I think I felt closer to Miltiades there in death more than I did in life. But grieving or not, I had to leave. No man can spend long alone in the solitary glades of that grim place. A creeping feel of unease gradually crept over me, growing to panic. I set off back to where the horse was tethered; walking at first before breaking into a jog then running full pelt.

Don't laugh, reader, or, at least, if you feel so inclined try spending some time alone there yourself. See if you feel like laughing then. The horse was fretful when I found him: whatever was there, he felt it too, and as soon as I mounted he broke into a canter. Behind me I could hear the shade of the Persian boy weeping for the manhood he never knew.

Once away the horse calmed and settled to a walk and we passed the temple of Hercules and the Deme boundary and at length, there ahead of us, lay the ancient homestead of Miltiades's ancestors: Brauron. I was relieved to have arrived but even here, safe within its precincts, I felt haunted. Not by the dead but by the living, now dead to me. For my mind was full of the memory of the night of bliss I spent with Elpinice in the olive grove beyond the estate walls.

So with nerves shredded and thoughts confused I rode through the gates to be greeted by the fierce barking of the family hunting dogs. But there was no relief to be found inside. Cimon had been hunting with his friends and afterwards drinking. He was stone drunk, barely recognising me;

able only to slur out an uncertain greeting. So the rumours were true. But that was nothing to what came next.

A woman emerged from the female quarters clad in a peplos and veil of mourning. The figure beneath the covering was haggard, emaciated and unsteady. Despite all that I recognised her instantly. Elpinice.

"Welcome, my brother will greet you tomorrow if his head has cleared."

No warmth or recognition of what we'd been to each other. In fact, the tone carried an edge of blame. But before I'd the chance to think of a reply,

"I will show you to where the purpose of your visit is waiting."

She turned and walked away down the passage leading to the andron. Confused, I followed.

The lamps were lit but the place carried an air of gloom. A day already disturbingly unworldly had become more so. She paused before the door of the andron and motioned for me to enter. As I moved passed her, she whispered,

"But I don't know what you'll be able to achieve."

Up close I caught the whiff of her breath: not perfumed as I remembered but unclean, foul as if some sickness resided within both her spirit and body. Thus disturbed and disordered I blundered into the ill-lit room, unprepared for what awaited me.

At the far end, beyond the effective range of the oil lamps, lying on one of the dining couches and shrouded in some form of bedding was the unmoving form of a man. I heard the door close behind me and the room seemed to grow darker.

I waited in the silence, wondering what was required of me. I began to detect the low pitched sound of irregular breathing. Then a muffled groaning: the type of noise made by those struggling to awake from the grip of a nightmare.

I felt I was myself drifting into a nightmare state, so unexpected was the turn of events.

The noises from the couch grew in intensity until with a shriek the bedding was thrown aside and the panicked figure sat upright. I found myself staring into the visage of the architect of the fleet and saviour of Athens: Themistocles.

Chapter Twenty-Three

Not very heroic, is it reader? And certainly something his enemies would have paid good money to know: but I've always been loyal. Not that I'm sure if that's a virtue or a sign of inflexibility. Maybe that's why the Gods sent me to Themistocles. After all, I'd seen Miltiades in a similar state more than once and been a comfort to him. I've been around enough powerful leaders to recognise the strain their ambition and the world place upon them.

They try to hide this, of course, but if you think about it, reader, it becomes clear that you don't challenge the existing order of things without paying a price. For Themistocles, Miltiades and, I suspect, many others that price is a darkness of the spirit that periodically turns the world black and freezes the soul. Then courage becomes fear, command melts into vacillation and anxiety hangs like a shroud smothering light and hope. I'd had more than my own share of such experiences so I had no trouble recognising the malaise and its symptoms.

There was no point trying to talk to him that night and from the blank look in his eyes and the smell of stale wine in the room he was in no position to speak to me. I summoned the housekeeper and had her prepare a particular potion Miltiades had used to clear his head when the black dog of despair shadowed him.

With difficulty I persuaded the great man to take it, and then I left the chamber. I waited outside the door and after some time heard the sound of retching which indicated that the potion was taking effect. So I stole away to the barn where I used to sleep at Brauron in younger and happier days.

It was a long and uncomfortable night but at least I had things to think on other than myself. I woke early to the familiar itching that sleeping in such a place induces, sluiced my head in the water butt and headed for the kitchens to find breakfast.

Cimon was already there; he said nothing, just nodded then continued to dip his stale crust into a bowl of oil. He was bleary eyed but otherwise looked in good condition. I wondered what to say but needn't have bothered, he spoke for me.

"It would be a good day to ride the estate boundary, don't you think, Mandrocles?"

With that last night was forgotten and whatever lesson there was to learn from it he'd taught himself. There was no need for me to say anything. Minutes later we were outside preparing the horses and shortly after rode through the gates, exchanging the sick rooms of Brauron for the healing air blown in from the sea. It was to be my last such day of peacetime careless country living for many years.

Cimon was a countryman at heart; if the Gods had not made other choices for him he could have settled as a contented rustic knight. You know; the type it's become popular to lampoon in the new and cynical comedies that have recently become so fashionable with the Athenian mob.

The estate was in good order and alive with activity in the early summer sunshine. The land we rode across could have been any demesne in Attica. Stony and thin soiled towards the coast where olives struggled amongst poor grazing for goats, but more fertile inland, good enough to support grain as well as vines. But Cimon's delight in the estate was focused on the pasture land that lay beyond the vegetable plots, close to the farm itself. This is where he kept his horses.

For a man whose military reputation was forged at sea he would have made a great cavalry commander. He loved horses, had a gift in training them and they, for the most part, responded to something they could sense in him. We spent ages in the rough corral as he showed me his colts, stallions and brood mares. It was past noon when he selected two we would ride to the far end of the estate, the part that bordered the Bay of Marathon. It was a day of freedom and delight like the first one I'd spent in his company, far away in the Thracian Chersonese where his father had ruled as tyrant.

Then he was a boy and that land was his inheritance, now he was a man, older than I'd been at Marathon, and the land was part of the Persian Empire. Any betting man with a good eye for odds would wager that this land was destined for the same fate. We didn't talk much: Cimon was the rare type of man who didn't need to say much, his company was enough. When sober, that is. We rode to the sea, swam in a creek, I can't remember much else; except …

Except for his one oblique reference to the preceding night.

"I'll be coming back to Athens with you, Mandrocles, I have to begin my work, and war changes the natural order, allowing young men of my age a role."

He smiled, as if to himself before adding,

"I'm to have the Athene Nike, Lysias will remain trierarch for the present, you will lead the marines. Themistocles reckons that between you, you'll keep me safe."

He touched his heels to the mare's flanks and sped away. I followed in his train. On our return, as we walked sweat-stained into the house, it was like entering a different world to the one we'd left that morning; Themistocles greeted us, saying to me,

"I give you thanks for the physic, Mandrocles, it was most efficacious."

He smiled as he said this but no further mention of his condition was forthcoming. Whatever it was that haunted him was gone. He was ready to face his destiny. Something else was missing too.

Elpinice, gone back to Callias, back to her duty like Themistocles and Cimon. She left a note, Themistocles gave it to me. Not much a few words, nothing about the past or love. But maybe something more than that. She thanked me, said her courage had returned. Although I'd done nothing really, it seems that the effect of my overnight visit had in a strange way liberated the three of them, woken them from nightmares.

Have patience with this rambling account of a visit to the countryside, reader, I promise you more action than you'll be comfortable with in what follows. But for now, humour me and think on this.

I think I accomplished more for Athens in those twenty four hours of doing nothing than with all the blood I shed in defence of the city of the Goddess. I only really understand this now looking back.

Strange, isn't it? Strange also that I never found out who it was that summoned me to Brauron. At the time I didn't think about this. Aeschylus gave me the message but of course he's long dead. Maybe I'll ask him when I reach Hades.

Whatever devils were toying with Themistocles's head in Brauron, he was clear of them. The next days were a blur of activity. He returned to Athens and convened a meeting of the five hundred on Pnyx hill. The fact that he hadn't the authority to call the meeting was no hindrance.

The city was frenzied, desperate to be led and walking up the hill to the assembly the noise, like a swarm of bees buzzing round the threatened hive, grew louder. It was to be my last night in Athens for some time and one to be remembered.

Themistocles gave them the leadership they wanted all right. He had two main points to put across: the first was that an Athenian delegation must leave next day for Corinth to put together a defensive alliance of free Greek states. Then, standing solid like an oak on the rostra, he moved to the issue at the forefront of his mind.

"Athenians, friends, patriots."

I noted the deliberate absence of any mention of the Demos: there was no room for factionalism or polis style trickery now. We were all in this together. He was, of course, helped by the fact that all of his heavyweight opponents were in exile. It was this that made his next appeal all the more surprising.

"We stand here today on the verge of changing the world. However we need for a moment to turn our attention to foreign shores. Foreign shores where Athenians with whom in the past we have had our differences are straining to catch an echo of our words."

He gave us a moment to let this sink in and for the more slow-witted amongst us to realise he'd moved onto another tack.

"Men who, admittedly, have made errors of judgement. But men who in the past have stood with us in the shield wall and dealt death-dealing blows to the barbarian invaders. Citizens, do you know of whom I speak?"

A disingenuous question if ever I heard one, but it was greeted by a full throated roar of assent.

"To punish these men for their intemperance was just

and right. But to punish them by denying them the right to defend their families, their friends, their City and the honour of the Goddess; is that not too cruel a penalty?"

Most of us had picked up where this was leading and shouted back.

"Yes, too cruel."

"Do I detect that you, wise citizens, like me, wish to make the city whole again, to close ranks against the barbarians?"

A great roar of 'yes'; even the stupid were up to speed by now.

"So friends, what must we do?"

He had the momentum now, even those with something to fear from the return of the exiles joined in the shouts of,

"Bring them home."

Never one to curtail the satyr play element of such gatherings, Themistocles squeezed the last oil from the olive. Hamming it up like a second rate chorus touring rural theatres he affected a slightly quizzical look. Then he shouted back,

"Bring them home? Bring them all back home?"

"Yes, all of them."

"Even Aristides?"

"Bring him home."

"And Xanthippus?"

"Bring him home."

"And Megacles?"

Just ahead of the beat some wag shouted,

"Even that fucker?"

And the crowd shouted,

"Bring the fucker home."

It worked like magic, an act of, what the poets call, catharsis, it brought us all together. The motion was passed, so they'd all come home. In this way we were better prepared than at Marathon: the whole city would be on the same side. It was a good piece of theatre, Aeschylus would have been proud. We drifted away and into the wine shops bars and brothels.

Later, sitting with the inner core of the crew of Athene Nike in the Bald Man's bar, I watched as a drunk and beaming Ariston finished his cup and shouted across the bar,

"And Theodorus?"

The crowded bar shouted back as one man.

"Bring him home, bring the fucker home."

¤ ¤ ¤

Corinth is a strange place. The town sits on a narrow isthmus between two sea gulfs guarding the only land route to the land of Pelops: guarding Sparta. It's the strategic key to the Southern mainland, which explains why Corinth swaps sides so often. The modern town lies at the foot of a huge spur of rock towering overhead. Ancient Corinth is at the top, complete with massive walls built during the age of heroes. The harbour front stretches along a series of creeks affording good protection for their fleet. For trade it enjoys the best position in Greece.

But, and it's a big but: the Corinthians can never rest easy knowing any war in mainland Greece is going to involve them even if they're non-combatants. I think this explains why they have a reputation for trickery and false friendship. Most of the time, despite our rivalry, we've stayed on good terms but I fear that soon the policies of Pericles the onion head will make war with them and through them the Spartans inevitable. But pardon me, reader, I get ahead of myself.

The night after the Pnyx meeting we overnighted near Salamis before pulling for Corinth on a smooth sea next day. The Athene Nike was near to its full complement of experienced men with a leavening of the most promising novices, so it was as close to an elite crew as the Athenian fleet boasted. Lysias was trierarch, Ariston at the helm, Themistocles in command: the Athene Nike not yet having been passed to Cimon as he'd anticipated. I commanded the fighting men but the bosun was a temporary fill in. This latter didn't matter so much as we swept down the coast of the Megarid with a following wind.

To my surprise, we changed course and pulled into the port of the town of Megara. I'd seen Themistocles exchange a whispered conversation with Ariston before the manoeuvre. For a moment I wondered if Lyra would be there. She wasn't, of course, but standing on the dockside was a familiar burly figure saying goodbye to young women with two infants. He waved casually to the boat as we stood offshore, not wanting to become entangled in the portside procedures. Then nimbly jumped down into fishing skiff and was rowed out to us greeted by shouts of,

"Bring the fucker home."

Thus relieved of blood guilt by war, Theodorus rejoined his mates. He looked none the worst for his experience and his brutal good humour strengthened us. I felt surprisingly strong emotion as I embraced him. He said to me through the grin splitting his beard,

"Remember, boy, just because you're now in charge of these useless landsmen passengers doesn't mean you don't do what I tell you to."

In Corinth I found out why Themistocles had been paralysed by fear at Brauron. Corinth was packed with refugees, agents of the Great King, representatives of the Greek states heading for the meeting in Sparta and representatives of the states refusing to go. Corinth seethed with deceit and treachery; no one was what he seemed. But on one thing everyone agreed.

The Great King was ready to eat up all of Greece. We were

briefed on this by Brasidas, acting as an agent of the Ephors after we met him in the house of a Corinthian democrat in the city. I'll give the Spartans this, once they decide on something they waste no time. To our surprise Brasidas had with him someone I'd no desire to meet.

Sitting between Brasidas and our host in the place of honour was one of the Aeginian worthies I'd last seen sitting next to Metiochus on the night of our humiliation in the temple complex. As my hand felt for my dagger, Themistocles crossed the room towards the man, who scrambled to his feet. They embraced. Brasidas with typical laconic oratory merely said,

"I thought it a good idea to bring you together before the conference convenes in Sparta."

Then he rose and said to the rest of the room,

"We'll leave Athens and Aegina in the capable care of our host."

He walked out of the room; the rest of us followed. I think he was enjoying himself. Later we sat in a corner of a scruffy wine shop dimly lit by the smoky light of a lamp guttering on poor quality oil. The place, poor as it was, was crowded but humming with noise so we could talk and not be overheard. I could see the wound still troubled him.

"You looked like you'd swallowed a wasp when you walked in, Mandrocles, good job Metiochus wasn't there."

"Metiochus? Him here?"

"So it's rumoured, not seen him myself and he's obviously not with the delegates from Aegina."

"Why?"

"You'll find out soon enough. How are you, boy?"

I don't know what I told him, can't remember what we drank or ate. What he told me drove everything else out of my head.

"In five days we, and the delegates from every state prepared to fight, convene in Sparta. Most states won't attend: too scared of the Great King."

He grinned at me then said,

"But that's not the worst of it. Some of the states sending delegates are at war with each other, like you and your friends in Aegina. But that's not the worst of it either."

I wasn't going to rise to this; I just sat waiting.

"Now your friend Metiochus, wherever he is, isn't alone. There are plenty of Persian agents here carrying plenty of Persian gold. Gold that they'll pay to some of the states that do attend as well as some that don't. Would you like me to give you an example?"

The lamp finally died, Brasidas shouted for a new one and more wine.

"Take Argos for instance: used to be a great power, stamping ground of Hercules. Now a poor subservient neighbour to us. And how those bastards hate us. Hate us enough to have sold out to the Great King, or so our agents say."

Across the far end of the bar some drunks started up a drinking song. Brasidas leaned across the table to be heard.

"But that's still not the worst of it."

I sat waiting for the worst of it, snatches of the song, a standard about an old man loving a flute girl flickering around my head.

"No, all that's rumour, probably true but hard to verify. The worst of it we can verify. Our agents have been monitoring it. Interested?"

For the first time it hit me that he was unloading this onto me; he was sharing it with me because he was scared and for me that was the worst of it. If men like him were scared, how could we expect men from weaker states to fight?

"The rumours are that the Great King has built a bridge of ships so his army can walk to Greece."

"Everyone knows that, Brasidas."

"Well, I bet they don't know this."

He took a swig of wine before,

"They've already crossed over, our men saw them."

"That's not possible, it's too soon."

He ignored me.

"Rumour is that he wants to strengthen his Phoenician fleet, the most powerful in the world, with others. Hard to credit that he thinks he needs them, isn't it?"

I waited.

"Ain't no rumour: the Egyptian, Libyan fleets and others from all over the empire are already there. They've sailed; it's started. It's started, Mandrocles, the greatest invasion force ever put together is already on Greek soil preparing to march on us."

He took a drink; he wasn't finished. The song and the bar may as well have been in another dimension. I waited in horror for what was to come.

"And this is the worst of it."

I saw he was struggling to control himself as he delivered what came next.

"A vast fleet and a massive army both packed with traitors. Packed with Greeks."

I thought of Metiochus; then he finished.

"Yes you heard right, packed with Greeks: there's more Greeks on their side than ours. And!"

Another pause for self-control, but he finished off on a typically chilling Spartan note.

"And that's only the ones we know about, there are probably others pretending to be with us, biding their time to see which way they're going to jump."

He dashed the jug off the table to the ground; I was surprised it didn't break.

"Look around us, Mandrocles. How many of these bastards in here will end up fighting against us?"

Neither of us wanted the answer to that question; we drank up and left. Brasidas walked away uphill towards the house where Themistocles was cutting deals with the delegates from Aegina and the Gods only know who else. I picked my way downhill through the maze of tracks and alleys, inhabited by the poor, sloping towards the docks. One of the few predictable rules in life is that the docks are always downhill.

I shouldn't have drunk so much, if I hadn't I wouldn't have been stupid enough to set out alone after dark in a strange city packed with enemies.

Chapter Twenty-Four

I suppose I should blame Brasidas, he'd set the example. But then for a Spartan it was typical behaviour. It wouldn't occur to them that anyone would be stupid or disrespectful enough to waylay them as they walked through a foreign and therefore inferior city.

The Gods never blessed me with that level of confidence and failed to compensate for the oversight by endowing me with an extra ration of common sense. Finding your way home at night in a city you know can be difficult enough; the back streets of Corinth are a warren and before long I was lost. Some of the filthy tracks had hovels packed so close together that it wasn't possible to see above the roof line to where the acropolis of Corinth was perched high up on its precipitous crag. This was disaster for me as I'd been trying to use sightings of the Acropolis to navigate.

A claustrophobic warren, it teemed with life hostile to any stranger stupid enough to wander through, particularly at night. The noise I made even though I was trying to creep silently sounded like the tread of an army. I was spooked as well as lost and in growing panic decided to follow the one source of noise I could hear growing in volume somewhere ahead of me. I reckoned whatever the noise was it must be emanating from one of the more ordered and well lit parts of the city, and from there I could find my way.

Yes I know you're thinking how stupid, reader, and of course you're right. Well I found the source of the noise all right. Whatever had been happening was in its last moments when I arrived. The sound of raised voices terminated and was replaced by the softer sounds of a scuffle. Emerging into a better lit square, I caught the dying acts of a tragedy.

One man was on the ground, legs twitching in the throes of death, blood gouting from a knife slash across the throat. The other was up against the wall, being questioned. A knife was pressed to his gullet, he was crying. I think it was that insignificant detail that held me there. For as I watched his helpless fear I remembered my torment in Aegina and for a moment I became that man.

There was a third man, a few paces back, cloaked and hooded, watching. He was enjoying it, a sardonic smile curling the ends of his lips. He was in charge; the other two looked back expectantly between questions for guidance. Whatever answers they were after weren't forthcoming. To me it was obvious the terrified victim wasn't withholding anything; he was too scared for that. Whatever they wanted he didn't know.

Another few seconds and he'd be dead, joining his friend on the floor. Such is life but the Gods love to surprise us: it suits their mercurial humour. The leader stepped forwards and in doing so his hood slipped back over his shoulders and I found myself looking at the very man I'd been thinking of earlier: Metiochus.

I've never had the reputation of a clever man, now I confirmed that judgement. Metiochus was still smiling, mocking the victim before his death. It was too much, something in my heart burst and a flood of bitter anger came flooding out. Like in the blood lust of battle, all sense fled except the lust to kill, the lust for death, sweet death, an enemy's death.

I heard the shouting of the battle paean before I realised it was me bellowing it. I was running at them, knife drawn, roaring.

They did what any sensible men would do in the circumstances finding themselves attacked by baying enemies in a hostile city. They ran, and quickly. I reached the spot in a few paces, slipped in the patch of blood, came crashing to the ground. The Gods got their joke. The fall brought me to my senses: any advantage of surprise I'd enjoyed was now spent. Pursuing them would have been fatal.

The whimpering man tried to help me to my feet. Apart from a couple of bruises and a speck of blood where the knife had pricked his throat, he wasn't badly hurt. I was thinking clearly again so I didn't need him to tell me,

"We need to get away from here; they'll be back with others."

I knew he was right.

"Can you get me to the docks?"

"You're Athenian? Quickly, follow."

He slipped between two buildings and down a passageway and I followed swearing that the next time I saw Metiochus I'd kill him. After a couple of turns we struck a paved street that led in a gentle curve down towards the boats. There were a couple of bars open with sailors drinking in them. It felt safer.

His name was Uliades and he was from Argos, which made me wonder what he was doing here if what Brasidas had told me was true. But my main concern was Metiochus.

"Now we're near the ships you can tell me what that man wanted with you."

He didn't need to ask which man I meant.

"Metiochus, he wanted what he wants from all he regards as renegades, information then my death."

I know my limitations, I wasn't going to waste time attempting to interrogate him myself, I'd leave that to Themistocles. I reckoned getting him onto the Athene Nike was enough from me and it didn't prove difficult. He more or less suggested the same thing himself.

We had to wait for Themistocles; he never came back that night so I had some time to get to know the man I'd saved. He claimed he was a supporter of the democratic faction in Argos, might have been true, but there again in circumstances like these everybody lies. I didn't know what to believe except what my first instinct had told me, which was whatever Metiochus was after he'd got the wrong man.

I did learn something about Argos, though, particularly their uneasy relationship with Sparta. From this I picked up that what, to me as an Athenian, was a clear cut issue facing all Greeks, if they didn't combine to resist the Great King. But I discovered that this looked far less clear from the perspective of other Greek states.

In Uliades's view, for some states the threat of Sparta was worse than Persian dominance and for others the spread of democracy from Athens was the greater evil. So we were going to fight a war in which many states, perhaps the majority, saw us as a greater threat than Persia. Notice any similarity with today, reader?

But it was only when Themistocles interrogated him next day that the real value of my intervention became apparent.

A day later we sailed down the coast of the Peloponnese, a journey I was all too familiar with, and into the Spartan port of Gytheion. On my previous two visits there'd been an element of subterfuge; now it seemed the whole world was looking to Sparta. The harbour was packed with vessels from all over Greece. Many had come to forge an alliance but there were also those there to spy for the Great King, and even some delegates who intended openly to oppose an alliance.

You will have heard the great tale of how the issue was decided in Sparta, or according to some versions, in Corinth, reader. Well, let me tell you it wasn't like that at all, that story of how Themistocles and the Spartans argued in public over who would command the fleet.

It was never going to happen that way, far too risky. No, everything that could be was planned then rehearsed after last minute deals had been struck. But it's the way of the world that nothing succeeds as planned and it was something unexpected that almost drove our fragile agreement with the Spartans onto the rocks.

It should have gone more smoothly. Themistocles had somehow patched things up with Aegina: they'd fight alongside us. He was going to spring this on the delegates during the assembly like a piece of drama, at which he excelled. But on a stage of this size, with the fate of the whole of Greece in the balance, nothing could be taken for granted. What we couldn't have predicted was the scale of the treachery, although the presence of Metiochus and men like him should have given us some clues.

The truth is the public debate was a farce. It achieved nothing and could have ruined everything. One of the sad things I've learned in life is that most of the good things have been brought about as a consequence of dirty dealing. There was one clear fact though: if Athens and Sparta couldn't combine, Greece was lost. So before the great assembly we met with the Spartan leadership to cut a deal in the house of Leonidas: the man who benefitted from the painful death of a brother and who believed the Gods worked through him.

They were all there in that austere and dimly lit room, the Ephors, two kings and others including a weak chinned individual who kept nervously arranging and rearranging his tunic. We were few, with Themistocles and Cleinias the only speaking voices. To my surprise I longed for the presence of Aristides, Xanthippus and even Megacles. In the event there wouldn't have been time for them to participate; it was a short and brutal meeting.

The rank-smelling, goat bearded Ephors banged their staffs on the ground and Leonidas began to speak. Even by Spartan standards of dictatorial arrogance it was an unfortunate beginning to a meeting of allies.

"Welcome, Athenians, and listen to how we shall fight this war. First let me tell you that the Great King has offered us favourable terms in exchange for our neutrality. Knowing all Greece looks to us for leadership and aware of our sacred obligations, we rejected his embassy and his ambassadors have joined their predecessors at the bottom of the well."

Pompous and offensive and typically Spartan but also oddly verbose. Where was the famous laconic application of brevity? We'd expected some attempt, at least the pretence of a friendly preamble. I looked towards Themistocles, he gave nothing away but I sensed he was troubled. But Leonidas had only just got warmed up.

"We will construct a wall across the Isthmus of Corinth and invite all loyal Greeks to fight under our leadership; we will make a fortress of the Peloponnese and find space for our allies who have had to abandon their homelands. We will force the Great King to fight on ground of our choosing and on our terms ..."

Themistocles cut him off.

"And how will you deal with the Great King's fleet once it has simply sailed past your great and doubtless impregnable wall, King Leonidas?"

There was an intake of breath from the Ephors; Leonidas, just begun on his peroration, looked daggers. Problem for him and the Ephors was that there was no answer to this question, at least not an answer that suited them. Something which couldn't be said for the answer Themistocles gave to his own question.

A number of years ago I gave an account of this exchange to young Herodotus to include in the stories he's writing about our heritage. So I remember it pretty well, even if he has subsequently altered details to suit the flow of his narrative. He's grown up into quite a clever man and got the main bits about Themistocles right, I'm pleased to say.

"Kings, Ephors, noble Spartiates, forgive my interruption, I'm a simple plain speaking man and mean no offence but let me answer my question for you."

Unparalleled on the field of battle but totally unused to being contradicted in their brutal slave state, they were at a loss and Themistocles took his advantage.

"Think on this, noble hosts: one of the problems with fleets is that walls don't stop them. So, after the Great King has sailed his vast fleet past your wall, as he of course will, he is free to land his troops anywhere in your Peloponnese homeland. This presents you with a problem as you will be unable to disentangle your army from your great wall, which will of course be besieged by the other Persian army which General Mardonius will have marched unopposed across Greece. A Greece which you refused to defend. And what do you think happens then?"

They didn't need to think, it had already struck them. But Leonidas made an effort.

"Is that not where your precious fleet earns its money, Themistocles?"

"If there had been a plan to defend all of Greece and not just your patch then you'd be right, King Leonidas."

The implications of this reverberated through the chamber. But Themistocles, although on unfamiliar territory, was a master of this type of engagement and pressed his advantage. Helped I think by the nature of the Spartans, who respect little but do respect courage.

"So, let me return to the answer of the question I posed."

I think Leonidas was torn between the desire to buy him a drink and the desire to kill him. I noted the chinless man adjusting his tunic now looked considerably more ill at ease.

"Think for a moment, great leaders of Sparta. Reflect upon what will happen on the other side of your great wall in the Greek states abandoned to the Persians. Remember some of these states, like Thebes, have already agreed to accept the Great King. For states like these, the fall of Sparta and Athens cannot come too soon."

He smiled a cold and bitter smile. In the pause Leonidas said,

"But Thebes is on the other side of the Isthmus; all the loyal Greeks will stand with us."

"You think so?"

It was clear in the ensuing silence that neither Leonidas nor the Ephors were sure. Themistocles took a sip of wine then pressed on, but in a more gentle tone, like a father explaining the harshness of life to a disappointed child.

"You see for me, I find it difficult to distinguish between loyal and disloyal Greeks. I merely see Greek states in a variety of difficult situations with hard choices to make."

Something was coming; in that room you could feel it like the silence before a summer storm, time seemed suspended waiting for whatever deal breaker or maker came next. Then the thunder.

"Take Argos, for instance."

I swear I saw the muscles in Leonidas's jaw tighten as he waited to hear the doom of his plans.

"Argos, which is of course on the same side of the wall as you are."

He paused and smiled at them before moving to the point.

"I have been speaking to an Argive friend, Uliades, a good man, a democrat, a man who wishes to fight with us. You Spartans are of course familiar with the political situation in Argos, your Peloponnesian neighbour. So you won't need me to tell you how they still mourn the recent slaughter of the cream of their manhood by the army of Spartans led by your late king, Cleomenes. You know how they resent your dominance."

"Get to the point, Themistocles."

Leonidas shouted this, the storm was breaking. In the last moment of stillness Themistocles mused, as if to himself,

"So I wonder how they'll react when egged on by the betrayed Greeks the other side of the wall. I wonder which port they will make available to the Persian fleet. Perhaps Nauphlio would be best situated as it is halfway between the wall on the Isthmus and the city of Sparta. A port with plenty of land to disembark and deploy an army, near to the ancient Argive fortress of Tiryns. I'd consider this possibility very carefully if I were you. From there, they would cut your army off from Sparta itself."

"You can't possibly know this."

"Oh, but I do, King Leonidas. I have it on very good account that the Great King has promised Argos hegemony of the Peloponnese after the defeat of Sparta. Not that it's only the Argives you have to worry about."

I believe at that moment Leonidas considered drawing a blade and striking Themistocles, but he controlled himself sufficiently to snap.

"Your fleet, it's the job of your fleet to stop that. That's what you promised. Listen Themistocles ..."

The storm had broken, now Themistocles was raising his voice.

"If you defended Greece, not if you betrayed it. Like you did back at Mara ..."

He managed to choke back the words that might have ruined everything. Leonidas was still shouting.

"You promised, gave your word you fucking Athenian renegade, you promised, you fucking promised. No one breaks their word to a Spartan and lives. No one."

"I can't deliver the fleet on your terms. No Athenian will agree once you betray us. We will evacuate our city and sail to one of our colonies, maybe in Italy, and leave the Great King to you."

They were screaming at each other; no one else moved. But there was something final and deadly in Themistocles's roar of anger.

"They have two and a half million men, not even counting the traitors. Stick to your plan, the wall will be bypassed; you will fight alone, be betrayed and wiped out. Sparta will disappear."

In retrospect I sometimes think that maybe that would have been the best conclusion, but back then we needed them. Funnily enough the same thought must have pulled both Leonidas and Themistocles back from the brink. There was another silence and Themistocles possessed the subtlety to let Leonidas speak first.

"So what do you want? What is your offer, Athenian?"

The last word was spat out with venom; Themistocles ignored this.

"I want to yoke the horses of Athens to the Spartan chariot. But; I need something from you that will enable me to do this. You must make, at least, a pretence of defending all Greece. You must send Spartan troops beyond the isthmus to slow the Persians down. Do that and we can build an alliance with most of the states that've sent delegates here. We can make it difficult for Thebes, Argos and the others to play the traitor. If it doesn't work, you still have the option of retreating to ground of your own choosing; the isthmus wall if you want. But defend our soil first. I know how it could work. Do this and Athens will sacrifice itself for Greece."

It's hard to tell how Spartans communicate. Sometimes they prevaricate for years. But not in that room. The kings looked at each other; the Ephors gently tapped their crooks on the ground. Only the chinless man seemed agitated, his eyes swivelling round the room. Then Leonidas stepped towards Themistocles and offered him his hand.

In that one gesture he changed the fate of all Greece and sealed his own. That's how it was done, reader, that's how the histories that young Herodotus writes are really decided. I know, I was there. But it was a close run thing. A great reckoning in a small room. All that stuff in the assembly the next day, that was just a show; a satyr play; but it's the way of the world that it's always the sleight of hand that's believed.

So they shook hands like the heroes of Homer after a contest. I think there was genuine respect between them. Themistocles was sweating and I caught a fleeting memory of him hiding under the sheets at Brauron. Sometimes we have to be all things.

There was to be one more twist, however. I can't swear to it but I think it was the nearest a Spartan has ever come to a subtle joke. Leonidas asked,

"So, we have your precious Athenian fleet then?"

"Yes, we fight together."

"Together, yes. But as you agreed under Spartan command."

Themistocles had nowhere to go.

"Yes."

"Well in that case let me introduce you to the commander of the Greek fleet."

He spoke one word; a name.

"Eurybiades."

The chinless man walked across the chamber and proffered Themistocles his hand.

Chapter Twenty-Five

So to the assembly of the Greeks. The great assembly. It was managed and choreographed like a play at the Dionysia. Except for the climax of course. No one saw that coming. But I get ahead of myself.

The conference of those Greeks hoping to form an alliance, and some who didn't, took place in a building the Spartans, with their customary self-aggrandisement, called the Hellenion. It was too small and shabby to deserve such a name and was cramped with poor acoustics. However, few of the delegates crammed in shoulder to shoulder worried much over that. The piece of theatre they witnessed once the prayers had been said and libations poured was far too dramatic to allow delegates the luxury of assessing their surroundings.

What would happen had been arranged between Themistocles and the Spartan kings. It was proposed by some minor, toadying member of the Spartan Peloponnesian league, I forget which, that the leader of the Greek army to face the Persians would be Sparta. This was approved, as was expected, by all except the Argive delegation.

Then the leadership of the fleet was raised. Themistocles took the rostra and in a short, high handed and provocative statement demanded that as most of the fleet would be Athenian it should have an Athenian leader. This drew the expected response from our rivals; Aegina and Corinth foremost.

There followed a period of unseemly squabbling as insults were bandied back and forth. Then, as it seemed an impasse had been reached, Leonidas took to the rostra. No one was going to heckle him so he was heard in silence as he delivered the speech that I suspect Themistocles had written for him. It concluded with,

"So I appeal to the Athenian delegates to put their rightful pride in their mighty fleet to one side and for the sake of unity and the freedom of all Greece, accept a non-Athenian as admiral of the fleet."

This was the cue for Themistocles to take the stage. With tears in his eyes he put on a display of such astonishing falsehood that I thought he'd have been shouted down. It was so obviously faked and staged that I'm surprised the gods didn't strike him dead there and then. But no: the delegates loved it, cheered him to the rafters. Particularly the conclusion, a masterpiece of hypocrisy, where he said,

"For me, fellow Greeks, as admiral of the Athenian fleet I realise it is my duty to put Greece before Athens. We have suffered for Greece before and will do so again. But let me make one suggestion: let the leader of the fleet be a Spartan so we have a unified command. I would proudly serve under a Spartan admiral."

Through the cheers that followed this, and before the puzzled eyes of the Aegiantians and Corinthians, Eurybiades was wheeled out to be greeted by embraces and tears of incredulous joy by Themistocles. Part of me wanted to throw up, but I suppose it solved things. And that's the account you now know and should believe, reader. Pure theatre. It should have ended there, but in life there's only so much that can be controlled.

There was movement at the back of the room, an area

where the least prestigious of the delegate's entourage were promiscuously mixed. It was difficult to identify who spoke but there could be no misunderstanding the tone and nature of the question shouted at the stage. The significance was increased by the question coming from someone associated with the Thessalian delegation.

Thessaly was on the direct line of march for the Persian army. It would be the front line soon; perhaps, as we debated here, it was already a war zone. The Thessalians were likely to offer earth and water to the Great King if their land wasn't defended. But the question was far more subtle.

"Can our noble Athenian ally tell us truthfully about the words of the oracle at Delphi that they have so recently received?"

If there was one thing that we'd tried to keep secret in Athens, it was that message from the Gods: the one that quite explicitly stated that if we resisted the Persians we'd be wiped out. Themistocles tried to buy time to allow him to understand the nature of this threat, for threat it obviously was. But there was no time.

"Let me refresh your memory, son of Neocles."

Then the Thessalian began to quote,

"Leave, flee to the ends of the earth! Abandon your homes and the towering heights that ring your city."

Themistocles grew pale; I saw the Spartan kings direct anxious glances at each other but they had no time to intervene.

"Has this jogged your memory, son of Neocles, or shall I give you a bit more? This section should be of interest to your allies."

He quoted again.

"Nor is yours the only towered city he will obliterate."

This was enough for Leonidas.

"Quiet, you have spoken out of turn. This is not the place to discuss the words of the Gods directed to a supplicant."

The man knew a threat when he heard one and shut up. But he'd achieved what had been intended: the room was spooked like a herd of wild horses by summer lightening. We never managed to get hold of the speaker, as he managed to lose himself in the crowd and slip away.

Leonidas promised that a further approach would be made to the Delphic oracle. Then he uttered the leaving prayer, thus closing the conference with the promise that all the delegates would reconvene in spring at Corinth prior to the commencement of the fighting season.

The delegates set off back to their states, in most cases more afraid than when they arrived and, as we know, several immediately made their peace with the Great King. I missed what happened next as the two kings and Themistocles convened behind closed doors. The taint of treachery was in the air and I suspected the hand of Metiochus at work.

But the next day, a haggard and drawn Themistocles brought the small group of Athenians together. It was a very short meeting.

"It has been decided that Athens will send a second party of supplicants to the oracle. Cleinias will return with the ships to Athens and speed up the preparation of our fleet. I will lead the supplicants. We leave at dawn."

So it was in this way I came to visit the most sacred and certainly the most frightening place in Greece: Delphi. Most sensible men stay as far from the occult as they can and for those desperate enough to approach the unworldly creatures who tend the shrines at Delphi and Dodona, the experience is neither comfortable nor reassuring. Themistocles occupied himself for the first hour of the journey cursing the stupidity of the religious city leaders having consulted the oracle in the first place.

It was clear from what he said there would be little religion in our visit: we were going to negotiate, if such a thing is possible, with the intermediary of the Gods. But, possible or not, we had to try it because what Greek army was going to march out to fight the Persians with the curse of the Gods hanging over it?

We had plenty of time to ponder this on the march up country towards the Gulf of Corinth. From there we would slip on board a ship and cross the gulf to where the sanctuary sits high up beneath the cliffs on Mount Parnassus. We travelled in secrecy but I think were watched. Despite this we maintained an easy pace, lived well off the country, and benefited from the mountain air and fresh streams.

The story of how the Athenians moved as suppliants towards the shrine carrying olive branches to placate the anger of great Apollo is well known. What's not so well known is that the bit about the olive branches is the only bit that's true and that was a ruse dreamt up by Themistocles to give the impression of piety. There was little piety in our expedition.

But there is something at Delphi, the ancient centre of our world. Something difficult to explain, something otherworldly and unsettling. The God is there but not in the way we understand. I would never go back. For the same reasons that I won't go back, I hesitate to write my full memory of the shrine. Some things are between us and the Gods. The Gods are seldom kind and never forgiving.

It's a hard slog uphill over rough ground and by the time we'd toiled up to the outer sanctuary where suppliants are received, weighed down by our bundles of olive branches, we were exhausted and sweating. The air was heavy and in the distance there was the faint rumble of thunder. We were admitted by a creature, male I think, muffled in a hood with a painted face. This was the first of a series of stages intended to disorientate the suppliant.

I've heard that the process at the Acheron Necromanteion

in the north, off the coast facing Corcyra, is worse. There the supplicant is drugged then follows the path of the dead. At least we were dealing with Lord Apollo, God of light and life.

After being led through a series of ill-lit chambers and asked to wait, Themistocles had had enough; he demanded to see the Phythia. On being told this was not possible by the hooded acolyte he raised his voice.

"When you tell her who it is that you are keeping waiting she won't thank you. I am ..."

He was cut off by a sharp female voice.

"I know who you are and why you're here. You are false dealing Themistocles, son of Neocles, and leader of the Athenians who the God has cursed."

A tall thin-faced woman in an enveloping robe of fine cloth had entered the chamber and I knew we were in the presence of Aristonice, Phythia of Delphi, seer of Apollo. Themistocles made as if to prostrate himself saying,

"I thank you for receiving us, gracious lady, we come to hear the voice of the God."

"You have already heard the voice of the God. I myself bestowed it on your fellow Athenians. This is not an Athenian market where you exchange goods you don't want."

I'm sure I saw the ghost of a smile round her lips as she said this. Themistocles replied,

"I understand, Lady Priestess. We bring fresh offerings."

"You have already had the only answer you will get."

Her manner and the acerbic tone in which she spoke indicated our audience was at an end. But this had little effect on Themistocles.

"All the same, Lady, I think the God would be angered were he not to receive our offering, and more offended if this holiest shrine of the Greeks were to be left undefended and thus ravaged by the barbarian horde."

"That sounds like a threat to me, son of Neocles."

As she said this I felt reassured: she too was in some way a politician.

"Never would a true Athenian dare threaten the most holy shrine of Apollo. We seek to enrich and protect it. But if we are not granted a second and more favourable oracle, then never will we return to Athens, but remain here till the end of our lives."

But it wasn't the end of the speech, with its implication of a threat, she picked up on. It was the promise.

"To enrich it?"

"Greatly, my Lady."

She dismissed her servants then said to Themistocles,

"The ways of the God are strange indeed, son of Neocles, I feel him moving through me as we speak. Dismiss your followers; we will converse with the God in private."

A servant outside the door escorted us out and led us to some simple lodgings where suppliants spent the night. I wandered round the shrine precincts, visited the temple the Athenians had built to give thanks for Marathon. The closeness had departed with the thunder and the air was chill and damp, moisture dripping from the leaves of the strange pale trees surrounding the shrine. Themistocles didn't return.

After eating a meal that would have disgraced a Spartan household we spent an uneasy night. There are wolves and bears in those mountains. We could hear them growling and howling in the dark. Heard other things too; things that survive only in ancient places remote and charmed by the Deities. Or maybe we dreamt it, for all of us were visited by strange and unsettling visions that night: forests and centaurs and gods of the night which never the sun shone on.

Next morning still no sign of Themistocles, we tried to elicit his whereabouts from the strange creatures that served the shrine but got nothing. There was a mist early morning so we sat lost in the sightless grey, waiting for release. Then, as the sun began to burn it off, he appeared. Not the tortured apparition we'd expected, more like a man who'd had a good night and plenty of wine. The latter we could smell on his breath.

He told us nothing, merely crawled into the rough booth that was our lodgings and went to sleep: a state he remained in till next day, condemning us to another night of nocturnal disturbance. But next morning, Themistocles was up early and took especial pains over his appearance and bade us do the same. Then, laden with fresh olive branches, we returned to the oracle. This time we weren't kept waiting but shown straight through and into the presence of the oracle. Aristonice greeted us in far better humour; her pinched and mean spirited face even wore the hint of a smile. She came straight to the business in hand.

"Your piety has been rewarded with a second oracle."

Themistocles bowed in gratitude and we stood waiting for what would follow. Her voice changed to that of the God's and she began to chant. Let me tell you, reader: even if you are one of those who foolishly laughs at the Gods, that change in the Oracle's voice would strike fear in you. As with all oracles, the message began with a preamble about the Gods and the past. But within a few lines we realised what Themistocles had accomplished during his twenty four hours with the priestess.

You know the prophecy as well as I do, reader, but I was there when it was first uttered by the mouthpiece of the God so imagine how we felt when we heard the lines,

" ... Far seeing Zeus grants a wooden wall.
Only this will stand firm as a bastion
to you and your children.
Do not rely on your cavalry, neither rely on your hoplites,

Rather in the face of this overwhelming host you must
retreat instead.
Turn your backs. Yet still shall you meet them face to face.
At divine Salamis the sons of women
will be destroyed by you
When the grain is scattered or
when the harvest is gathered in."

I still get a tingle when I hear those lines and find myself transported back in time to Delphi. Aristonice handed Themistocles a parchment and uttered one last sentence directed only towards Themistocles.

"I will wait with pleasurable anticipation for what you have promised on behalf of the Athenians to the servant of the God, son of Neocles."

Then she turned her back and walked out, swinging her stringy buttocks, and I'm pleased to say I never saw her again. It took some time for it all to sink in, not that we needed to work it out for ourselves. Themistocles was in great high spirits over what he'd achieved and talked all the way down the mountain towards the sea sparkling below us in the sun.

"Couldn't believe she'd give us all of it, Wooden Wall; real divine inspiration that was. How much more clearly can you say ships without using the words?"

He laughed so hard at this he almost slipped off his mule but recovered himself in time to continue.

"How can we lose now that the God has spelled out our battle plan for us? How can any of the allies, including those Spartan bastards, question how we use the fleet?"

And he was right; the Oracle interpreted correctly presented the essence of Themistoclean strategy and he wasn't about to let us forget it. I think he considered this his finest moment but I only fully understood the genius of it later that day as we sat in a tavern on the harbour front. We were killing time, waiting for the ship that would take us to the isthmus and the road home. Listening to him in that tavern even the dimmest of us realised the full magnitude of the God's message.

"Not only the ships but where we'll deploy them."

He raised his hands in the air and chanted solemnly.

"At divine Salamis."

He lowered his arms, took a huge slurp from his wine cup, ineffectually wiped at the stain from the spillage on his tunic and belched loudly.

"And the best of it, the best of it: it gives us a free hand, no time limit, you understand me?"

More wine spilled then he was quoting again.

"When the grain is scattered or when the harvest is gathered in."

He waited for a response scanning our faces. We weren't going to interrupt his flow.

"What other time is there. Everything is either before or after. We can act when we decide the time's right. The God thinks of everything."

Now we were laughing with him. We could see what this oracle had delivered to Athens and to him in particular. We should have stopped drinking but it was a special day. We had a couple of hours before the ship was ready so he ordered another chou of the finest the tavern could find. Maybe we should have quit then, maybe the God was listening: nemesis follows hubris.

Later, as we were flicking the lees from the dregs in our cups in a game of Kottabos, Themistocles muttered,

"Problem with oracles is they're subject to a range of interpretations."

We waited for what he was going to follow up with.

"So the great thing about this one came in the first line before all that waffle about Cecrop's land and holy Cithaeron."

Even through the clouds of drunkenness he must have noted our blank expressions.

"The first line, didn't you get the first line."

We said nothing.

"All right, listen, I'll quote it for you."

He raised his hands above his head.

"I shall tell you in words that can bear no distortion."

He dropped his hands.

"See, see, 'Bear no distortion', the Gods telling them that there's only one way to understand this, it isn't ambiguous, the real meaning is nailed on."

He favoured us with a pathetically pleased-with-himself smile, like a child, said,

"So no one can argue with it, see."

Then went outside to be sick.

Shows just how wrong you can be, doesn't it, reader?

Chapter Twenty-Six

The news and the exiles arrived at about the same time. The news eclipsed the return of the exiles. Mardonius was on the march, moving quicker than anyone could have predicted. With him marched the uncountable Persian host led by the immortals. An army three times larger than anything a united Greece could ever raise, and it would be faced by a disunited Greece. An army that marched towards us lusting for blood and revenge for Marathon.

Mardonius was headed for the high pass over the mountains of Thessaly. The pass, once traversed, descended into the soft underbelly of Greece. From that pass the road led straight south to Athens. Between them and us were a few vacillating states, like Thebes who we couldn't trust. These bastards would betray us and within months Athens would burn.

Two days after the panic had taken hold we sailed back from Delphi into Athens, into a city racked with fear. A city preparing for the type of war it had never previously faced. A crowded city packed with refugees and riven by rumour.

There was a little comfort; we'd been reinforced by the returned exiles, Xanthippus, Aristides. Most of them had returned to stand with us, but not Hipparchus. There were many political fences to be mended.

I tasted the flavour of this in the New Year at a gathering in the house of Themistocles. A large group of his faction mingled with Xanthippus's, Aristides's and Megacles's followers. But it wasn't city rivalry on the agenda; there was something more serious to occupy the gathering. News had come that morning from Sparta that Mardonius scouts and skirmishers had crossed the border into Thessaly.

Old resentments were buried; the men of Marathon needed to stand together. There's nothing like an external threat for promoting alliances. The erstwhile rivals hid any grievances; these could wait for the end of the war, if any of us lived to see the end. Most of us doubted we would, so what we promised today didn't really matter. Aeschylus and I weren't needed; we wandered off to find somewhere to drink, as there wouldn't be many more chances – the fleet was to be mobilised.

That morning a message had been sent to the Spartans enquiring of their intentions. But events bypassed it. Along with their warning of the advance of the Persian skirmishers they'd sent a message direct from Leonidas to Themistocles: short, like all Spartan messages, and thus easy to quote.

"From Leonidas, King of the Spartans, to Themistocles, son Of Neocles Athenian.

Greetings,

I go direct with such men as are available to Tempe to hold the mountain pass against The Great King in obedience to my word. Do you the same. Gather your fleet to support us."

So we had, at most, a couple of nights of freedom in Athens and then we'd be off to war. A war we'd fight at sea, packed into triremes, living on top of each other. That night we avoided the bars where we'd be likely to find the crew of the Athene Nike. We headed for the part of the Ceramicus furthest from the whores. These days of course the seamen drink and live in Piraeus, but then it was different – although the first signs of that shift were beginning to appear.

We wanted a quiet bar but there weren't any: war leads men to congregate in places where they can both drink and share their fear.

Not that Aeschylus was interested in sharing his fear, he didn't fear the type of things the rest of us do. We found a place near the old shrine of the Goddess on the road leading to the wall. The shrine wasn't much used now and exuded an air of neglect. But someone had left flowers at the feet of the ancient and worn figure of the Goddess. I remember that after a dry spell there had recently fallen a sharp shower, and the little square smelt of damp earth.

Aeschylus wanted to learn about what it was like to be a supplicant. Go see his play of that name, reader; it's still performed in some of the rural demes. Because in that play you'll see what we talked about that night. In many ways it's a women's play ending with the appeal to the gods to 'grant victory to the women's cause' but, as in all things, he had another purpose. After one small jug, when he'd extracted from me as much as I could remember from my time with the oracle, he said,

"Not much time left, Mandrocles, you need to make things right."

Must have been obvious from my expression I had no idea what he was talking about.

"She's back, Mandrocles, you should go to her."

"Where, when?"

"Back about a month. Living in her old place for now. Things have happened."

He wouldn't specify, thought it should be left for her to tell me. I wish he'd spelt it out. If he had, things might have been different. Don't know how I felt, only that I wanted to see her.

It was almost like the old days: Demetrius favoured me with an evil squint as he let me in, his face had acquired another scar; there was a comforting sameness about that. There was another girl in her room and they were sitting on the bed together playing with an infant. She looked confused to see me and hastily handed the child back to its mother.

The mother must have been confused too; she looked surprised to be handed her own baby, which began to cry as she carried it out. I've never been good in situations like this. I knew there was something I was missing, something I needed to say but couldn't think of; instead I remember mumbling something like,

"All right, Lyra? You look nice."

She started to cry. She did look nice but she was different, life changes us all. Later, when we'd overcome the strange diffidence and I undressed her, I felt it. She was heavier, her breasts and belly particularly. But I liked that and when I entered her it was like coming back home. When we'd finished, she had Demetrius bring a flask of wine and we lay back to talk. I'd always liked to lie holding her and hear her talk after the act that men call 'the little death'.

Her tale of having to go to the Megara to look after family didn't quite make sense to me. Every time I questioned her about it she became distressed and then started to cry then said to me,

"Do you want the real truth?"

I didn't, well I did really but I was trying to be kind. Everyone knows a whore has to make things up as she slips from one situation to another. I didn't want to put her in that position. I just said,

"No, love, let's just sleep."

She looked disappointed: strange that. But settled her head onto my shoulder, I was tired, happy I drifted straight off. Looking back I ...

I don't want to write any more about that, I won't.

¤ ¤ ¤

Next day Cimon made his entrance into the legends of our city. It is a story still told to the young to encourage them in their duties. It has many versions and is set at different times. I'll tell you how it really happened and when you've read this you will feel, deep in your soul, that this was how it was. Cimon was wild, his friends were wild, aristocratic roaring boys drinking, whoring and fighting. But like all of us back then we understood our duty to the Gods and to the city.

What we needed in those desperate days was to heal our divisions and fight as one. Something we'd only done once: at Marathon. There we'd fought on foot like gentlemen hoplites. Now that wasn't our role. Greece needed our ships.

But there was bad blood between hoplites and seamen between the young aristos who served in the cavalry and the sons of the Demos. Remember Theodorus had been exiled for gutting a young aristo. There was resistance from the landed classes towards fighting from ships like low born pirates.

People believe the idea came from Themistocles, but for once I disagree. I think it was pure Cimon; it was an example of nobleness of spirit, and no one would accuse Themistocles of that. Those two days when we mobilised our fleet there was the atmosphere of a festival.

The public ways leading down from the city to the Piraeus were packed with all of Athens. Athenians love a crowd and no one was going to miss waving our new fleet off. It was before the traditional sailing season but we knew that whatever was going to happen would happen quickly.

We were provisioning for the expedition, triremes haven't

space to carry much and whereas a few ships may be able to survive by living off what they can find along the coast, that's not possible for a whole fleet. So we were to be supplied from a fleet of merchant craft, mainly pentecontors. Ariston was threatening the captain of the ship which would supply our squadron. There was a standard belief among trireme crews that the merchants adulterated the food and watered down the wine in order to increase profits.

The merchant captain was protesting his honesty while Ariston prodded his well-padded belly with a knife when there was shouting from higher up towards the city. Then a voice directed at me,

"Mandrocles, you've gotta see this."

Then we were off, provisioning forgotten as all of us legged it up to the city. Got there just in time, too. In time to see a group of aristocratic youths carrying their horse harnesses emerge from the Agora. All Athens stopped and turned out to watch. It was a beautiful day as we often get at this time of year when summer begins to perfume the air. Hot too, so the crowd sweated and stank. At first we were too far back to see much, so shoved our way through the crowd to the front. That's where I saw him: Cimon.

His father would have been so proud; it was just the kind of stunt he excelled at. The crowd were shouting questions at them but always received the same answer.

"We are going to make a dedication to the Goddess, follow if you want more."

We did want more, all of us, so the crowd surged after them as they began to weave their way through the packed streets leading up to where the great ramp led into the Acropolis. We had no trouble fighting our way to the front and that's the position we maintained until the show was over.

In the old songs of the fight at Troy the heroes are

described as Godlike. Well. let me tell you: Cimon was God like that day. Taller than his companions, broader too with his thick curly hair lying long over his shoulders. It could have been the young Achilles returned to us.

They processed onto the ramp in high spirits shouting out to each other and laughing. The city needed something like this to take off the edge of constant worry. At the top of the ramp, after a brief stop to honour the small shrine that used to stand there, they took the well-worn track that wandered through the forest of steles and statues leading to the ancient and lovely temple of the Goddess Athena.

You'll have to imagine this, reader, it's all gone now, all destroyed and vanished. What has replaced it and what is still being built although bigger, richer and grander lacks the simple dignity and sense of Godhead of the ancient Acropolis. There was no flashy marble gleaming white, just grey limestone hewn from the Attic Mountains. Six great columns at the front and back and twelve along the sides.

However there were fine marble sculptures adorning the temple. The finest of these depicted a battle between the Gods and giants. In this, mighty Athena was prominent. Back then the temple was hung with shields dedicated by soldiers returned safe from the wars. Cimon and his troop, with due reverence to the Goddess, approached the colonnade of the temple where the shields hung.

Aware of the watching Gods the crowd was shushed and in this sudden deep silence Cimon approached the Goddess. For a moment he stood before her, head bowed in reverence. Then, lifting his arms in supplication, he dedicated his horse trappings to her, hanging them before her statue. Then, turning, he walked to where the nearest shield hung.

As he lifted the shield the sun caught it, flashing off it in a dazzling beam that illuminated the shadowed face of Athena. I swear as this happened the Goddess opened her eyes and smiled on him. Not just me; we all saw her so it must have happened.

Holding the shield he turned and faced us in the silence as, behind him, each of his companions in turn dedicated their horse bridals and took down a shield. None of us missed the significance of this gesture. When they were all arrayed, shield-bearing, behind him, he shouted out across us and down towards the city.

"We know our duty to the Goddess and the city. We will man the wooden walls. We will fight from the ships alongside the people."

I didn't realise he had such a stentorian voice; it would have graced any parade ground. He turned to his companions and shouted,

"To the ships."

They replied,

"To the ships."

They came down off the temple and began to make their way down through the city and to the harbour with the crowd surging behind them, shouting,

"To the wooden walls. To the ships."

At Piraeus each of them chose and boarded a separate ship. Cimon, who as leader got to choose first, chose the Athene Nike, to the delight of its crew. A city faced with destruction needs moments like those, but moments like those come only from great leaders.

The euphoria was short lived.

We were betrayed. However good the reasons for the Spartan army to be seen as defending all Greece, there was no sensible military logic in attempting to defend Thessaly. The emotions of the Greek assembly infected our minds and distorted our logic. A mixed force under Spartan command was marching to guard the way to the mountain pass at Tempe. From the outset everything that could have gone wrong did so. But there were also strategic reasons that weighed against us. The fleet and the army were too far apart for one to support the other.

That wasn't the worst of it. The worst of it was our lack of military sense. A good commander knows and chooses his ground. We had no idea of the ground. We were told by our Thessalian allies there was only one route through the mountains that an army could use, narrow and steep sided. Our leaders never bothered to verify this, just moved the whole of our makeshift force to defend the pass at Tempe.

There were two passes. Two passes and we hadn't bothered to check, hadn't bothered to scout it properly. But there was worse news to follow: the Persian army was moving at a speed we'd not predicted. There were even some optimists who claimed that it would be impossible for such a great army to live off the land during their march. These fools claimed that army would exhaust all food supply and drink the rivers dry.

Whoever it was charged with the provisioning of that army must have been a genius. Their whole army was at Tempe almost as quick as our small force and was neither starving nor parched but in prime condition to fight. At the same time, anyone standing on the windswept crags of Mount Athos could have seen the entire Persian fleet – over twelve hundred strong – sweep round the peninsula to support the army.

Euainetos, the Spartan commander of our force at Tempe, had about ten thousand men with him and was able to trust less than half of them in battle. Once informed of the existence of a second pass, which was being approached by a substantial Persian force even as the news was being delivered to him, he took the only sensible decision any commander could.

He got his troops out of there as quickly as possible, abandoning Thessaly without having struck a blow. The Thessalians then took the only sensible decision any state could, although in truth this had been the preference for more than half of them as soon as war was even rumoured. They went over to the Great King, an act that other states now followed. The whole of northern Greece was abandoned.

In the fleet we had our own problems. We managed to put together a Greek fleet of about two hundred and seventy triremes, with some merchants following with supplies. But we had to sail early and the weather was poor. For experienced seamen it wasn't too bad although we all feared the type of late winter storm that could wreck a fleet. But for the rookies being tossed about in their unstable craft half a mile from shore, it was far worse. The gunwales swam with vomit as the green faced recruits heaved up their guts into the sea. We never came close to the army, having to pull up onto a beach in southern Thessaly rather than risk riding out a storm at sea.

That's where we were when we heard the news that northern Greece was abandoned without a fight. It's also the place where, huddled by a camp fire, I first heard the name of a place that was to acquire a terrible and bloody name. The news of Euainetos's retreat reached Sparta at the same time as a message to them from the oracle of Apollo at Delphi. Not a particularly helpful message either. It informed them they had a choice: they could lose a king or their city to the Persians.

The two Spartan kings, Leonidas and Leotychidas, conferred with their allies including Themistocles at Corinth. Here many of the allies attempted to resurrect the plan to abandon the rest of Greece and fight from behind a wall built across the Isthmus of Corinth. I wasn't there; I don't know how the debate went, but I do know what plan emerged. We would withdraw our forces to make a stand at the next narrow pass further south in Phocis.

This plan must have been cobbled together by the two kings and Themistocles. The fleet was given orders to retreat south to Artemisium and prevent the Persian fleet from sailing down the coast and to support a Greek army. A Greek army led by Leonidas, the senior of the Spartan kings. He would lead a Spartan army and a mixed force of Greek allies. Lead them to a strange place with a strange name. A narrow defile on the road to Athens with high cliffs on one side and the sea on the other. A place where hot stinking springs bubble out of the earth. Hot springs that gave the place its peculiar name.

Thermopylae.

Chapter Twenty-Seven

Right from the beginning we made heavy going to Artemisium, rocked by gales and caked with salt spray. The Athene Nike pitched and rolled and she had the best crew in the fleet; the Gods alone know what it must have been like onboard the other triremes.

Themistocles sailed with us as commander of the Athenian contingent, which comprised the heart and lungs of the fighting ships. Somewhere behind, towards the rear was the Spartan flag ship on the deck of which Eurybiades was, no doubt, heaving up his guts into the disturbed waters.

It was the best place for him; he'd no feel for fighting at sea and led in name only. This had been made clear to him by the leaders of all the other contingents. I think he was relieved. Even for a Spartan he was cautious and whatever the situation all he could do was react, and he was slow at that.

It wasn't that he lacked courage; just that he was lost once he boarded a ship. At least we'd sorted out the practical issues of command before we went into action. There was no such problem in the Persian fleet. Their Phoenician fleet commanders had generations of sailing fighting ships in their blood.

The Athens we'd left behind was a graveyard, devoid of men. We'd managed to build Themistocles the ships he'd demanded but we hadn't the men to crew them. Think about it. To put crews on board the Greek fleet, ours and the reserve fleet left guarding approaches to Athens called for sixty thousand men. Far more men than we had.

The cream of the crews sailed with us to Artemisium. But the triremes we left in reserve were undermanned and sailed by inexperienced men. We'd had to draft in recruits from Chalcis and the brave and willing Plataeans to sail the fifty-odd ships held in reserve. They were mainly hoplites farmers with little, if any, seagoing experience.

So it was a desperate and forlorn venture. But at least Themistocles and Leonidas had patched together a plan between themselves. We'd stop the Persian army at Thermopylae and stop the Persian fleet at Artemisium. We would fight two back to the wall defensive engagements. If it worked, the Persian army would be held and the Persian fleet would be prevented from supplying it.

The Gods help us if either fleet or army was outflanked. Our commanders reckoned the fleet would be the easier to outflank as the Persians, if checked by us, could sail right round Euboea and come up behind us. That's why we'd had to divide the fleet, leaving almost half to guard the straits between Andros and Euboea and the approaches to Sounion.

Our worst fear was that they'd find a way to get to Athens; our city was deserted, and any man capable of fighting was on board a trireme. While the men of fighting age were with the fleet our women and children were unprotected and, if taken, could expect little mercy.

And this being Athens there was the usual strong possibility of betrayal. Not all the exiles had returned, some were with the Great King and somewhere beyond our horizon Hipparchus was pacing the desk of a Persian warship.

After two days beating up and down the narrow channel dividing the mainland from Euboea in the unseasonably strong winds, we pulled the triremes up onto a flat stretch of white sandy beach about ten miles long. It was a relief to be on dry land. On the way we passed Thermopylae; there was no sign of Leonidas and the Spartans. The pass was unguarded.

Unsettled, we dispatched a squadron to scout the waters ahead for Persians. Themistocles dispatched a fast skiff under the command of his most trusted agent Habronichus to Thermopylae to find our land forces. In the meantime we set up camp around the ships. Round my camp fire were Themistocles, Cimon and Aeschylus and some hoplites who'd fought at Marathon. For all its murder and bloody grimness war, at least, brings the best company.

The site had fresh water; a network of small streams drained through patches of marsh into the sea. Ahead of us were the islands of Skiathos and Skopelos and the narrow straits through which the Persian fleet would have to sail. We ate a poor meal of barley porridge seasoned with a thick sauce of cheese mush and onions then settled down to sleep.

Sleep wasn't easy as the wind rose in the night and howled through our flimsy shelters. Aeschylus used the experience to imagine the Greeks by their ships at Troy and scribbled snatches of verse through the night. But for the rest of us there was only one question reverberating round our heads in the dark. Where were the Spartans?

Two days later the skiff reappeared, sailing into the teeth of a gale. A risky business that; so we knew that whatever message they carried must be urgent. Themistocles must have felt that too. As soon as Habronichus leapt from the prow onto the beach Themistocles shushed him up then led him away inland where he and the other commanders could speak unheard, without rumour and misconception spreading through the fleet like wildfire.

They'd wasted their time; when they returned to us their

faces told the story and it wasn't a happy one. Themistocles said nothing, merely ordered that the Athene Nike prepare itself to sail. The weary Habronichus reboarded his vessel and set off back for Thermopylae. Within the hour we were following.

Let me tell you about Thermopylae, reader; even if you've been there, which I doubt, don't skip this bit because you couldn't have seen it through our eyes; the eyes of fear. Thermopylae was perched directly above us. We moored up at the base of some steep sloping bluffs and slogged up to the pass. If the Gods ever created a perfect spot for a small, vastly outnumbered force to stand and hold that was it.

The Greek army had arrived and was making camp behind a battered ancient wall. They were in the process of strengthening this wall at a spot where the pass was only wide enough to let three ox carts, packed together side by side, struggle through. On the landward side the cliffs rose sheer and to the seaward the land fell straight to the sea. In other places the pass narrowed to the width of one ox cart. The place has a strange feel and sound is strangely distorted. Hot springs bubble out from under the cliffs, shrouding Thermopylae in a faint smell of rotting eggs.

Leonidas himself greeted us as we disembarked; he looked different, there was a light in his eyes as if a God had touched him. This version of the man was not the one I remembered from my time in Sparta. Maybe it's true what they say about Spartans being unable to cope with the freedom and temptations of life outside their repressed state. Leonidas greeted Themistocles like an old friend, it wasn't an act either; it was clear that he was genuinely relieved to be reassured that the Athenian fleet would meet its promise to hold the sea straight.

Amongst his officers I was delighted to see Brasidas, and while the two leaders went to Leonidas's headquarters tent he showed Cimon, Aeschylus and me around the camp. At the rear of the camp there was a Theban contingent; Brasidas pointed them out.

"We've put them where they can do least damage. They don't like being here any more than we like having them."

Cimon asked,

"So why bring them?"

Brasidas shrugged.

"I'd have thought that the son of Miltiades and companion of Themistocles would have understood the treacherous art of politics. They're here to make sure their friends back in Thebes don't go over to the Persians."

He spoke bitterly, and looked tired. Whatever ailment he had was quickly sapping his strength, I wondered how he managed to get himself drafted into this army. I think Aeschylus must have been thinking the same; he asked,

"But you've an unassailable position here, numbers count for nothing in this gorge, the more men, the more cramped the fighting space. It's far better than we had at Marathon."

Brasidas smiled.

"Well said, poet, perhaps we'll make a Spartan out of you after all."

Aeschylus ignored this and moved on to the point that I think had occurred to all of us while he was speaking.

"In fact, the only way a determined body of fighting men could be dislodged from here ..."

Brasidas finished it for him,

"Would be if their flank was turned and they were attacked from the rear."

"That would mean another pass through the mountains."

"Right again, poet."

Brasidas wasn't smiling now and I think Aeschylus realised what was to come, asking,

"And?"

"And what?"

"Is there another pass through the mountains?"

"Yes, unfortunately there is. A route we weren't informed about when we made our decision to hold the line here."

He pointed directly above us to where a ridge line of cliffs dominated the skyline.

"Just the other side of that ridge, about half an hour's march to our rear, there's a hill track. It's just a goat track really; steep and difficult going but passable all the same. As yet we think the Persians don't know of it."

None of us wanted to push him further and we didn't need to.

"And in case we are betrayed and they do manage find it we've put our Phocian contingent, whose ground this is, to defend the track where it's most difficult."

It sounded convincing but there was something in his manner that didn't quite ring true. Cimon changed the subject.

"The Spartan contingent seems smaller than the others."

For a moment I thought that we were going to hear some Spartan boasting that one Spartan was worth ten of anyone else, but we didn't.

"Yes it is."

Cimon asked,

"How many?"

"Three hundred."

We stood in silence looking over the small campsite, trying to work out its strength including Thebans who couldn't be trusted and the Phocians in the hills guarding the track. But whichever way you looked at it, there weren't enough of them. Eventually, almost as an afterthought, Brasidas muttered,

"But we're only the advance guard: the ones who could be mustered straight away. The main army will follow. It's probably already en route. Once they get here even the gods would be hard put to shift us. Let's go back to my tent and remember Marathon over some good Spartan wine."

The wine wasn't any better than I remembered, sour and overwatered, but it was good to sit and drink with an old friend. Interesting too, being able to watch how the Spartans live in their war camp. Some were practising with sword and spear; others were oiling and plaiting their long hair. What none of them were doing was fraternising with the other Greek forces.

We ate with Brasidas and his tent mates that night. It was of a better standard than we'd ever had in Sparta. One of the tent mates, also strangely enough called Brasidas, explained why. He was a grizzled man who'd had several teeth knocked out by a sword jab, giving his mouth a shrunken sour look.

"We're not going to run short of supplies here. We came in the way Xerxes's army will and we've stripped every bit of food out of that area, burned what we couldn't carry. So the bastards either wait for supplies or starve to death on the march."

He laughed, which twisted his mouth into an unnatural angle which the lamplight emphasised. His mates roared with laughter though. He was evidently what passed for a joker in the Spartan ranks. But it was a good-spirited night. Partly because we were friends of Brasidas but mainly, I think, because we'd fought at Marathon.

Later we walked back through the camp to the ship, stopping briefly by the wall they were strengthening. Somewhere beyond it in the darkness was the full might of the Persian army preparing to attack a crumbling wall defended by only three hundred Spartans and a ragbag of troops who distrusted each other.

The night in that pass was disturbed by strange noises.

Maybe just the wind gusting through rock crevices and across the ridges but I think ghosts walked in the night at Thermopylae even before the battle.

Next day as we were preparing the Athene Nike to sail, Themistocles and Habronichus returned from Leonidas's tent where they must have stayed the night. Leonidas and some of his officers came with them, but not Brasidas I was sorry to note. Spartans are not prey to the emotions of other men, but it was clear that between Leonidas and Themistocles there had sprung up a respect and trust which bordered on friendship. They embraced before Themistocles climbed aboard and we pulled away from the shore.

Leonidas and his men stood and watched us leave. Above them towered the cliffs leading up into the high mountain and somewhere up there lay a path that bypassed the pathetic little wall they were trying to defend.

I was relieved as we pulled away from Thermopylae; even then there was a reek of death about the place. Once out in the channel the rotten smell of the hot springs was replaced by clean sea air. But the mood on board didn't lift as I'd expected. Maybe that was down to Themistocles. Whatever he and Leonidas and had talked about obviously hadn't been optimistic for the Greek cause. No point in asking Themistocles.

But I'd learned enough about him to know that having few close confidants, he needed someone to unburden himself to. Someone who could be trusted and was of no account and therefore couldn't use the information for personal gain. I'd also learnt that there's nothing like feeling yourself alone at sea to loosen a man's tongue.

Towards sunset I was sitting in the prow with Cimon and Aeschylus, watching the sun sink red in the west as we were approaching a mooring for the night. The winds had dropped but it was still too risky to consider sailing through the dark to rejoin the fleet. Themistocles, who'd sat like a stone figure in the trierarch's chair, suddenly said,

"So what do you make of the chances of our small band of Spartans?"

Cimon answered him.

"Their lives depend on factors outside their control. I wouldn't want to be with them at the mercy of events beyond my control."

He'd summed their situation up perfectly; I couldn't have come up with an answer like that. Themistocles looked surprised and asked,

"And what factors would those be then, son of Miltiades?"

He always retreated into this formal and pompous style when put off his guard. Cimon replied,

"Well, when are the reinforcements going to arrive? And when is the location of the track over the mountain that outflanks their position going to be revealed to the Persians by a traitor?"

Themistocles grunted something then said more clearly,

"I doubt if the whereabouts of the pass will remain a secret for long, and I'm not much more optimistic about the reinforcements."

Aeschylus said,

"So, it's the old tragedy then: the great betrayal."

He almost sounded pleased as if what he was hearing strengthened his bleak view of life and its purpose. Cimon protested.

"They promised to support him with a full Spartan army, without it the strategy is doomed."

I saw Themistocles and Aeschylus exchange a glance. Themistocles said gently,

"That's the way it will happen though, I don't think there will be any help. They're on their own."

"The Spartans would never betray their own like that."

For such a successful leader as he became, Cimon always had a weakness in that he tended to take statements at face value. Particularly statements made by Spartans. He never learned and look where it got him.

Themistocles leaned back in his chair and wearily spelt it out.

"It's not a betrayal, more a matter of common sense and logic. When Leonidas was in Sparta offering to lead the advance party they promised him support and I'm sure they meant it."

Above us in the darkness a burning star flashed across the heavens to disappear beyond the mountains. We paused a while to appease the gods, then Themistocles made his point.

"But now Leonidas is stuck at Thermopylae, miles from Sparta, and the Ephors having listened to the counsel of his rivals will see things differently. All the ones who wanted to stay and defend the isthmus will be talking that strategy up while the advocate of holding the Great King at Thermopylae is miles away and can't argue against them. If I were one of the Ephors or Leotychidas I think I'd be inclined to agree with them."

Cimon came back at him.

"But what about the alliance, what about us?"

"Never expect much from agreements, young man, they always change. I was surprised to get Leonidas here, I don't expect him to be reinforced any more than he does now. No, I think he'll have to fight alone. They won't throw more men's lives away and weaken Sparta for the alliance. Think about it, now our fleet's engaged: they've already got what they wanted even though it's cost them a king."

"But the strategy to stop the Great King here, what happens to that?"

"I don't think there was ever a chance of stopping him here."

Cimon looked on the point of tears as he asked,

"So what are we doing here with our fleet?"

Themistocles replied quietly,

"We're buying time. Time for Athens to make the only decision it can and in buying time we'll buy experience for the fleet. Next time we'll fight them on grounds of our choosing. If things go badly with us here we can withdraw."

"And Leonidas?"

"No, there's no withdrawing for him. He'll have to stand and die."

Then Aeschylus, who had said nothing, spoke.

"There is something about him, I felt it. He's in love with death and he knows Thermopylae is where he'll find it. That's why he's not bothered to put a Spartan officer in charge of the Phocians who are guarding the pass."

I was compelled to ask,

"But that seals his fate?"

Aeschylus gave a bitter laugh.

"Exactly, he gets his place in the heroic legends. Betrayed and fighting to the end, the man becomes a myth."

"And the alliance?"

Themistocles answered.

"His sacrifice achieves the purpose of strengthening the alliance. The Spartans stand and die for it miles from home and we get a heroic martyr thrown in, and let me tell you ..."

But he never got the chance to; there was shouting ahead and out of the gathering gloom we saw the lights of a ship bearing down on the Athene Nike.

Chapter Twenty-Eight

So he never got to tell us whatever he was going to, and we never got to beach the Athene Nike and camp that night: the ship tearing hell for leather towards us was carrying a message. The skirmishers of the Persian fleet had been sighted and the main body wasn't far behind. The moment of our testing had arrived.

There was good news as well. Bad as the weather had been in the narrow straits where our fleet was pulled up onto its sandy beachhead, the weather out in the open sea was far worse. The great Persian fleet had got caught up in a storm off the coastline of Magnesia. The more experienced commanders had anticipated this and pulled their squadrons into sheltered inlets or beached them. But that's difficult for a fleet spread out along thirty miles of treacherous and hostile coast.

For the squadrons with less experienced or diligent commanders it was a very different story. A storm at this time of year in these waters rears up out of nowhere: there's not much time to save yourself if you fail to recognise the early warnings. About half their fleet either didn't recognise the change in the weather or failed to act on it. When the storm broke they had no choice but to try and ride it out at their sea moorings.

Not a position you ever want to find yourself in, reader. In a bad blow even strong, well-sailed ships, if clustered, get swirled about and smashed against each other like they're being stirred in a pot by a hungry giant. The Persians in the open sea were tossed about and ground together like kindling shredded for a fire. Each ship's splintering timbers become a lethal hazard to its neighbours. Enemy or not, no sailor likes to think of seamen tossed about like grains of chaff in the murderous maelstrom of towering wave, howling wind and fractured beams and spars.

In the morning, with the storm blown out, the surface of the waters resembled a murky wood soup. We learnt this from the crews of a couple of Chian triremes pressed into the Persian service who took opportunity of the confusion to escape and defect to us. They reckoned the Great King must have lost upward of four hundred ships in the blow. Evened up the odds a bit and Themistocles made sure the story spread rapidly throughout our camp.

I never worked out how many ships they lost, but after the Athene Nike was sent out on a reconnaissance a couple of days later I understood pretty well how many they had left. We reckoned we were up against at least eight hundred triremes and maybe twice that number of support ships and troop carriers; well over twice our number.

And, reader, remember back in those days, despite our experiments with extending the outrigger to accommodate a few more hoplites, their ships were bigger. Much bigger and carrying more fighting men. Get boarded by one of those fuckers and you were outnumbered and it was backs to the wall. So any optimism we'd felt because of the storm was wiped out when we saw them approaching the islands of Skiathos and Skopelos. There they'd establish their fighting station, pinning us back into the narrow channel, outnumbered and outmanned.

Wasn't just us taken aback at the size of their fleet close up and sailing our waters. No, whatever fears we harboured, our leaders had them worse. Of course the popular story today is of the heroic Greek fleet, secure in their ability, confronting the overwhelming Persian numbers. You probably believe the account where Themistocles and the other leaders brought us together and inspired us with the example of the Spartans at Thermopylae.

It wasn't like that, nothing like it: the way things really were we almost didn't confront them at all. Even amongst the Athenians there were as many of us who wanted to cut and run for Athens as there were those who wanted to stand and fight.

But the greatest threat to those who wanted to stand and fight came from the leader of the Corinthian contingent, a man named Adeimantus who rarely let a day pass without threatening to withdraw his ships and sail back to Corinth. There weren't any public meetings; that would have been far too risky, exposed too many rifts and uncertainties.

Whatever differences and arguments the leaders had, they conducted in private; they weren't stupid. But the detail leaked out like piss from an old hound and you won't be surprised to learn that as in any dealings between Greeks, they included elements of threat and bribery. It was said that Themistocles had to offer Adeimantus three talents in silver to remind him of his obligation to fight alongside his fellow Greeks.

While this was going on and as the Persians conducted their manoeuvres in full view, our camp was riven with rumour. Rumours that the Persians had sailed round Euboea and outflanked us, that the Spartans were beaten, and most popular, that we were about to strike camp and run for it back to Athens. These rumours spread among the tents like wildfire.

Then the Gods smiled on us; we had one last stroke of good fortune. I was sitting bored and morose watching Aeschylus scribbling. Before I forget, reader, I should point out that we owe a considerable selection of his writing to the nervous boredom of life in camp waiting for action.

He was particularly preoccupied with the indifference of the Gods to our suffering and their spiteful response to any perception of our happiness. I think his great Promethean trilogy was engendered on that windswept beach at Artemisium. Then we heard the cheering spreading from the southward tip of the camp.

Heard it without understanding, but beginning to cheer ourselves all the same. Then it got passed on: the news. The news that the detachment the Persians had sent round the far side of Euboea to cut off our retreat and attack us from the rear had been caught in another storm and badly mangled. Too badly broken up to carry on. An islander brought us the news and that night some of the Ionian Greek ships in the Great King's fleet slipped anchor and came across to us. Things were turning round, we began to believe.

It was then that Themistocles acted. Then that our leaders brought us together on that beach in the squadrons we'd fight in. There, they filled us in on Themistocles's plan. We'd expected it I think but, shivering in the predawn chill as the surf growled on the shingle, the world felt like it was lurching. Each trierarch addressed his crew. Lysias was no great orator but we respected him.

"The time's come now, boys, what we've been waiting for."

He faltered and we knew something big was coming. Then after a pause it came.

"We're going out there to meet them."

Theodorus couldn't help himself; he spat out,

"What? Us taking it to them?"

"You've got a problem with that, rowing master?"

Wasn't really an answer to that so Lysias continued.

"They won't expect it and anyway we need space for the way we're going to fight, can't afford to be boxed in."

Now we were interested.

"We've not enough experienced crews and they outnumber us, so –"

He paused and we waited.

"So we're going to use the manoeuvre we we've been practising: the hedgehog."

We hadn't been practising it very well. It was a manoeuvre where the fleet formed itself into one great circle with the rams pointing out like the quills of a hedgehog. We understood then why we needed to fight in open water; get tangled up with each other and the formation becomes a shambles, fights the enemy's battle for them.

"So we go off, one ship after the other, follow my leader round and round and you'll be pleased to know Athene Nike's the leader."

There were grumbles of 'what about the Spartan' but deep down I think we were proud to be chosen. There was another cause for pride.

"And Themistocles fights from Athene Nike."

The rowers picked up their oar loops and cushions and we eased the ship of the Goddess into the water. Lysias touched my head for luck and climbed aboard. Sailors like tradition and value luck even more; they all followed suit and then I, as last man, climbed onto the deck. So it began.

Artemisium was different to the other great battles in our death struggle with the Persians, in fact it was different from every other engagement I fought in and there have been plenty of them. It wasn't so much a battle as a series of running fights that spread over more than three days, although the Athene Nike was only there for two of them as you'll soon discover, reader; but I get ahead of myself.

It was mid-afternoon before the fleet was sufficiently organised to move in rough formation through the straits; the weather was hot and sullen and the swollen waters beneath us rolled ominously. We sweated and worried in our impatience; Themistocles more than anyone.

He had good reason to worry; we met no opposition and sailed on through the relatively open waters towards the Persian fleet moored at its station at Aphetai. Where were they? Were we being drawn into a trap? By late afternoon you could feel the indecision and doubts of our commanders like a physical presence. But by now we'd come too far to turn back. Then we saw them.

Pulling out from creeks, inlets and harbours on the opposite coast were the disparate elements of the mighty Persian fleet. It seemed they'd been less prepared for fighting than we were. Equally clear that they were attempting to surround us and would hit us all along the circumference we were trying to construct as we moved into hedgehog formation. There was no order; the fighting would be random and disordered. And that's the last coherent thought I had in the next forty eight hours.

It took all the skill of Ariston, Theodorus and his rowers to prevent us getting fouled by our own ships; the sun disappeared behind a haze of light cloud, the waters beneath began to roll. During the wait we marines tried to stay still, not fidget, not disturb the equilibrium of Athene Nike. There was plenty of time to enjoy the customary stench of loosening bowls and bladders, the grunts of oarsmen, the slap of oar blades on churning water.

Then they were close enough for us to see their faces and the first arrows whizzed overhead. I didn't need to say anything to our Scythian bowmen; they knew what to do, they'd played before. Then it was our turn; I looked at the marines in the prow and stern and we pulled down our helmets. A last glance at friends before disappearing into the solitary world of limited vision and loneliness that a helmet brings.

Cimon looked excited; Aeschylus showed no emotion at all. We tried to brace ourselves as best we could against the roll of the ship as we formed a small protective shield wall round Ariston and Themistocles, sitting in the two chairs from where they'd attempt to control the ship. Though my slits of vision I saw Persian triremes speeding across the water at us. There were plenty of them moving fast while we had to maintain our slow holding pattern.

This was the first sea fight where we'd not been able to use our prime weapon: speed. At first their speed worked against them as instead of hitting us together in force they made contact in ones and twos. Our numbers counted and they lost ships.

But, as the rest pressed behind them, the pressure on our formation at the points of engagement pushed us into each other and out of formation. We were being squeezed. I sensed this rather than saw it; all I saw was what was right in front of me and that was a space of open water between The Athene Nike and the nearest Persian: no one engaged us. But we were scraping against other Greek ships. I heard Ariston shout,

"S'no fucking good, can't maintain this; we have to break formation."

There wasn't a response but Themistocles must have understood what he meant, anyone with eyes could see that we were being pressed into a huddle of Greek ships. Much longer and we'd be immobile and defenceless waiting for the superior Persian numbers to swarm across our decks from one trireme to the next. We waited in agony for a command from the only man who could give it.

Then Themistocles's voice.

"Do it. Break formation."

The boat began to pitch, we stumbled into each other for support, Theodorus was calling a different stroke, Lysias was shouting to the nearest Greek triremes.

"Break the circle, take them one on one."

For those of us with some space it wasn't too difficult but I'd have hated to be on board one of the Greek triremes that was engaged and tangled up with an enemy. Our speed increased. I heard Ariston shout,

"Ramming speed."

We seemed to fly across the water; turning my neck to look straight ahead I saw a Persian trireme side on to us trying to shift as quick as it could. I remembered to shout a command to brace and then we hit with a terrible noise of breaking timber. I was flung across the deck with the impact so hardly noticed our back stroke as we withdrew and the terrible bronze ram tore itself back out of the guts of the crippled Persian.

We'd hit her on the downroll, just below the waterline near the stern. A fatal blow and the sea was rushing in to the jagged gape in her side. She went down at once, dragged from the stern and the startled crew, who minutes before were safely free from the combat, were dragged screaming down with her.

I stumbled to my feet to reorganise the fighting men, one stayed prone on the deck, head at an awkward angle, neck broken. The sea was filled with ships in the bloody disorder of a series of running fights. Now it was the superior number of the Persians that disadvantaged them as we moved from compression to space and they fell back onto each other. Chaos, how the Gods love it.

In their panic they did more harm to each other than we did to them, it's like that fighting at sea: in an instant everything can change. We stood off picking our targets amongst the disorganised enemy, any ship limping and isolated we went for. Couldn't do as much damage as we wanted: we kept getting in each other's way. The only other damage the Athene Nike managed to inflict was on a crippled Persian pentecontor already engaged at the bow by one of our unreliable Corinthian allies.

We ghosted up onto its stern. The trierarch was standing by his seat shouting orders to his men in the prow, who were struggling to repel borders while his helmsman and rowing master were trying to disengage their ship. I gave the orders for throwing spears and we spitted the three of them; then our archers poured in their shafts. At this range it was murder. The light was fading and both sides were happy to disengage but we came away the happier: we'd been lucky.

I had trouble getting my fighting gear off because of damage to my right shoulder. I only noticed it after the fighting had ended. That night, camped up on the beach, a fast boat brought a message from Leonidas. The Persians had attacked and been repelled, so both the army and the fleet could fight again the next day knowing their rear was protected.

Next day after a poor night's sleep disturbed by the cries of the wounded and dying we were back in the ships early enough to watch the sun rise from the deck. My right shoulder was a nasty mix of purple and livid yellow; I'd not be throwing any spears, that's for sure. We went for the same tactics; bring them onto us then when they fouled each other because of their numbers go for them. The only way to learn how to fight at sea is by doing it and we were learning quickly.

The day followed a similar pattern but the fighting started earlier and by noon the sea between Artemisium and Aphetai was filled with skirmishing ships. Any battle plan only lasts until the moment of the first engagement, but Themistocles was quick to pick up what was possible to co- ordinate from the deck of a trireme. He kept the Athene Nike towards the rear of the Athenian contingent so we didn't engage, which for me was a relief as I doubted my ability to wield a sword in my right hand.

From this position Themistocles attempted to direct the actions of as much of the fleet as he could. As the light began to fade, both sides again disengaged and returned to base claiming victory. But it was more of a victory for us as we'd taken on the full might of the Persian fleet for two days and lost fewer ships. As Themistocles said that night after we dragged the ship up onto the beach,

"Our ships are quicker to break formation than theirs. If only we could lure them into a position where we want them, where they have to come at us. Then I think we could force them into an engagement where there was no possibility of retreat, where we could destroy them."

But that was the last bit of optimistic thinking we enjoyed that night. When Lysias came back to our campfire from the officers' meeting, he was glum-faced.

"The admirals think we can only fight like this one more day: they can field fresh ships from their reserves, we've already committed all ours. "

He was right, and anyway triremes aren't built to withstand continuous days of fighting. They soon get the stuffing knocked out of them. We knew this from the state of the Athene Nike, which was still taking on water from the damage done during our ramming action the day before. But we could tell from his expression that wasn't the only bad news. This was confirmed when Cimon asked him,

"But what about the Spartans? They're depending on us to secure their flank."

Lysias didn't answer, just gazed at the fire. Cimon repeated, "What about the Spartans?"

Lysias took a slug of wine, spat in the fire before grunting,

"There's been no word from Thermopylae."

We sat thinking through the implications of this as the flickering fire cast weird shadows. The whole camp was silent. Presumably there was a conversation like this round each ship's company fire. Somewhere across the bay the Persians were sitting round the campfires they shared with traitors like Metiochus and Hipparchus. Their conversation would be more cheerful: they faced neither of our major problems.

Lysias would have made a good Spartan; he was as laconic as they were. Eventually he said,

"So we can fight one more day, then we leave the Spartans exposed. Or ..."

He faltered, Cimon prompted,

"Or?"

But I think we'd worked out the answer before Lysias said,

"Or there are no Spartans anymore and we're already out-flanked."

We turned in shortly after; the conversation had taken from us any energy we still possessed. But the night wasn't finished with us. Sometime later, I'm not sure how long although the stars had shifted position, I was shaken out of a disturbed doze by a hand placed over my mouth. A voice said,

"Ssh, keep quiet, Mandrocles, get up and follow."

It was Ariston. I blearily struggled to my feet and followed him scrunching across the shingle to where a small knot of men stood by the Athene Nike's stern. I recognised Cimon, Lysias and, to my surprise, the Spartan admiral Eurybiades looking tired and I think a little drunk. Themistocles began speaking as soon as I we arrived.

"The message we expected from Leonidas has not come: there's been no boat so I've ..."

He managed to correct himself in time.

"That is we, rather, that is Admiral Eurybiades, has

decided to send our best and quickest ship overnight to Thermopylae to ascertain the position. There they are to inform King Leonidas, if he still lives, that we will hold one more day then withdraw. That will give him time to make his own dispositions."

I glanced towards Eurybiades, he looked as if he was about to be sick, didn't even make a show of commanding. Themistocles continued.

"But if Leonidas is dead and Thermopylae is in the hands of the Persians, come directly back and warn us of the new danger we face. It is a desperate voyage at night for a damaged trireme but yours is the crew I trust most. The fate of Greece depends on you so may the Gods protect and go with you."

Chapter Twenty-Nine

That nightmare mission to Thermopylae was like entering a large crowded room at night lit only by a dim lamp in one corner. You sense there is much going on but can only see the little that surrounds you. In fact, that's true of our voyage through the night to Thermopylae as well; we knew there were rocks and shallows lurking in the darkness but couldn't see them. That's why the journey took so long, with Ariston grumbling the whole way that we shouldn't be sailing these waters at night. But despite his fears he got us there, albeit at a snail's pace.

Sometime after dawn, the sea fret we sailed through lifted and we saw the mountains above the pass. Even from a distance we could tell the narrow pass was a seething mass of activity, but which way things were going there we had no idea. War is confusion seen through the eyes of ignorance, and at a distance that confusion is compounded.

It takes nerve sailing into a mooring which may well be held by your mortal enemy but we had no choice. Our one consolation was that as long as there was still fighting then there was still hope and the closer we got the clearer it became that there was fighting, and hard fighting at that. By the time we pulled up to the shore we found chaos: it was like the worst pit of Hades. Lysias took the only sensible decision he could.

"Helmsman, keep the boat offshore and in readiness to pull away at once if threatened, no one leaves their place at the rowing benches. The marines will remain on board. If we don't return within two hours or you hear no word, get back quick as you can to the fleet and tell the commanders that the pass is lost and they are outflanked."

Good leadership, that. Ariston was impressed; all he said in reply though was,

"Aye, trierarch, and the Gods go with you."

We jumped to land and the Athene Nike pulled a short way off into the channel ready to run for it at the sight of trouble. Three of us only, although I think Aeschylus would have joined us given the chance. Cimon, as the son of the hero of Marathon, led the party out of respect to Leonidas, or in the event of his death to whoever now commanded the Spartans. Lysias and I comprised his retinue.

We scrambled up the steep track and arrived on the pass about seventy paces behind the wall. The place was scarcely recognisable, strewn with broken weapons and broken men. It was clear that most of the non-combatants had withdrawn. In fact apart from a contingent from one of the allies clustered together by the cliff face and looking ready to surrender the wall was undefended. There was plenty of evidence that it had been defended in the wounds disfiguring the bloody scattered dead.

The noise of fighting came from beyond the wall, the Persian side. This we couldn't understand; it seemed impossible to believe that the Spartans had gone on the offensive as that would be suicide. We had no alternative but to follow the noise of battle, picking our way through the dead and dying and cross over the wall. Thermopylae is a terrible place.

We made our way through the detritus of war to the wall but as we reached it the howl of battle ceased, except for the groans of the maimed and dying that is. Our arrival by good fortune coincided with one of those lulls that occur in all battles when weary men driven beyond endurance pause to draw breath. So we had some moments to observe the carnage that had raged in the pass.

Two lines of Spartans with a small reserve stood with their backs to us. At a glance it was clear that the dead Spartans we'd walked across combined with the ones on the ground this side of the wall far outnumbered those still standing. Those still standing were ragged and bloody.

But beyond them, on a patch of ground slippery with blood and entrails, lay corpses. Heaped into piles, mostly Persian but with some Spartans and a knot of other Greeks lying dead together. It's hard to describe that horror even now, despite all the other scenes of slaughter I've seen since. Beyond the dead packed densely together in the pass were the Persians, stretching back beyond where the eye could see. I recognised the black garb of the immortals at the front.

I could see they were using the pause to bring fresh men from the rear up to the forward battle line, a luxury not afforded to the Spartans. At Marathon we'd forced the immortals to run; they wouldn't run from here. We'd arrived in time for the death throes of the battle. We knew now what message we had to take back: the fleet had to withdraw. The stricken field was lost and with it perhaps the war.

Lysias and I were turning to leave, to get away while there was still time, when one of those strange twists of fate occurred. A Spartan turned and saw us, shouted something. There was a command and both lines, keeping formation, backed towards us.

I've never liked Spartans, never trusted them and for good reason, but there, there in that blood soaked patch of ground strewn with the mutilated dead and dying, they stood in their element; and for an instant I saw something magnificent. Cimon saw it too, except for him it came to define and ultimately ruin his life.

None of them was without a wound but as we stared at these creatures entering their own deaths the ranks parted and a man from the front rank approached us. In my memory, looking back it seemed to have all happened in silence but with the noise of the dying that can't have been the case.

Then Leonidas stood before us, huge and grim like the God of war. Bare armed but wearing body armour behind his great shield. He was streaked in sweat and blood, cut about all over. His massive arms were slippery, streaked with grime, oil and blood. But it was his eyes you saw before everything else.

His eyes were somewhere else, not with us, like those of the temple servants who imbibe the fragrant smoke in order to receive the words of the Goddess. Cimon's eyes were on him, fixated. And to be fair to Cimon, I too felt a compulsion to stare at Leonidas, but he himself broke that spell.

"Welcome, Athenians, I expected you earlier in answer to the message I sent."

Speaking for Cimon, Lysias replied,

"We got no message, lord. Themistocles, son of Neocles, sent us to enquire if there is any way in which he can aid you."

Sounds unbelievable, reader, doesn't it, that in those circumstances men should address each other as if they stood before the assembly. But I promise you that actually was what Lysias said. Leonidas replied,

"No, there's no aid he can send us, we're beyond aid here. As for you, you've seen all you need. You see how things stand with us."

We knew and that should have been the end of it; our

duty was to get the information back to the fleet. Lysias and I were already turning to go when Cimon asked him,

"But why leave your defensive position?"

It was a good question but not for there and then, we had to be away. Then a remarkable thing happened. Leonidas threw back his head and laughed as his mouth opened wide I could see the blood running over his lips and into his beard. The men around him began to laugh and through the laughter he said,

"If you care to hang around long enough on the other side of the wall, you'll see why we've decided to enjoy the change of scenery over here."

They laughed harder at this. I think Leonidas saw the hero worship in the young man's eyes and decided to go easy on him. He controlled the laughter and said,

"Soon a second Persian army will come up behind us; in fact I'm surprised they're not already in sight. So instead of waiting to be finished off like rats in a trap we decided to come out here onto open ground for our last stand and give them a lesson in how Spartans sell their lives."

I could see that Cimon wanted to join them; his hand went to his sword hilt. Leonidas must have seen it too; he said,

"Your place is not with us, son of Miltiades, your duty is to warn the fleet and tell the rest of the Greeks how Spartans died, obedient to their word. So you'd better get off to your ship. I'll pass on your respects to your father when I see him later today in the depths of Hades."

I'm not even sure Cimon was listening to this. He asked,

"But how could they get behind you?"

"How? We were betrayed, boy, some treacherous Greek led them through the pass I expect."

"But it was guarded."

Leonidas ignored this; his gaze was returning to the battle, he said to Lysias,

"Tell Themistocles what you saw here. Tell him I kept my word and I expect him to do the same."

Lysias began to reply but Leonidas wasn't listening anymore. There was a howling from the Persian ranks and he turned and rejoined the front rank, throwing back a strange last comment.

"If you want to bid farewell to your friend, you'll find him at the foot of the wall."

Cimon didn't react; I think he still wanted to die with them. But I knew what Leonidas had meant. I moved back to the wall and after a few moments picking my way through the dead and dying I found him: Brasidas. He wasn't dead; well not quite dead but close, soon his spirit would fly wailing to join the other dead. The broken off stump of a javelin protruded from his shoulder, his leather corselet was gashed and pierced, most of his blood was seeping into the dry earth he lay on. He was conscious, recognised me.

I began to loosen the straps on the corselet to make him more comfortable. He stopped me.

"Don't, Mandrocles, the hurt's too bad, my guts will spill out, don't want that, I'm a dead man anyway, rather die looking like a soldier."

His lips were dry and cracked I tried to give him some water, he didn't want that either.

"No, not with a stomach wound. Fought well here; made up for the stain on our reputation at Marathon."

He coughed up more blood and began to choke, then with a great effort of will that I think took the last of his spirit he said,

"Never had a son. You're a good boy, Mandrocles, fought well at Marathon, was proud of ..."

Then his eyes glazed over and he was gone, the only Spartan friend I ever made. Lysias touched my shoulder.

"We have to go now, Mandrocles."

I staggered to my feet; none of this seemed real. I felt like I was walking through a dream. Cimon still stood twenty yards in front of the wall watching the Spartans; he wouldn't come when we shouted, so we had to fetch him. As we were pulling at him a remarkable thing unfolded before us. The seventy or so surviving men with Leonidas at their head charged at the massed Persian ranks. Suicide.

The Persians let fly a dense black cloud of spears and arrows. Leonidas stumbled, turned half round and crashed to the ground along with half his men. There was a desperate struggle around Leonidas's body like something out of the heroic poems of Troy. It lasted less than a minute and the remaining few Spartans, with the body of their king, withdrew to a small mound upon which grew a desiccated stump of a tree, the only other living thing in this arid, deathly pass.

There they stood in a circle with the king's body in the centre. The Persians massed round them, then stopped; the two sides stared at each other. The ragged Spartan survivors with their broken spears and jagged swords protecting the body of their king, and the thousands of fresh Persian troops who'd been fed through from the rear for their turn to fight.

We grabbed Cimon and legged it for the boat and just in time because on the road behind the wall on the Greek side, we could see the skirmishers of the army that had come over the mountain pass heading straight at us. At the top of the path down to the Athene Nike, Cimon shrugged us off and turned to look back. We turned with him. That's how we came to see the end.

Don't expect to read what the stories say, reader. Don't expect the myth about the Spartans fighting to the end with fists and knives because their weapons were broken. Believe me, you can't fight thousands of men, hefting long spears, with fists and knives. You can't do that because you can't get beyond the spear points.

The way it ended, the Persians didn't use their spears. These fresh troops didn't even need to get their hands dirty. They just watched as their Scythian archers launched volley after volley of shafts into the small circle of men standing on the mound. The Spartans disappeared under the rain of arrows; it took only seconds.

The other Greeks we'd seen earlier huddled behind the wall threw down their weapons and waited for whatever fate had in store for them. It was all over, the pass was taken, the battle lost, the fleet outflanked.

We scrambled down the track, into the sea and were hauled over the side into the Athene Nike, which pulled away from the shore with Theodorus calling the stroke. I don't think the Persians even bothered to fire any arrows after us. Cimon was weeping.

And that's how it happened. I was there, I know.

The famous story about the Persians threatening to block out the sun with their arrows and the Spartan reply that it suited them to fight in the shade; I don't think that happened and they didn't fight with fists and teeth at the end, that certainly didn't happen. They stood and were mown down like grass for fodder.

The courage, though? Well, that's a different matter; we saw that. Or was what we saw merely pride? Perhaps the two go together. Whatever; they ended up doing what Spartans do best: dying hard. They died very hard.

The Persians thought so too. They'd fought against them for three days and what they probably thought would be not much more difficult than a stroll though the meadows cost them more lives than they could ever have imagined. I think that's why they mutilated Leonidas's corpse the way they did. Emasculated him in death the way they couldn't while he lived.

Then they cut off his head and stuck it on a spike to

watch over the pass he'd defended so well. I believe his spirit watches it still.

The real legacy of the three hundred was that they showed Greece they were prepared to die for a cause. They created a myth and the legacy of that myth, inspired other Greeks who otherwise would have given up. I still hate the bastards, but ...

We didn't talk much on the voyage; there are things that kill the desire to talk. We sat there, each man wrapped in his own thoughts. Sometime later Aeschylus tried to get me to explain what I'd seen and felt back there. He was looking for material to use in his plays. But I couldn't. I just couldn't; so think yourself lucky, reader, because you're the first one I've ever told.

The voyage back was more difficult, it started out fine but darkness fell as we hit the stretch of water where the currents are most treacherous. We nearly snagged on a small island in the shadows, and after that had to pick our way very slowly. So it was late when we got back, the early hours of the morning, the time when those near to death give up the struggle and ghosts stalk the earth.

The fleet was back on its beach and they'd been hard engaged. We knew because before we even heard the rasp of the surf across the pebbles we could smell the smoky residue from the funeral pyres on the shore. Once you've fought with the fleet, that's a smell you never forget. The sentries challenged us; we beached the ship and were taken to Themistocles.

Themistocles hadn't turned in for the night; he was sitting with the leaders of the other contingents huddled round a small fire outside his command tent. In the flickering half-light he looked weary and wore a cut across his left cheekbone from the day's fighting. We didn't need to say much: he could read everything in our eyes. In fact it was he who spoke first.

"So, it's over then, they're dead?"

Lysias answered for us.

"They fought well, we caught the end of it."

A faint grimace from Themistocles. He asked,

"And Leonidas, did he still live when you arrived? Did he have a message for me?"

"We saw him. He sends his regrets but your flank is now exposed and the fleet's position is no longer defendable. He died well."

I think Lysias had been rehearsing this speech ever since we left Thermopylae. He didn't need to say more. The news of Leonidas's death drew groans from the others round the campfire, particularly Eurybiades the Spartan.

Themistocles asked,

"Anything else?"

"He bid me tell you he kept his promise and urges you to ..."

Themistocles signalled him to stop, got to his feet and spoke to the other Greek leaders. I remember his words and set them down here; they are worth your attention if you want to know true leadership.

"Leaders of the free Greek fleet, we must prepare our ships to leave. I hate the thought of leaving Artemisium to the enemy and slinking away like a thief in the night. But we are now the only hope. We must preserve the fleet as all Greece depends on it. Today was bitter, we had worse of it, but remember: over three days fighting we've bested an enemy twice our strength and learnt much."

He pointed towards our battered fleet on the beach.

"At sea we have nothing to fear from the Persians, and next time in waters of our own choosing we will destroy them however many they are. On that day, we will revenge the sacrifice of Leonidas and his noble Spartans. Then it will be Persian women who weep and mourn. Now get your ships away from this place, leave campfires burning to confuse the enemy. Well fought, generals; Greece is grateful."

And that was how he answered the dead Spartan king and kept his side of the bargain.

It should of course have been Eurybiades saying this but he went off as instructed like all the others. There was no rest for the crew of the Athene Nike during what remained of the night; no sooner had she been beached than she was dragged back into the sea. We rowed dead tired and next day when we passed Thermopylae, keeping a good distance, we saw the smoke from the mass burial pyres and smelled the terrible smell of men's bodies roasting.

But worse than that was that despite all we sacrificed, we were retreating to the city of the Goddess. Retreating to a city we couldn't defend.

Chapter Thirty

The boy, Ephialties, has gone to help with the harvest; he will be gone some weeks, good for him I think, but I will miss him. I am not entirely alone; his grandmother, the old woman, is here to ensure that I do not injure myself by eating too little or drinking too much. She has grown stout and short of breath so we spend time sitting together, particularly early evening when there is much to watch below us on the streets of Piraeus. We don't speak much: we don't have to.

Whatever I might have done differently it's strange to reflect that this is how we have ended up. What fools life makes of us, still, a better ending than Aeschylus would have thought possible under the rule of the Gods. I wonder why I prevaricate and bother recording such commonplace reflections.

But no, even that is dishonest. I am trying to put off writing what comes next. You, reader, will understand this whoever you are. You will understand it because although I don't know you I do know that you are an Athenian and therefore something in you will feel the same dread of anticipation that I do.

You could feel that dread pouring out of the city in waves as we approached the harbour at Piraeus. However bad things had been for us, imagine the feelings of the women, children and old left in the undefended city. A city into which rumour and fear entered with each indrawn breath, engendering a frenzy of panic.

The most terrorstruck were already leaving; laden merchant ships, their decks crowded with refugees, passed us heading for Salamis and points beyond.

We pulled into the crowded harbour and queued for a mooring; we could see ships from our reserve fleet already there, all the sea power of the Greeks crowding into one threatened city. Standing on the quay waiting for Themistocles, worried and uncertain, were Xanthippus and Aristides. I watched as he was rowed from his temporary flagship stuck further out in the slow moving mass of warships to join them. I saw him scramble up to the quay and be embraced by his former enemies: war, it seems, turns everything on its head.

When the Athene Nike finally reached her berth and we'd pushed our way through the crowds on the harbour front to Aeschylus's bar, it was dark. But no one was going home, the city was waiting. Waiting to see if it had any future or, as some of the rumours said, it would be abandoned and its people would migrate to found another city amongst the Greeks in Italy. Tomorrow these and other matters would be debated by the assembly and the Demos on the hill of the Pnyx. Cimon set out for the house of Callias to find his sister.

I remember Aeschylus speaking some lines at me, perverted lines where he took the image of nature and growth and turned them to blood: he was rambling about something 'Blossoming like a sea of blood' and 'Pain flowering on a man'. Maybe some other time I'd have been interested but not now, when we stood on the verge of destruction.

I thought of going to look for Lyra but where would she

be? Was she still in Athens? Anyway I was dead beat so after a couple of drinks with Aeschylus, who fortunately had talked himself out and was on the point of slipping into sleep himself, I went up to the sleeping loft. That night I dreamt of Thermopylae and Brasidas.

In the morning the streets were still full; throughout the night there'd been the sound of people on the move, of cries and whispers. Somewhere out on the sea and marching across the mountains towards us were the fleet and army of King Xerxes, now reunited. So all our effort and the blood of Leonidas and his Spartans had been for nothing. All I knew for sure was that the men of the fleet were ordered to stay close to the ships, except for a contingent who would be at the assembly to make sure that whatever motion Themistocles proposed was carried.

Strangely the streets were eerily empty next day. Even the refugees streaming in from the surrounding countryside were avoiding the city, heading straight for the port. The city was emptying so the only crowds were at the gates and on the harbours. We made our way up to the Pnyx without any difficulty, but arrived to find a sullen, brooding atmosphere.

The proposal to evacuate the city and move the women and children to Troezen, birthplace of Athenian hero Theseus, was put by Themistocles and supported by Aristides and Xanthippus. It was heard in silence but before the motion could be passed a greybeard who I didn't recognise got up to speak. He put one question.

"What about the protection of the wooden walls?"

Themistocles replied,

"The wooden walls are the ships, we're using them."

The greybeard replied,

"The wooden walls are not ships. Since the birth of the city, the shrine of the Goddess Athena has been protected by an ancient and sacred thorn fence. The shrine has never been desecrated; the fence has protected it. That fence is the wooden wall."

Themistocles, frustrated by this as time was running short, snapped back at him.

"The wooden walls are the ships, I should know, I was there at Delphi when the oracle gave us the message."

"So, you have suddenly become a pious man have you, son of Neocles? To those of us responsible for the sanctuary of the Goddess your recent posing as an expert on the oracle has come as a surprise."

Aristides, seeing how this was going, interjected.

"No one will dispute religion with a man of your pedigree, Teisamenus, but within days, maybe hours, the advance guard of the Persians will be here. Themistocles speaks true: we can't fight them in Athens, our only chance is to flee until our fleet and the Spartans prevail."

"So, you too have become a seer, young Aristides? Well let me be plain, the oracle spoke clearly, the ancient wooden walls of thorn will protect the city if we have faith and rebuild them."

I've found in life, reader, that you can argue with any but the mad and those whose religion has convinced them of their own rectitude, however extreme. None of Themistocles's political tricks would sway the man and his supporters. Precious time was slipping away. You could feel anxiety and impatience running through the crowd; men were looking down towards the sea as if they expected the Persian fleet to appear at any moment. It became clear how intractable the impasse was when a decrepit accomplice of Teisamenus asked to be heard and spoke in a surprisingly commanding voice.

"No argument will sway us, but if the virtue of our pleading does not persuade you then perhaps this will. There are other reasons why we will stay with the Goddess. Many of us are too old and infirm for a sea voyage and the precarious life of exile that follows. We did not quit the city when the Great King tried to destroy us. If I remember correctly it was you who counselled us to stand and fight back, Themistocles, and at Marathon we won the victory. The Gods were with us then and they are with us now. You run if you want to. We will remain and defend the Goddess."

There was even a faint cheer for this and at that moment Themistocles knew he wouldn't win them over. He put the motion to the vote and it was carried, but not by much. Thus was the city divided. Those of us for whom wooden walls were the ships headed down to the harbour while the rest went up to the Acropolis to prepare the defences. Themistocles had the decree which he'd written the night before read throughout the city. It was a surprisingly long document loaded with justification but its message was clear: prepare to leave the city immediately.

Whatever they tell you now about the courage of the Athenians in leaving their city let me tell you now, reader, the God Pan spread fear like an infection. I knew what it would be like, I'd had my fill of close escapes; I remembered the panic and slaughter when we'd had to pull out of Khardia back before Marathon. And I wasn't disappointed: there was now a mad dash for the harbour front.

Our fleet wasn't prepared; triremes aren't designed to carry large numbers of people and the only way they can is to strip out two rows of rowers and pack the hold. This makes them even more unstable and slow. We couldn't afford to convert all the triremes as we'd be defenceless if the Persians sent a fast squadron ahead. There was worse news for me: the Athene Nike, minus Cimon who was too precious to risk, being named for the Goddess was to be the last ship out. So I got to watch the tragedy at close quarters.

The crush at the water's edge was intense as women and

children pushed for the boats. Every so often a surge, occasioned by a rumour the Persians were murdering and raping their way down to the harbour, led to the weakest slipping beneath the herd of trampling feet. The first ships to fill and sail were merchant pentecontors and a stream of them, crawling with refugees, struggled low in the water towards the harbour mouth. The Gods will need to help those on board if even a moderate wind begins to ruffle the sea.

Where the fighting ships were berthed it wasn't quite as bad; the marines kept such order as they were able so the crowd couldn't surge over the decks. The only way to deal with so many was to moor the ships side by side and feed people across the decks of the ships nearest the harbour to the one furthest out. When that one filled, we had to beat the crowd back until the next ship was ready to load.

I'd been there hours, shepherding crying and terrified families across the deck of Athene Nike and onto 'The Breath of the Gods' tied up next to us, when I heard a voice call my name. Looking down into the mass of humanity I saw the scarred face of Demetrius, the gate keeper for the flute girls.

"Mandrocles, look, Lyra."

I looked closer and saw her standing by him like a young bird shielded under its mother's wing. He forced his way a little distance through the crowd towards me and tried to hold Lyra in front of him. She was shouting to me but in the press of noise and confusion her voice didn't carry. Then she tried to raise something above her head like she was trying to show it to me. A small bundle wrapped in cloth. I was trying to see what it was when there was another surge in the crowd and she and the bundle were swept away.

I wanted to follow her, find her, I knew there was something of significance I'd missed but it was too late; she'd disappeared in the surge for one of the boats further along quay. I prayed Demetrius would see her safe to Troezen. Then the inevitable misfortune struck before our horrified eyes; the press of desperate people gathered sufficient impetus to sweep across the decks of that line of triremes, the crew were overwhelmed and the two outermost ships, one of which fully loaded, capsized and went straight down.

For a moment there was a brief agonised silence before the mass of screaming and shouting struck up again: pure fear, hysteria. There was less control here than on a battlefield, as sailors fought to hold the crowd back and the crowd tried to storm the ships.

Then a different noise, harsher and grating. A column of fully armoured hoplites with Xanthippus at the helm forced their way brutally between the screaming people and the ships. Shields and the flat of swords were used indiscriminately and gradually an empty but bloody strip of dockside was established between the weeping crowd and the ships. More troops fed into this space and the women, children and slaves were pushed further back. There was a standoff but at least in that stasis the pressure on the boats was relieved.

There wasn't time to wonder what would happen next as a blast from a series of horns like the ones that announce the spring Dionysia, only louder, reverberated round the Piraeus. Now there was silence.

A funnel of space was created in the rank of the troops and a voice I recognised bellowed,

"Athenians, the daughter of Miltiades, the hero of Marathon and saviour of Athens, is making her way to the ships. Do you wish to impede her passage?"

There was no answer but the crowd stayed still and silent. Through the narrow passage way in the hoplite ranks a high born lady appeared, leading a small gaggle of mothers with their children. Tall, and dressed in a modest peplos but with head uncovered so the crowd could see her. Elpinice.

Grave and calm as the goddess Athena herself, she approached the crowd leading her small following. As she drew near they gave way before her. From the deck of Athene Nike I saw this face on. In her bearing she could have been Miltiades. As the crowd gave way she smiled to the right and left, head erect, and you could feel a relaxing of tension spreading from her through the frightened masses.

The voice, Themistocles of course, roared again.

"Athenians, let the Lady Elpinice show you the way to safety on the ships. Let her show you how Athenians should behave in the face of danger."

She passed through the throng and people stretched out to touch her and kiss her hand as she progressed to the most central of the dockside triremes, one of the boats Callias had built. Once on board she didn't, as I'd expected, make her way across the decks of the triremes moored to it and onto the next to depart. She climbed into the stern and turned to watch the crowd. So under the supervision of those calm penetrating eyes and directed by the hoplite officers the embarkation recommenced.

Of course this being Athens it didn't go smoothly, there was pushing and shoving, but the previous ruinous anarchy was gone. All the same it took through the night and well into the next day before most of those willing to go were aboard. Elpinice stood at her station throughout. Then, when there was only a single line of triremes left at the harbour side, Cimon joined her and their trireme pushed off towards the harbour mouth.

The next hours were the worst as, one by one, the other triremes departed and we were left in the uncanny silence of a deserted Piraeus. We were waiting for the men tasked with sweeping up stragglers or the lame and halt up in the city. The Piraeus may have been like a ghost town, but sounds were beginning to drift down from Athens, and not reassuring sounds.

Shortly after midday a fast skiff entered the harbour and shouted a message across to us that the advance of the Persian fleet had been sighted and was little more than an hour away. I hate the waiting most; it gnaws away at you, breaks down your nerves. We were tired and now we were scared, the Athene Nike was attached to the dock by only one rope and Theodorus had the rowers ready for the first stroke.

My hands sweated and I couldn't keep still. I thought back to the first time I'd seen Athens: the day I'd stood on the deck of the old Athene Nike with Miltiades, Cimon and Elpinice waiting for permission to disembark. The city of the Goddess had seemed so strong, calm and safe. Now I was back on board waiting to escape, homeless again. What bitter humour the gods enjoy.

It ended quickly, a small group of armed men came skittering down on to the harbour. They were breathless and frightened. Their swords were bloody and some of them wore wounds. They were shouting, gabbling at us.

"Persians, Persian skirmishers are in the city, couldn't hold them off; right behind us."

They scrambled over the side as we were casting off. On reaching the harbour mouth we saw not more than half an hour away the forward squadron of the Persian fleet. Everything we feared was happening. The officer of the rearguard, a man I recognised from Xanthippus's household and who'd been on the fateful mission to Aegina, clasped my arm and wheezed,

"Didn't think you'd wait, owe you lads for this, Luck Bringer."

Then he turned and vomited over the side. The sea gets to you like that. I'm going to have to put the next bit off, reader: the emotion is too raw. So in the meantime let me clear up another myth about the old days: that story about Xanthippus's dog.

You know, the one about how there was no room for animals on board and so Xanthippus's faithful hound jumped in the water and swum after the boat all the way to Salamis and when it got there it just had the strength to lick his hand before it fell over, dead of exhaustion.

It's all made up you know, part of the myth these families create about themselves. I know it's not true because we were last out and there certainly weren't any dogs swimming in front of us.

The Persian ships were either too tired or disinclined to give chase so we followed our distant fleet with its human cargo. Lysias was wiped out and dozing in the trierarch's chair; the last two days he'd had no sleep. The rowers were resting and Ariston steered us, catching the offshore breeze. I was half asleep myself but, as officer of the hoplites, had to stay awake while Lysias caught some rest. Aeschylus was talking to me as much to help me stay awake as anything else.

He was talking about how crowds behave; comparing the women on the quayside to the followers of the God, Dionysus. When in frenzy they tore King Pentheus into little pieces. He began to chant some lines from the idea of a play he was working on, can't remember them now.

Then he stopped.

"Mandrocles, look."

I turned and followed the direction he was pointing: back to Athens. He always had better eyes than me; at first I couldn't see anything. Then I could; smoke. Wisps of smoke over the lower parts of the city. I said,

"Looks like something's happening around the Agora."

"Not there, look up, look at the Acropolis."

I did; now I saw what he saw. Above the crowning glory of our city the sacred temple of the Goddess Athena herself, smoke, clouds of black smoke.

"Athens is burning, Mandrocles; Athens is burning."

Cheshire. Samos 2012-14

Lightning Source UK Ltd.
Milton Keynes UK
UKHW040658280220
359508UK00002B/289